America's Founding Heritage

Second Edition

W9-CNA-967

America's Founding Heritage

Second Edition

Frank W. Fox
and
Clayne L. Pope

Brigham Young University Press
Provo, Utah

Cover image courtesy Brigham Young University History Department, from a poster by McRay Magleby advertising the Birth of the American Republic lecture series in 1976.
Cover design by Robert E. M. Spencer.

ISBN 0-8425-2614-5

Printed in the United States of America
10 9 8 7 6 5 4 3 2 1

Contents

Introduction

As far back as we can peer through history, humankind has lived under some form of government. Families, clans, tribes, city-states, nation-states, and a variety of other groupings have always devised some means by which individuals can live together in an orderly fashion. The need for government seems to lie in the socializing nature of the human species, coupled with the instinctive desires to seek pleasure, avoid pain, and express the self as an individual. Through government we wrestle with the issues that push us together and pull us apart.

In an ideal world, government would resolve dilemmas successfully, and we would recognize public order as a universal blessing; the system would always be fair, reasonable, moderate, compassionate, wise, forgiving, and helpful. In the real world, alas, government often becomes an instrument of tyranny, at least for some. The horrors of history—from Pharaoh oppressing the Israelites to Hitler incinerating Jews—are essentially the work of government.

The problem, then, is this: how can we enjoy the benefits of government without incurring its dreadful costs? Humankind has proposed many solutions—the majority of which has failed. On most of the planet, at least the past century has been as rife with oppression as any of its predecessors; and the advancements of science and technology have served to make bad situations worse. Think of various problems in Africa, Latin America, China, India, and the Middle East. Think of Stalin's Russia, Pol Pot's Cambodia, and Big Daddy's Uganda, to name a few.

Most resolutions to the problem of government have resulted abruptly from war and conquest, or else have evolved slowly over time from historical experience. Once in a while circumstances have made it possible for the problem to be solved by conscious intention. A single individual, or more likely a small group of them, deliberates about what a better form of government would look like, how its elements would fit together, and what the result would be. It happened just like that in the fifth century BC, when an Anthenian tyrant named Cleisthenes, for reasons still somewhat unclear, sat with leading men in Athens and created a democracy with various assemblies, law courts, and voting districts—an extraordinary feat. We speak of such an instance as a *founding*.

Foundings are amorphous events, difficult to define precisely. Still, they typically involve a variety of elements, such as an outline of government, a body of law, definitions of citizenship, modes of participation, and some evocation of divine approval. They may create an identity for some new group, together with a sense of homeland, derived from the Latin *patria*. Additionally, a distinctive culture might ensue from a successful founding. Finally, the process is generally attended by a certain amount of upheaval, for foundings rarely arise in quiet times.

While a founding *could* result from foreign conquests or palace coups, we tend to insist otherwise. A true founding, as we conceive it, must address itself to the problem of government posed above, attempting to create a polity that will benefit everyone. We don't think of William the Conqueror as founding England but as merely invading and subduing it; when William's heir King John and the local landowners signed the Magna Carta in 1215, *that* was a founding.

Accordingly, foundings rest on ideas and beliefs generally accepted by the controlling community. We refer to these as *principles*. William the Conqueror had few principles other than his own claim to the English throne, but the document signed by John and the nobles was filled with them:

38. No bailiff for the future shall, upon his own unsupported complaint, put anyone to his "law", without credible witnesses brought for this purpose.

39. No freeman shall be taken or imprisoned or disseised [dispossessed] or exiled or in any way destroyed, nor will we go

upon him nor send upon him, except by the lawful judgment of his peers or by the law of the land.

40. To no one will we sell, to no one will we refuse or delay, right or justice.

Principles are unifying elements. All who accept the principles of the Magna Carta become English in a sense and subscribe to the English founding itself. This fact helps us to understand something else of importance about foundings, something we call *heritage*.

When a founding becomes successful and its political culture truly works, future generations look back to it as a reference point and come to regard it specifically as heritage. The concessions wrung from a reluctant King John made little difference in 1215—John continued many of his errant ways—but in time they were accepted as the foundation of Anglo-American institutions. (Compare, for example, the three articles listed above with certain principles in the U.S. Bill of Rights.) History moves along; but principles are timeless.

The United States of America resulted from one of these founding instances. Its Founding represented a historical circumstance in which it became possible to intentionally design a government, and in the process a nation-state came into being. The American Founding was an enormous task, for it brought the Founders to confront questions as complex and diverse as:

What promotes internal peace and security?
What protects against foreign intermeddling?
What fosters public happiness?
What ministers to our sense of justice?
What invokes divine approval?

Between 1770 and 1800 the American Founders wrestled with these questions in a direct and primary way. After 1800 they continued to ponder them—for the Founding itself had created new difficulties—but with less fervor. They also began to look back and see that they had created that mysterious thing we call heritage.

In the twenty-first century we continue to feel the power of the Founders' achievement. Often, though, we are not altogether certain just what we feel. For some Americans, the Founders have become demigods (to use Jefferson's term) and their work has become a cosmic given, beyond the scrutiny of mortals. For others, the Founders have become all too human, and should have known better than to do some of the things they did. Both sides in the present-day culture wars often reduce the Founding to an abstraction, forgetting how very real it was. Modern thinkers may not realize the Founders were fallible humans, caught in one of the strangest of situations. The Founders ran risks, took chances, struggled with baffling difficulties, and did not know the final outcome of their labors. To call them "dead white men" is not just a sneer, it is a statement of fact. They never thought to include women, never apologized for slavery, never admired Native Americans. They lacked all sense of postmodern political correctness—and any benefit of our hindsight. Perhaps the best we can say for them is that they created a Founding that worked and a heritage we can be proud of. In doing so, they found a somewhat satisfactory solution to the political problems that have plagued the ages.

This book seeks to tell that story.

Chapter 1

The Problem of Government

In the introduction, we saw that government is a fundamental necessity, but one that can become perverted into oppression. In this chapter we will zero in on this problem of government, and attempt to understand it.

Sovereignty

For government to do its job effectively, it must possess *sovereignty*. Sovereignty is ultimate political power—the final say within a jurisdiction. Entities that lack sovereignty may find their names on a map, to be sure, but they are not accepted as full-fledged nation-states. Without the ability to make final decisions, the self-sufficiency we call nationhood cannot exist.

Once in a while we catch a glimpse of what that means. In 1957, over the issue of school desegregation, Arkansas Governor Orval Faubus decided to have a showdown with the U.S. government. He closed Central High School in Little Rock, vowing that no order of the Supreme Court could open the school to African American children. A reluctant but determined Dwight D. Eisenhower nationalized Faubus's own National Guard, and for good measure sent in the 101st Airborne Division of the U.S. Army, with orders to open Central High to white *and* black students, by whatever means necessary. It was an object lesson in sovereignty.

Human nature has shown itself vulnerable to corruption by the possession of such power. Human beings have many good qualities, as witness mankind's noble achievements, but they obviously have a dark side as well. For every product of beauty and progress created by humankind, there has been any number of deplorable atrocities such as gulags, ethnic cleansings, political brain washings, and reigns of terror. Power lurks behind many of the horrors we find in history. "Power corrupts," Lord Acton famously observed, "and absolute power corrupts absolutely."

The Human Predicament

Sovereign power and its ill effects give rise to the *Human Predicament*. Throughout history, kings, tyrants, dictators, and other despots have used such power as they commanded to exact pain and hardship upon their subjects. Those subjects, in turn, became restive under the yoke and soon began plotting to remove it. If their revolt was crushed, even worse pain and hardship were sure to follow. If it succeeded, the result was often no better—and sometimes actually worse—than the tyranny that occasioned it.

The other side of tyranny turned out to be anarchy. The various groups who joined forces to depose the evil king or slay the powerful Caesar would never quite agree on a common course of action and often wound up fighting among themselves for control. Sometimes

THE HUMAN PREDICAMENT

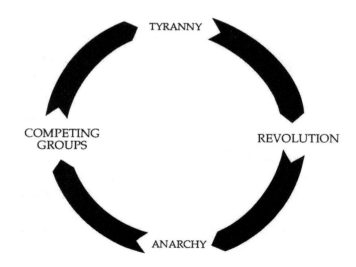

TYRANNY

COMPETING
GROUPS

REVOLUTION

ANARCHY

the fighting would go on and on, an endless cycle of violence and terror, as first one group and then another made its desperate bid for power. Other times the infighting would be mercifully short—for some *new* tyrant had emerged victorious.

Of the two sides of this dreadful coin, tyranny was often preferable. Tyranny, after all, has a constituency in those groups that back the tyrant and stand to benefit from his rule. Anarchy, on the other hand, benefits no one. So it is that, say, a Saddam Hussein in Iraq or a Pol Pot in Cambodia wound up in power, supported by *some* of the body politic. There were worse things than seeing someone *else* dragged off to the killing fields.

The Human Predicament offers a sad description of certain forces in the ancient world, with its chronicles of war, conquest, and revolution. What seems sadder is that we can still tune into such events on the six o'clock news. It is, to name a few recent examples, the stories of Afghanistan, the Congo, Cuba, Haiti, Iran, Iraq, Lebanon, Liberia, Nicaragua, and Yugoslavia. There will assuredly be some new illustration by the time this book is in print.

The fact of the matter is that many people on planet Earth have had to choose between or suffer under one of two alternatives, tyranny or anarchy. It has been the Human Predicament indeed.

The Good Society

Here and there within this tapestry of sorrow we see some notable exceptions, societies that broke all the rules. These mavericks were reasonably stable and orderly, yet with no strongman-style tyranny. The societies were reasonably prosperous, too, and their citizens enjoyed freedom from want. They developed strong, vibrant cultures, producing many of the world's memorable achievements. The societies were peaceful to their neighbors and yet pointedly held in respect. Their citizens were in charge of their own lives, and those lives were graced by opportunity and possibility. One thinks of Renaissance Florence in this regard, or of the Dutch Republic that came into flower in the days of Queen Elizabeth, or of that collection of entities that somehow merged into Switzerland.

But the prime candidate is usually thought to be classical Athens. True, it was not a Good Society in all particulars. The Athenians practiced slavery—made a virtue of it in fact—and they had an over-

The Acropolis in Athens was built during the flowering of Athenian culture and the development of democracy.

whelming compulsion toward empire. Nevertheless, given the limits of time, place, and culture, what the Athenians produced was dazzling. They enjoyed a respectable, though not lavish, prosperity. Their energetic political participation enriched and ennobled the lives of many citizens, and in this positive atmosphere creativity abounded. In the high season of the Athenian democracy, Sophocles wrote *Oedipus Rex*; Herodotus and Thucydides became the fathers of history; Socrates and Plato expounded philosophical idealism; Aristotle laid the foundations of science; and Phidias built the Parthenon.

For our purpose, the Athenian example is particularly worth remembering because of its influence on the American Founding. The Founders, virtually to a man, had studied classical Greece as part of their own education, and they knew aspects of it by heart. They knew Pericles' speech to the Athenians, warning of the dangers of empire. They knew Plato's *Republic*, extolling the importance of virtue, or *aretē*, as the backbone of republican morality. They knew what happened at the end, too, when the excesses of democracy led to the Peloponnesian War, when faction had contended with faction in the Ecclesia, and finally, when Socrates was tried and convicted for corrupting Athenian youth—a conviction based on spurring them to reach for unattainable ideals. The Athenian example, alas, became one to avoid.

All of which highlights the problem. What made such exceptions of these Good Societies possible in the first place? Why were they so rare? Why were they so fleeting? Over the millennia, political thinkers have attempted to grapple with these questions. We need to examine some of their general findings.

Political Legitimacy

One way of escaping the Human Predicament was to convince people that their government was *legitimate*—that it didn't rule their lives arbitrarily, that it was grounded in something higher than stark necessity.

In the ancient world, this was usually accomplished by assuring people that their rulers enjoyed the approval of the gods. Thus, according to myth, Zeus dictated the laws of Crete to his own sons, Minos and Rhadamanthus, who went on to found Minoan civilization. Ancient Sparta was established by the hero Lycurgus, acting under the direction of Apollo. Ancient Rome was famously founded by Romulus and Remus, whom the gods saved from drowning and arranged to be suckled by a she-wolf.

In the modern world, this notion developed into a theory called "divine right of kings," which means something like this: just as God organized the world into families and placed the father in charge, God organized society into kingdoms and made each king the father of his subjects. Rebellion against the king was thus held to be a violation of the Fifth Commandment—and rebels were shown no mercy.

Yet religious precepts could be invoked against kings too. For example, the enemies of King James I, an ardent divine righter, argued that God spoke to all through Holy Scripture, and it was up to believers to govern *themselves* according to the written word. These ideas, significantly, made their way into the American colonies.

There were other answers to the legitimacy problem. Some claimed to be in touch with God directly, and thus ruled by *theocracy* (think of modern Iran, for example). Some claimed to be in touch with history, or some other metaphysical force, and justified their rule accordingly (as in the former Soviet Russia). Some claimed to be smarter, wiser, or wealthier than their fellows; others said they could trace their lineage to distinguished ancestors, grounding their rule in *aristocracy* (ancient Sparta).

Ultimately, since the eighteenth century, the most compelling answer to the legitimacy question has been that of consent. That is to say, we legitimize government by the consent of the governed, expressed by means of free election. To the modern mind this seems obvious. It was by no means so until quite recently, however. Government by consent comes down to *self*-government. To some, self-government seemed like no government at all—a veritable oxymoron.

Freedom

Ideas of freedom appear to be as old as humankind. Yet many of them are elusive, with no settled historical meaning. When Moses begged Pharaoh for the freedom of his people, he didn't have the same thing in mind as, say, a Fourth of July orator today. He meant that *the people as a whole* ought to be free from oppression and bondage—and free to do only as God directed them. That another kind of freedom might exist became evident when Moses returned from Sinai to find a golden calf and a host of drunken revelers.

Freedom in ancient Greece had still a different meaning: the privilege of taking part in the political process. In the Athenian democracy, where every adult male enjoyed such a privilege, the Greeks began to glimpse yet another dimension of freedom, one that would become relevant to the modern world. In a famous speech to fellow Athenians, Pericles pointed out that they not only exercised political power, they also exercised self-sovereignty, for the one quality was necessary for the other. Having a stake in the political process required the individual to be in command of his own life, and vice versa. Only free and autonomous men could participate in the free and autonomous society.

The Granger Collection, New York

Pericles, a fifth-century bc Athenian general, believed self-sovereignty and political power were essential for freedom.

But didn't such autonomy imply anarchy—individuals going their separate ways? The

Greeks worried about this too. Athenians were discouraged from amassing large fortunes because it might distract them from public duty. One could only be virtuous, the Greeks believed, with an eye to the fortunes of the *polis*. They eventually resolved this contradiction (between the individual and society) by appealing to law. True freedom, as they came to understand it, could only be achieved by allowing citizens to govern their own lives—but they must do so in accordance with the law.

Human Nature

The deeper issue was whether men were meant to be free at all. Some philosophers—and virtually all rulers—concluded that they were not. It all came down to the question of human nature and how it was to be understood, a question which was by no means simple. While the nature of horses was easy to fathom—all of them followed the same general rules—human beings seemed entirely different. So many factors impinged on human behavior, and they varied according to time, place, circumstance, and conditioning. If there were general rules for explaining the human animal, what were they?

For the Greeks, understanding human nature came down to understanding the precise virtues of which such a nature was capable. If, for example, the virtue of the horse was to run fast, good horses ran faster than bad horses, and *all* horses aspired to run faster than they did. The striving of the horse for speed was mirrored in the striving of human beings for their own kind of excellence. Thus, the athlete aspired to physical prowess. The warrior aspired to vanquish foes. The orator aspired to spellbind his audience. Virtue, or *aretē*, explained everything.

This striving for human excellence was tied both to the question of freedom and the question of government. If human beings were made free, they would naturally want to ennoble their lives by striving for greater and greater virtue, and they would naturally want to govern themselves by means of the virtues they had mastered. Plato, for example, identified four cardinal virtues in the civic realm, which he called wisdom, courage, temperance (in the sense of moderation), and justice. Free citizens would cultivate all four, he believed, especially with benefit of a proper education, and as a result they would govern themselves well. They would select the wisest, the most

VIRTUE OF STATESMANSHIP

Statesmen who put public ahead of
private interest, exhibited enormous
personal integrity, and exercised wise,
practical, and far-sighted leadership.

PUBLIC VIRTUE

Virtue of the common citizen, encompassing
four separate elements to restrain abuses of
political power.

courageous, the most temperate, and the most just among them and make these their guardians.

That was one way to analyze human nature and solve the problem of government. There were others. The Christian world, to name a second example, had a different understanding of humankind and different ideas about governance. Jesus spoke of virtue too, but the qualities he mentioned—meekness, patience, humility, long suffering, compassion, love for one's neighbor—were unlike the heroics of Greek *aretē*. Yet Christians stunned the world by showing such virtues were real.

Christian communities dominated Europe from the time of the Caesars to the time of the Renaissance, and in many of these the problem of government was effectively solved. Ordinary Christians simply did what they were told and left matters of public concern to someone else. If the someone else happened to be lord of the manor, the very power conferred on him by Christian meekness tempted him to the kind of excess we have seen elsewhere. It was not a good solution to the Human Predicament. But then, as it turned out, neither was the Greek solution.

The Granger Collection, New York

David Hume by Allan Ramsay, 1776. Hume, a European Enlightenment philosopher, believed men were motivated by self-interest rather than virtue.

During the European Enlightenment, there was yet a third understanding of human nature, and a different set of implications for government. Enlightenment thinkers, while allowing for Greek excellence and Christian humility, noted that most human beings, most of the time, were characterized by self-interest. (Indeed, the Greek athlete eager to win his laurels and the Christian saint anxious to win salvation had that much in common.) Self-interest meant that, after all was said and done, high ideals were less reliable than ordinary comforts at explaining the behavior of *Homo sapiens*.

Here was another way of understanding freedom and government. It affirmed that people ought to be free to pursue their own self-interest, and government shouldn't stand in their way. On the other hand, just as there was something noble in the idea of Greek *aretē*, there was something ignoble in the idea of "me first," "I want mine," "what's in it for me?" or any of the other ways we have come to think of self-interest. Many people were obviously short-sighted and irresponsible, desiring creature comforts, sensual pleasures, bright images, passing fads, a quick buzz. Could such trivial individuals handle freedom? Or manage self-government?

Four Alternatives

In the world of the American Founding, and certainly in the world that was to follow it, thinkers worked out several alternatives to the problem posed by freedom, government, and human nature. While the following describe only four of the possibilities, these four are important. The American Founders considered all of them in some form, and they were tempted by more than one. Later on, as Founding became Heritage, Americans would have occasion to revisit the choices, which continue to shape our political dialogue today.

GEORGE III.
King of Great Britain &c.

Library of Congress

An engraving by Joshua Reynolds of King George III, the British "tyrant."

Autocracy

Authoritarian forms of government—including monarchy, dictatorship, and other kinds of despotism—begin from a rather straightforward analysis of human nature. People are like children, this analysis holds, and hence they must be carefully directed and controlled by the state. Government is not only necessary, it is critically essential, for it alone can bring order to human life. As for individual freedom, that can be forgotten. Freedom of the state may be important, but the freedom of the individual is precisely the problem, leading down the path to chaos and anarchy.

The American Founders believed they were dealing with just such a view of the world in the form of British tyranny. While they reacted strongly against it—in fact, mounted a revolution against it—the Founders weren't totally convinced it was wrong. They had seen chaos in their own streets before the Revolution, the so-called Boston Massacre being a prime example, and the issue of "people in the streets," as historian Gordon Wood put it, continued to haunt them. Alexander Hamilton frankly espoused a strong dose of monarchy in the constitutional mix, precisely because, as he said, "your people is a beast."

Classical Republicanism

The alternative embraced by the classical republics—and by present-day conservatives—began with a kinder view of human nature. Human beings are not necessarily corrupt, according to this view, but they are corrupt*ible*. If they are taught proper moral values, and if this teaching is constantly reinforced, they *might* be able to govern themselves. However, because individuals can be corrupted, so can government. Thus, constitutions must be carefully designed to

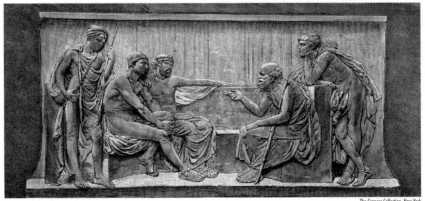

The Granger Collection, New York

A nineteenth-century bas relief of Socrates teaching in the Athenian agora.

constrain governmental power and refine its moral influence. Under the proper constitution, government can encourage a moral climate conducive to the Good Society.

The framers of the U.S. Constitution generally operated from this perspective. They included many features in the constitutional structure—separation of powers, checks and balances—that frankly assumed human corruptibility. At the same time, they framed provisions of the Bill of Rights—freedom of speech, freedom of religion—specifically to strengthen moral agency. They believed in the virtue of the people as a whole, and thought of the Constitution as mobilizing such virtue on behalf of the public good. Yet they also believed in the bad intentions of some and did not hesitate to use the power of government to constrain unseemly behavior.

Libertarianism

On the whole, the prime value embraced by libertarians is that of individual freedom. They believe that all institutions of society, including government, need to be cognizant of that value. Libertarians have no illusions about human nature, recognizing that some people are as bad as others are good. But nothing that society can do will make much difference in particular cases—people are what they are. Government should be limited to securing the rights of individuals, period, leaving the rest of life's fortunes up to them.

Library of Congress

Thomas Jefferson by Rembrant Peale, 1801. Jefferson believed "That government is best which governs least."

Few of the American Founders would have called themselves "libertarians" as such. Yet most of them prized the libertarian's strong espousal of freedom, as we will see.

When Jefferson said "That government is best which governs least," he was embracing a libertarian point of view. Later on, U.S. presidents such as Andrew Jackson would echo Jefferson's sentiments and point out that Americans were at their best when they were free of government restraint. The economics of the market system would dovetail with libertarianism and be accepted as an American article of faith. Let the individual alone, said the free traders, and watch him or her dazzle us.

Liberalism

Of all four alternatives, liberals—we use the term in its contemporary sense, not its traditional sense, which was more or less synonymous with libertarianism—have the warmest view of human nature. For liberals, human beings are essentially good, if only their fundamental decency could be freed from poisonous influences. The intolerance, greed, poverty, and conflict in the world does not stem from the human heart but from social institutions, such as private property or competition, which focus the mind on the wrong things.

As with human nature, liberals take a kindly view toward government, which they see both as a weapon against those poisonous influences and a tool for releasing human potential. Their view of individual freedom is more complex than the other alternatives. For the most part, liberals see freedom as a good thing—indeed, a battle cry of the oppressed and downtrodden. But too much freedom, or freedom of the wrong kind, exacerbates the social problem, as liberals see it. The freedom of, say, a factory owner to pay his workers a starvation wage is certainly not conducive to justice. Accordingly, liberals generally confine their regard for liberty to the political realm; in economics, government should take a hand. Of course no one should be free to accept intolerance, greed, bigotry, poverty, or war.

The American Founders knew liberalism by a different name. They saw reflections of it in Plato's *Republic*, which most of them had read, and in Jean Jacques Rousseau's *The Social Contract*, a political bestseller of the time. Rousseau had experienced a marvelous epiphany while still a young man, and as a result had come to see that human beings were born entirely virtuous, acquiring their depravity only through corrupt institutions. Do away with such things as established churches or private ownership and the world would also do away

The Granger Collection, New York

Jean Jacques Rousseau by Quentin de la Tour, ca. 1840. The Founders applied many of Rousseau's "liberal" ideals from *The Social Contract* into the new government.

with vice, crime, and squalor, Rousseau believed. While few of the Founders would have accepted such idealism whole-heartedly, most of them resonated with Rousseau's focus on justice. The words "with liberty and justice for all," from the Pledge of Allegiance, would become a theme of the American Founding, and later of the American Heritage, echoing through Lincoln's Gettysburg Address, through Franklin Roosevelt's New Deal, through Martin Luther King Jr.'s "I Have a Dream."

While the Founders made no conscious choices among these alternatives, all four presented them with options, viewpoints, ways of thinking about nationhood. Questions of human nature and liberty were tied together, and both were tied to the question of government.

Political Economy

In the twenty-first century, we commonly divide the study of politics from that of economics, while recognizing that the two often work together closely. In the world of the American Founding there was no such distinction. For example, in considering the Human Predicament—that choice between tyranny and anarchy—how could the Founders separate economics and politics? Tyrants imposed their will for the sake of gain as well as power, and the factions that upset the Greek *polis* were often rooted in material interests. What was oppressive about despotism was not just the lack of political choice but the grinding poverty of whole classes. And revolutions were not just about liberty, they were about equality and opportunity as well.

To a considerable extent, then, the problem of government becomes a political-economic problem, with perspectives from both disciplines. There were economic systems in the world that precisely mirrored the political systems accompanying them, and vice versa. The American colonists felt the hand of British oppression not just in Parliamentary high-handedness or the denial of jury trial, but in "unfair" restrictions on their trade, in government franchises and monopolies, in closing the frontier to hopeful settlers.

The TORY'S Day of JUDGMENT.

American colonists' aggression was often sparked by economic oppression, as this image depicts an English stamp tax agent strung up on the liberty pole.

There is another connection, too. The problem of government is, after all, a problem in controlling human behavior. If self-interest is the prime mover of such behavior, there are obviously economic as well as political ways of moderating it. Government sets boundaries on human activity by means of laws, courts, and the policeman on the corner. An economic system may accomplish similar ends through its rewards and incentives. If interest is balanced against interest in the marketplace, for example, the result for society is not much different than if the balancing were prescribed by the legislature.

Some economic systems tend to produce a rough-and-ready equality, others a marked *in*equality. Each condition has political implications. The social justice that liberals seek is usually described in terms of economic equality, the rich and the poor faring more or less the same, while vast inequalities seem not only unjust to some but also politically dangerous. Struggles between the haves and have-nots were particularly destabilizing in Plato's Athens, which is one reason why Plato recommended that the Guardians in his ideal republic possess no property whatsoever. In our own time, of course, struggles over economic equality led to the great communist revolutions of the twentieth century.

There is one further connection between economics and politics in the shaping of a founding. Property itself has a double meaning. Economically speaking, property in the form of capital—land, machinery, liquid assets—is what makes the world work. Politically speaking, property creates power. The owners of vast wealth often get their way in the political world, by one means or another, while those who are penniless often get pushed around. Political independence often depends on economic independence, a fact well appreciated by the American Founders. For a citizen to stand up and be counted, especially on an issue of controversy, he or she must be beholden to no one.

For these and other reasons, the economic dimension must always be considered in addressing the problem of government.

Founders' Tool Kit

The founders of successful political states have a kind of tool kit to draw upon, consisting of ideas, concepts, and institutions that have worked well in the past. We should be aware of some of the most important tools in the kit:

1. Structure

After carefully studying the constitutions of various Greek city-states, Aristotle concluded that some of them worked a lot better than others, and that political *structure* often accounted for the difference. For, as the philosopher noted, people seemed to behave differently in different structured relationships. A small legislative body, for example, tended to be more cool and deliberative than a large one, which was moved more easily by passion and rhetoric. Same players, different game. And often a different outcome.

2. Participation

Encouraging participation of the citizens themselves helps to shape a political society in beneficial ways. Even if they did tend to be more stable, the Greek *poleis* (plural of *polis*) run by tyrants or oligarchs could not match democratic Athens for energy or creativity. For when the ordinary citizens can vote, hold office, and take part in political deliberations, they acquire a sense of ownership. The public world becomes their own world.

3. Law

The ancient Greeks left the world another important legacy in the domain of law. Law had existed before, of course, notably in Israel and Mesopotamia, but the Greeks learned that laws of a certain kind had a profound effect on the political process. General rules, known to all, made by common consent, and applied impartially reduced the scope of arbitrary action in the political arena. When such rules existed, the rulers themselves felt bound by them, and all players had a better chance in the game.

4. Custom and Tradition

Successful foundings can draw upon elements of custom and tradition, even when these fail to make good sense. The English, for example, had the idea of "sanctuary," holding that a hunted fugitive, upon entering some holy place or touching some sacred object, could not be taken directly into custody. To be sure, this custom may not have made for good law enforcement, but it did create a concept of privacy—places that the authority of government couldn't violate—which would become part of the American Founding centuries later.

5. Moral Sense

Almost without exception, successful political societies depend on shared values, common notions of right and wrong, an innate human *moral sense*. Government has a lot less to worry about if there is agreement on such fundamentals. For some, this raises a troubling philosophical question: is there really such a thing as moral truth, something to which all polities must adhere? While the question is sometimes answered negatively, history affords few examples of enduring nations based on "anything goes."

6. Founding Myths

We have seen that when the gods participated in a founding, it stood a better chance of success. Not all *founding myths* necessarily invoke the divine. Some are simply based on a shared belief, such as in America where a poor boy can go from "rags to riches." While this particular belief may not be statistically valid, it operates much in the way that myths of old did, creating a sense of identity and belonging. Founding myths often provide the real sinews of nationhood.

7. Leadership

Could there have been an Israel without Moses, a Rome without Caesar, an Athens without Solon or Cleisthenes? While we shy away from such thoughts in the modern world—how about a Soviet Union without Stalin or a Nazi Germany without Hitler—history affords few examples of leaderless foundings. It may sound democratic to say "the people came together and decided to act," but in point of fact "the people" almost always respond to initiatives from the bold, the daring, the visionary. The American republic would be no different.

There were other tools in the tool kit, and we will have occasion to examine some of them later. Suffice it to say, the creation of a new political society was no simple task.

The Social Compact

Some philosophers of the European Enlightenment envisioned foundings as a *social compact*. That is, people living in a "state of nature," before government, in a sense came together and worked out a common agreement about the sort of political world they wanted to live in. We see many of the tools in our kit reflected in this key idea.

The social compact remained largely theoretical. With few exceptions, there were no historical instances of free and autonomous individuals meeting to forge a nation-state. Yet the concept was still credible. In the history of, say, France or England, through wars and conquests, revolutions and accommodations, the French and later the English had indeed worked out something like a general agreement about their identity, their common purpose, and the manner of their governance. The very fact that they called themselves French or English, that they took pride in those labels, and that they were not constantly seeking to overthrow their respective monarchs suggested a tacit accord among them.

The Granger Collection, New York

A nineteenth-century engraving of Americans gathered at the Constitutional Convention in 1787 to draft a social compact and create a government.

The social compact had startling implications for the American Founding, where from the beginning nothing was tacit and everything was deliberate. The American colonies were *created*, basically from scratch, by groups with specific purposes in mind, and foundational issues were raised at the very outset. As the colonies grew to maturity, their charters were revoked in some cases, replaced in others, renegotiated in still others, so that Americans grew up thinking about constitutional questions. There was evolution and development, of course, but it was always with an eye to getting matters straight, nailing them down, working out satisfactory arrangements.

When the great controversy with Britain began in earnest, the air was filled with rhetoric about the social compact. Who had agreed to what? Under what circumstances? By whose authority? With what justification? Over and over, it was "the English constitution" this and "the rights of Britons" that and "the laws of nature" something else. How were things established? Americans asked. How *ought* they to be established? And where do *we* fit in?

The most important implication of the social compact was that the American people, as a people, gradually came to see that they could create whatever political society they chose, state by state or together as a nation, according to their hopes and dreams, their ideas and values, their understanding of the past, their conception of the future, their sense of common destiny. When some fifty-five of them gathered in Philadelphia in the spring of 1787 and regarded one another across baize-covered tables, there was no thought that they were mere spectators in the drama of life—they were on center stage, before a hushed audience, with the thrill of a rising curtain. They meant to tackle the problem of government once and for all.

Chapter 2

City upon a Hill

The United States of America grew from a set of colonies "planted" by Great Britain. These colonies were established by a variety of groups for a variety of purposes, and there was a good deal of learning as the colonizers gained experience. Some of the colonies were business ventures, aiming to promote corporate (and by extension, national) wealth, precisely as a company might set up an outpost in Antarctica today to explore for minerals. Others were sanctuaries for groups seeking religious freedom. Still others began as feudal fiefdoms for great nobles of the realm. One colony, Georgia, was set up as a refuge for the poor, while another, New York, was captured from the Dutch in a maritime war. In time, the significance of the colonies broadened, deepened, and took on peculiar overtones. To understand these new connotations, we need to reflect for a moment upon the discoverer of the New World, Christopher Columbus, for he cast a long shadow on the American future.

Columbus

The Genoese mariner we know as Columbus has been accused of power-madness and gold fever, the destruction of Native Americans, the building of an empire, and the despoliation of the natural world. In some respects, he stands guilty as charged. His character mirrored both the irony and paradox of Renaissance Europe; he was a complex and many-sided man.

Library of Congress

A sixteenth-century engraving of Christopher Columbus, the "Admiral of the Ocean Sea."

We forget, however, that Columbus was also an idealist and a visionary who believed that God was guiding him. What's more, history supported this belief. He had amazing luck in catching the right winds, the right tides, and the right ocean currents in crossing the Atlantic and returning to Spain, and on more than one occasion he emerged from fearful scrapes by what seemed like miraculous means. He survived shipwreck, mutiny, blood-soaked rivalries, bad food, exotic illnesses, and political betrayal, only to die at home in bed.

When it became clear that he had reached, not India, but a "new world," Columbus began to emphasize his discovery's beauty, bounty, and salubrity:

> This island is fertile to a limitless degree. In it there are many harbors on the coast of the sea, beyond comparison with others which I know in Christendom, and many rivers, good and large, which are marvelous. Its lands are high, and there are in it very many sierras and very lofty mountains. All are most beautiful, of a thousand shapes, and all are accessible and filled with trees of a thousand kinds and tall, and they seem to touch the sky. . . . Some of them were flowering, some bearing fruit, and some in another stage, according to their nature. And the nightingale was singing, and other birds of a thousand kinds in the month of November there where I went. . . . In it are marvelous pine groves, and there are very large tracts of cultivatable lands, and there is honey, and there are birds of many kinds, and fruits in great diversity. In the interior are mines of metals, and the population is without number.

By the time Columbus had reached the mouth of the Orinoco River, he believed he had located the Garden of Eden.

These perceptions also reflected the world from which Columbus had sailed. Europe was tired at the end of the fifteenth century. Corruption, dishonor, and violence lay everywhere—the world of Shakespeare's *Romeo and Juliet*. Protracted wars had devastated both England and France. The Catholic Church was divided and discredited, and soon it would be engulfed by the Protestant Reformation. Turkish warlords had pushed their way to the Danube. Given this troubled state of affairs, it was unsurprising that artists and writers of the time dwelled almost obsessively on escapist themes, and especially on the idea of mythic lands beyond the sunset—Avalon and Lyonesse, the Golden Cities of Cibola, the Fortunate Isles, the Isles of the Blest, Utopia. These were all imagined places of beauty and bounty, where life was long and full of promise. Poets supposed that if someone could discover such a paradise, it might enable jaded

The Granger Collection, New York

This 1835 American engraving depicts Columbus landing in the New World, which he believed was the Garden of Eden.

Europeans to start over again, rediscover innocence, and return to first principles. Consider, for example, the report of another navigator, describing the islanders of Hispaniola:

> They go naked, they know neither weights nor measures, nor that source of all misfortunes, money; living in a golden age, without laws, without lying judges, without books, satisfied with their life, and in no wise solicitous for the future. With neither ditches, nor hedges, nor walls to enclose their domains, they live in gardens open to all. Their conduct is naturally equitable, and whoever injures his neighbor is considered a criminal and an outlaw.

Inspired by similar dreams, Christopher Columbus came to believe he had been led to America, and that America might have a role to play in the moral life of Europe. We should keep the Columbian legacy in mind as we see how Britain's colonies began to grow and develop.

Corporate Communities

English settlement in Virginia was conceived as a corporate undertaking. The idea was for a joint-stock company of merchants to send a work party across the sea, set up operations, and then develop a profitable enterprise such as fishing, furring, timbering, or gold mining. Because there would be no official local government in far-away Virginia (the name referred to the entire coastline), the Virginia Company had to exercise powers of government among its American operatives, and it acquired the authority to do so through a royal charter. This document, which was signed and sealed by King James I in 1606, sketched out the organization of the company and described its civil authority. Right from the beginning, Americans would live under a constitution.

Life in Jamestown, as the first settlement was called, proved to be much tougher than anyone had imagined. The elements were harsh. Supplies were scarce. Incompetence and disorder often prevailed. The sort of people who liked to style themselves as adventurers were not often those accustomed to hard labor, and in any case they weren't sure whether to plant crops or search for gold. In the starving time that followed the exhaustion of their immediate supplies, wave

By 1622, Jamestown had become an established colony and discovered its cash crop—tobacco.

upon wave of settlers perished from illness or malnutrition, and in such numbers that there were often few left to dig the graves. The colonists struggled to develop some sort of profitable enterprise, and they failed repeatedly. Costs mounted. The Virginia Company teetered on the edge of bankruptcy. On top of everything, there was an Indian war.

A clash of cultures between Europeans and Native Americans was inevitable. Almost everything prized by the one was scorned by the other. Matters came to a head—as they would in most of the colonies—over land. For the Europeans, land was property, a purchasable and exploitable resource, the basis of all human wealth. For the Native Americans, land was sacred and free as the air or the water. Otherness also came to figure in. Europeans assumed that any people so different from themselves must be inferior, which gave them further justification for exploiting and dispossessing them.

When the Indians had had enough, they mounted a bold surprise attack and almost drove the invaders into the sea. The English counterstroke was equally vicious, and in the end it pushed the Indians out of the tidewater and into the wilderness. The Virginia Company declared bankruptcy in 1624 and was taken over by the English crown. That might have spelled the end. But Jamestown was no longer a company outpost in the narrow sense, nor were Virginians any longer mere adventurers. Somewhere along the way, John Rolfe and other settlers had finally come up with a business enterprise that worked—the cultivation of tobacco. It was a difficult undertaking, involving a lot of guesswork, and neither Rolfe nor anyone else knew exactly what they were doing. Yet they learned quickly, while their countrymen in England took up the smoking habit. Virginia, which had been a charnel house and burial ground and the worst investment imaginable, was suddenly in the black.

Nova Britannia.

OFFERING MOST

Excellent fruites by Planting in
Virginia.

Exciting all such as be well affected
to further the same.

London
Printed for Samvel Macham, and are to be sold at
his Shop in Pauls Church-yard, at the
Signe of the Bul-head.
1 6 0 9.

The Granger Collection, New York

This 1609 pamphlet advertised Virginia as a land of economic opportunity.

Tobacco was a labor-intensive crop, however, and labor became the basic difficulty of colonial agriculture. One solution to the problem was indentured servitude, where farmers in Virginia would pay the passage of those willing to come over in exchange for an agreed-upon term of service. After, perhaps, seven years of hard and unremitting toil, the indentured servant was released from his obligation, given some land, some seed, perhaps a few tools, and was now free to seek his own fortune.

Another solution to the labor problem was to import African slaves. These too were viewed as indentured servants—at first. But their indentures never quite seemed to run out. A combination of racial prejudice, fears of "otherness," and unabashed greed operated to hold the blackamoors, as they were called, in perpetual bondage.

Slaves excepted, many willingly came to Virginia in pursuit of their fortunes. No matter how bad things got, the privilege of tilling one's own land, living in one's own house, and taking charge of one's own life was a powerful draw to those who had been landless and essentially homeless for generations. Even after the failure of the Virginia Company, emigrants continued to come over as simple farmers, humble artisans, or lowly indentured servants. The English saw America as a place of opportunity.

It was also a place of self-invention. Many small farmers in Virginia became large farmers, even "planters," for land was cheap and easily acquired. These self-made planters began putting on airs of gentility. A bigger house, an imposing barn, furnishings imported from London, a carriage rattling down the dusty country roads— these were symbols of a social station to which only birth could admit one in the Old World. It wasn't a common phenomenon, but it became an important one. Where cheap land was available, virtually anyone could pry open the doors of social advancement.

When the troublous times ended and the Jamestown beachhead grew into the Virginia colony, it presented its inhabitants with a ticklish problem of governance. The old company governors had been replaced by a royal governor appointed by the king. The governor, in turn, appointed a council from a few prestigious local families,

Meeting of the Assembly in the Settlement of Virginia.

A nineteenth-century engraving of a meeting of the colonial Virginia House of Burgesses.

and together governor and council ran the day-to-day affairs of the colony. But there was an important innovation. Virginians themselves wanted to have a voice in their own governance, and willy-nilly they had begun electing representatives to meet in an annual assembly they called the House of Burgesses, passing ordinances, approving taxes, and now giving the royal governor—who after all was an outlander—a local perspective on things. Crown officials were never entirely happy with this arrangement, and more than once they tried to throttle it. But the arrangement persisted, mostly because the colonists themselves strongly supported it.

In a rough-and-ready way, the governing institutions of England (now Great Britain) were coming to be mirrored in New World practice. The crown-appointed governor took the place of royal authority back home. The governor's council acted like the British House of Lords, backing up royal authority and exercising a sort of veto power. And the House of Burgesses behaved quite a bit like the House of Commons in Westminster, discussing, debating, often dragging its feet, and, above all, jealously guarding the power of the purse.

In time, Virginians began to gain hands-on political experience, again, like their counterparts back in London. They learned the standard parliamentary procedures and, with practice, a few parliamentary tricks as well. They learned how to threaten; how to cajole; how to bargain and negotiate; how to hold governors in line by subtle means, such as controlling the amount of their salary; how to counter the thrusts of royal policy. Above all, Virginians learned how to represent the interests of their various constituencies. Tobacco planters, let us say, had a clear and cogent interest in policies that were friendly to their particular enterprise, and the representatives they sent to the House of Burgesses came to understand just how to make the weight of that interest fully felt.

So it was that Virginians came to enjoy the blessings of liberty. It had happened without conscious intention, a somewhat free dividend of the colonial experience. Settlers more or less ran their own political institutions, and in consequence they were able to run their own private lives as well. Royal government in Virginia was too tenuous and too far from home to be harsh or tyrannical. It could only function in cooperation with those it presumed to govern, and thus it wound up doing their bidding most of the time. Of course there were exceptions, and life in Virginia was still punctuated by the occasional crisis. Gradually, however, Virginians began counting their blessings. They had found something in America that was deeply and primarily important to them.

Covenant Communities

Virginia, the oldest British colony in the New World, became a model for other corporate communities. Indeed, the Virginia experience came to be reflected in all of the colonies to a certain extent. Americans still acknowledge the importance of Jamestown, but they identify even more deeply with a much smaller colony on the rocky shores of Cape Cod. Every Thanksgiving that sense of identification is symbolically renewed. It lies close to the heart of something we think of as quintessentially "American."

The group we call Pilgrims was actually a small congregation of separatists seeking to distance themselves, physically and spiritually, from the Church of England, which often failed to please religious purists. This particular group, the followers of Robert Brown, was certainly that. According to Brown's teachings at Cambridge University,

Pilgrims going to church. The Pilgrims established Plymouth as a covenant community based on their religious beliefs.

"God's people"—those whom he had specifically chosen for salvation—would always be very small in number, and they would *never* be mired in the corruptions of an entity like the English Church. Inspired by Brown's teachings, the Pilgrims packed up and left England to its fate. After a sojourn in the Netherlands, where once again they saw compromise and corruption all around them, they made a second exodus, this time to the distant shores of the Atlantic, landing at a place near Cape Cod that they christened Plymouth.

Unlike the Virginia Company, which had enjoyed the patronage of the English government, the Brownist Pilgrims were literally on their own. They too faced starvation, harsh winters, and problematic relations with the Indians. Like the merchant-adventurers, many Pilgrims succumbed to the trials of New World life. "Yet it is not with [us] as it is with other people," wrote William Bradford in his *History of Plymouth Plantation*, meaning that no matter what happened they would never throw in the towel. Their courage in the face of staggering hardship is one reason why we honor them still.

The settlement at Plymouth operated as a "covenant community." One of the Pilgrims' primary beliefs was that God's chosen people covenanted with him—*and* with one another—to live according to the divine plan governed by God's will. As they formed congregations, these covenants tied them together. The salvation of each was bound up with all the others.

While religious in nature, the covenant had a secular dimension. It was almost precisely analogous to the social compact discussed in chapter 1. The mutual promise to "bear one another's burdens" made it possible for the members of a congregation to form their own government, decide on its organization, and determine how each saint would participate in it. In doing so, they made use of many of the tools described in our tool kit. A fundamental equality before God made it possible for them to govern themselves—for there were no permanent rulers set over them.

The deepest meaning of Thanksgiving today is its symbolism of divine protection in the face of monstrous difficulties. That the Pilgrims possessed such confidence in God was due in no small measure to the strength of their beliefs and to the kind of polity they were able to build on such a foundation. Like Columbus, they found more on the western side of the world than they had expected. They believed they were a chosen people and that God's special protection was a daily manifestation in their lives. That quality of "chosenness" seems to have become part of the broader American experience.

The settlers of Plymouth became forerunners of a much larger migration of dissidents from the Church of England, who ten years later settled further north. We refer to this latter group as the Puritans.

While the Puritans shared some doctrinal beliefs with their Brownist cousins, the Puritans were not complete separatists. They wanted to reform the Church of England, not sever all ties with it, and even though they felt unwelcome back home, they were not completely on their own in America. Accordingly, the Puritans' model of colonization bore some likeness to that of Jamestown, based in a joint-stock corporation seeking to establish commercial activities across the Atlantic. The Puritans secured a royal charter, just as the Virginia Company had, and with it came a title to a vast stretch of the northern coast. It was another case of American opportunity beckoning.

The Puritans made the most of it. Some of them set to farming, clearing the stony soil, and planting a variety of crops. Others embarked upon fishing, fur trading, and timbering ventures, which led toward shipbuilding and then navigation. Still others took up mercantile enterprises, and Puritan merchants became some of the best in the world, trading local products in an expanding transAtlantic network. Like their English compatriots in Virginia, the Puritans eventually discovered ways of making the New World into a complete world.

Business aside, however, the Puritans were a people of exceptionally strong beliefs, and many of those beliefs have become associated in one way or another with aspects of the American Founding. It is noteworthy, for example, that the Puritans brought their charter along with them rather than leaving it back in London, for once it crossed the ocean their colony became a self-governing republic. Beyond this, Puritan New England—the colonies of Massachusetts Bay, Connecticut, New Haven, and Rhode Island—became in some sense the birthplace of many American ideas and institutions, perhaps even the cradle of the American character.

To begin with, Puritan towns were all covenant communities, precisely like Plymouth, and as such they were politically viable from

The Beginnings of New England by Clyde O. DeLand. Puritans believed they glorified God by building up their community and helping each other.

the start. Each town (formed by a separate congregation) worked out its own power structure, its own machinery of government, its own body of law. In each there was provision for general participation in the political process—very different from English practice of the time—by way of voting or holding office. In putting their town governments together, the Puritans drew upon biblical precepts, English law, and a strong foundation of shared values. If nothing else, Puritans believed they knew the difference between right and wrong.

Puritan religious beliefs would also affect American nationhood. In particular, we must consider three of these: God's Elect, the Christian Calling, and Moral Self-Governance.

God's Elect

In the theology of John Calvin, who inspired the Puritans more than anyone else, God chooses in advance those who will be saved and those who will be damned. The latter, which accounted for most of the people on earth, were sensuous and sinful, and nothing could be expected from them but trouble.

The saved, on the other hand, were obliged to illuminate an otherwise dark world. The very fact that Puritans had come together, recognized one another, organized themselves, and were now undertaking this monumental mission for the Lord attested to their cosmic importance. The elect, as they called themselves, must go on to build the godly community, and it truly must be *godly* in every way.

This meant that for the Puritans almost everything had a moral dimension. Farmers, merchants, and factory owners were enjoined to deal fairly with one another, with employees, with customers, and with the public at large. Sin was everybody's business, vice, everybody's problem. If the Puritan community was tainted by drunkenness, fornication, heresy, or witchcraft, no one could turn a blind eye. Accordingly, politics was not so much about power and privilege as it was about good and evil, right and wrong.

The Christian Calling

Calvin scorned those Christians who attempted to reach an exalted state of holiness by retiring into the monasteries and convents. All people were sinners, he taught—at least until they received God's grace—and one of the worst sins was supposing that one could emulate God through a life of self-denial.

Instead, Calvin believed that Christians should be "workers in the world." They should face up to their flawed humanity and be content to live the life of mere mortals. Instead of emulating God, they ought to glorify God by showing forth his great works. Building the godly community was the principal task before them.

Workers in the world pursued a "calling." Some were called to be brick masons, others to be ironmongers, still others to be merchants, and so on. All were obliged to rise early in the morning, work hard, save their money, and invest it wisely. And all, of course, must walk uprightly before the Lord.

If God was pleased with this manner of worship, he would manifest it by enabling the faithful to prosper. So if one looked around and saw well-tended orchards and freshly painted barns, if one beheld bustling towns and busy wharves, if the balances on the ledger books remained safely in the black, these were signs of God's pleasure. His kingdom was very much of this world.

Moral Self-Governance

Puritans believed in universal standards of right and wrong. All must live a righteous life, and they must do so, moreover, largely on their own. Each man must be responsible for his own actions and those of his family—with an eye on his neighbor as well. There was no penal system in Puritan New England, apart from a few implements of public humiliation, so law and order were more or less up to the individual.

It was but a short step from moral self-governance to political self-government. The very reason that Puritans could trust ordinary citizens to vote wisely and hold political office was due to this similarity. Just as the ancient Greeks had believed all citizens could recognize "the Good" and act accordingly, American Puritans believed that all of God's elect could recognize fundamental truth and shape their lives to it. Politics was held on course by a strong sense of individual accountability.

Puritan ideas and institutions remained influential in America long after Puritanism itself burned out. For one thing, the Puritans had relevant things to say about the problem of government, as discussed in chapter 1. For another, the Puritans had mirrored the assumptions of Christopher Columbus about the world he had discovered. It was a blank slate, they believed, a *tabula rasa*, on which mankind could begin the human story anew—and this time get it right.

City upon a Hill

Let us choose a single example for the purpose of illustration. While still aboard the *Arbella*, Puritan magistrate John Winthrop made a speech that invoked a remarkable image. "We shall be as a city upon a hill," he said. "The eyes of all people are upon us." This may have been the first iteration of what was to become the idea of America.

What Winthrop meant was that he and his fellow Puritans were going to show the world what God could write upon that *tabula rasa*. His city upon a hill would be nothing less than a vision of the world as God had intended it to be, the world recast according to holy principles. In a later speech, for example, Winthrop delved into the nature of liberty, explaining the difference between natural and civil

The Granger Collection, New York

John Winthrop said that the Puritan community would become "as a city upon a hill" and "the eyes of all people are upon us."

liberty. The difference would be crucial to that city upon a hill. Given natural liberty, men were free to do precisely what they pleased, Winthrop argued, and the sad state of the world reflected the choices that most of them made. In the Puritan commonwealth, by contrast, men would enjoy civil liberty, where one was free to do only that which was good, just, and honest.

Winthrop's city upon a hill was a little like Plato's ideal republic. It was to be as near to perfection as a flawed and sinful world would allow. It would include many of the attributes that political philosophers had imagined of the Good Society:

- Reasonable order, created by the people themselves.
- Reasonable prosperity for everyone.
- A strong, vibrant culture, prizing such things as science and literature.
- Peaceful toward others, yet strong and well respected.
- Citizens in charge of their own lives, yet in pursuit of common goals.

Freighted with such qualities, Winthrop's city upon a hill was what we might call a founding myth. It tapped into the power of several other myths, stretching far back into history. One of these was the myth of the Garden—that Eden which Columbus believed he glimpsed at the mouth of the Orinoco—promising a return to some lost golden age. A second was the myth of the Promised Land, the land of milk and honey that God had held before the eyes of ancient Israel. And a third was the myth of the New Jerusalem, that heavenly city of the future in which the Judeo-Christian saga would achieve ultimate fulfillment. Combining all three, the city upon a hill provided a way for Americans to think about their country, and in the process provided them with a unique sense of identity.

Something like the city upon a hill seems to have been in the back of patriots' minds when they resisted the Stamp Act, cast tea into Boston Harbor, and opened fire at Lexington Green. It was reflected again in the determination of the Philadelphia delegates to push ahead with their task of writing a constitution in spite of daunting difficulties. It may have been on Henry David Thoreau's mind when he wrote about living deliberately, and on Ralph Waldo Emerson's when he wrote about self-reliance. It explains the willingness of Grant's troops to charge the Confederate fortifications at Cold Harbor, knowing in advance that most of them would be killed. It helps us to understand America's participation in the war against Hitler, and its determination to stop Soviet Communism at all costs. It also helps us make sense of the difficult and costly war against Saddam Hussein.

The city upon a hill helps us to better understand English settlement across the Atlantic. It was not simply a story of colonization. It was a story of the westward movement of something vital that had characterized European civilization. America offered hopes and dreams to ordinary people—those whom the world had almost entirely overlooked. We see this in the eager push into the Virginia tidewater and in the confident towns that sprang up in New England.

Despite the wish to preserve their European heritage, colonists in America were already living a different life. They were working out new kinds of political institutions. They were breaking new ground in economics. And they were applying religious metaphors to both.

Chapter 3

The English Legacy

The irony of the American Revolution was that it claimed to be a revolt against British tyranny and yet it sought to recover lost or threatened English rights. This irony affirms the importance of English/British ideas and institutions to the American Founding. At the same time, it affirms a deep-seated fear that the qualities of a free society, be they European or American, may be lost easily.

We saw in chapter 2 that early in their colonial career Americans began developing rough facsimiles of English political institutions, such as representative assemblies. There was much else of importance in the English legacy. In this chapter we will examine three critical elements of that legacy and think about their relevance to the American Founding.

Lockean Liberty

The idea of freedom has long existed in political discourse, going back at least as far as the ancient Greeks. Until quite recently, however, freedom had other meanings than the one we use today, most of them focusing on participation in the political process. During the seventeenth century—the century of American colonization—there developed in England a wholly new concept of freedom, the freedom of the individual to live his own life and be his own person without interference. As opposed to the older idea of freedom *in* society, this was freedom *from* society.

This development was the result of an intellectual revolution that drastically altered our assumptions about the world. From today's vantage point, we look back and wonder how people could have practiced slavery in the American South, how indentured servants could have been treated like cattle, and how laborers could have been shot down in the streets for going on strike. The answer in all three cases is that we are looking back across the gulf created by the liberal (meaning freedom) revolution. True, practice was slow to catch up with theory but when it finally did so, our lives were changed forever.

The new idea of freedom—rechristened "liberty"—became bound up with both the American Revolution and the American Founding. Yet it flowed from the pen of an Englishman and addressed a situation that could have developed in no other country but his. We need to pause and examine what happened in seventeenth-century England and understand why that era of turmoil and conflict still shapes our lives today.

The Granger Collection, New York

King James I by Daniel Mytens, 1621. The Stuart kings of England, including James I, believed kings ruled by the pleasure of God and did not have to answer to anyone.

England's Time of Trouble

When Queen Elizabeth I died without heirs in 1603, the English throne fell to her next of kin, King James VI of Scotland, who became England's James I. The new monarch arrived in Westminster with a pronounced Scottish accent and some disconcerting ideas. James Stuart—and virtually all of his heirs on the throne—had no background in, and still less patience with, troublesome law courts or foot-dragging parliaments. As far as James I was concerned, kings ruled by the pleasure of God alone and never had to answer to anyone.

Stuart claims of ruling by

the "divine right of kings," as the doctrine was called, were destined to clash repeatedly both with the English law courts and the English Parliament. Certain judges in the law courts would maintain that the law was primary and fundamental, and that the king himself was bound to obey it. Certain members of Parliament would maintain that their institution alone could make changes in the law and that no taxes could be levied without parliamentary approval. Neither the courts nor the Parliament bought into the divine right of kings.

Tensions between the two sides mounted slowly, decade after decade, and ultimately led to civil war. In 1649, Parliament emerged victorious from the war, and beheaded Charles I—the Stuart monarch. For the next ten years, Parliament ruled England in a kind of legislative dictatorship. However, when Charles II was restored to his father's throne in 1660, the bickering and wrangling resumed. Stuart kings continued pressing for divine right prerogatives, and their opponents continued disputing their claims. Thoughtful Englishmen wondered about the positive and negative outcomes of this seemingly irresolvable issue. Some came to realize that England lacked a true constitution, for there was no final authority to embody the realm's sovereignty.

When James II assumed the throne in 1685, matters seemed destined for another showdown. In addition to the divine right bias of the Stuarts, James II had become a Catholic, and his reign threatened a resurgence of the religious wars of an earlier time. At this point a strange thing happened. A nobleman of the realm, Sir Anthony Ashley Cooper, Earl of Shaftsbury, began to organize the opposition to the king *politically*—as we might think of doing today. The "Whigs," as Shaftsbury's compatriots called themselves, were in essence England's first political party. They were also the spiritual ancestors of the American patriots, many of whom would call themselves by the same name.

But they opposed the king on what grounds? After all, James II *was* the ruler of England, Catholic or not, and the fact that most of his subjects loathed his person and feared his rule might be irrelevant. Lord Shaftsbury's personal secretary, a young man named John Locke, went to work on this problem. Locke was highly intelligent and extremely well educated, with a philosophical turn of mind. He developed a pair of treatises that addressed the entire question of rulers and their claims to authority. Locke questioned whether the doctrine of divine right was valid. If not, then what was it that legitimized a sovereign's rule?

The Second Treatise

Locke's *Second Treatise on Government* became one of the masterworks of Western civilization and a direct inspiration for the American Founders. It argued, compellingly, that the authority of all legitimate government is not God or history or genealogy, but rather the people themselves. It was a careful argument, meticulously crafted, and we should know its outlines well.

Locke's first point was that in the original "state of nature"—a hypothetical condition assumed to exist in the absence of government—human beings must have lived in perfect freedom and general equality. In such a world, moreover, all had the same rights, for "rights," by their very character, could not be granted by man, but only by nature. All had the right to live their lives, enjoy their liberty, and make the most of their property, as long as they did not disturb the rights of others.

Library of Congress

A lithograph of John Locke. In his *Second Treatise on Government*, Locke argues that all humans have rights and government should protect those rights.

Some few did disturb the rights of others, however, and so there was a manifest need for law and for a common judge to hear and decide disputes. Accordingly, Locke's second point indicated that individuals came together and agreed to establish government. There was no divine mandate for this social compact, only a simple need. Government was a human invention, made to serve a human purpose.

The character of that purpose was Locke's third principle. Government could have but a single end, he argued, and that was to protect the rights of citizens. (After all, why else had they created it?) Those rights could never be surrendered or abridged, for they had been granted by nature, but they could be disregarded. Government's job—its *only* job—was to make sure that didn't happen.

Government, then, existed only by the *consent* of the governed—Locke's fourth principle. The government must look to the people for its legitimacy; it could not presume to govern in God's name. There had to be accountability of some kind—elections, representation, parliaments—by which the governed had a chance to have their say.

Fifth and finally, if government violated the terms of consent, if it lost track of what it was supposed to do and whom it was supposed to serve, the people had the right, indeed the duty, to alter or abolish it, even if that meant revolution. Revolution was a powerful word in Stuart England, but John Locke employed it advisedly. If James II broke his compact with the English people, they had every right to cast him out, which is precisely what they did.

In 1688, shortly after the *Second Treatise* was written (but before its official publication), the English people rose against their king and expelled him from the country in a bloodless revolution. They then invited James's daughter Mary and her husband, William of Orange, to assume the throne as joint monarchs—*subject to the will of Parliament*. Thereafter, as they made clear, monarchs would rule England only by the active consent of the people.

Englishmen regarded this revolution, known as the Glorious Revolution, as a true founding. It confirmed what judges of the realm had been saying about the supremacy of the law, and what representatives of the people had been saying about the supremacy of Parliament.

XXVIII. WILLIAM *the* THIRD *and* MARY *the* SECOND, *from* 1688 *to* 1702.

WILLIAM the hero, with MARIA mild,
(He James's nephew, she his eldest child)
Fix'd freedom and the church, reform'd the coin;
Oppos'd the French, and settled Brunswick's line.

King William III and Queen Mary II, eighteenth-century English woodcut. William and Mary were the monarchs of England but subject to the will of Parliament.

It cemented the place of rights in English government. Above all, it confirmed Locke's theory of personal liberty, for if government only secured the rights of its citizens, the citizens were bound to enjoy their freedoms in abundant measure. They could do what they wanted with their lives. They could enjoy their liberty to the fullest. They could buy, own, improve, and sell their property. They could, as Jefferson would put it, pursue happiness.

In the turmoil that led to the American Revolution, the colonists would look back to the Glorious Revolution and John Locke's formulation of political truth. They had come to live in a Lockean world, one in which government literally was created by the people and rights seemed natural and fundamental. When Locke pointed out that the people had the right of revolution if the monarch let them down, they took it seriously.

The Rule of Law

Locke believed that these truths were derived from nature, reflecting the world as God had created it. This argument went back to the ancient world. The classical Greeks, followed in turn by the classical Romans, spoke a good deal about what they saw as "natural law." Natural law was the moral law, the law that resided in the human heart, the law that reflected our innate sense of right and wrong. It followed that natural law would protect natural rights. If there was, for example, a natural right to life, then there was a natural law against the arbitrary taking of life; and if there was a natural right to liberty, there was a natural law against slavery; and so on.

According to legal theorists like Cicero, the laws handed down by the great lawgivers, such as Moses or Hammurabi, were accepted by the people because they embodied natural law principles. The laws enacted by legislative bodies should, in principle, do the same. No legislature in the civilized world would dream of passing laws that condoned arbitrary murder, nor would judges smile benignly at theft, robbery, or burglary. In consequence, there came to be something mystical, almost ineffable, in the idea of law. Obedience to the law, under any and all circumstances, was the great political value of the ancient republics.

Such ideas persisted in seventeenth-century England. The great law courts that applied and slowly developed the English "common law" often took the view that they were "discovering" natural law principles. In consequence, the law was often regarded as a companion to freedom. Let us consider a couple of legal principles by way of example.

Who should be able to bring criminal charges against someone? If there is no *prima facie* case of wrongdoing—such as a thief caught in the act—the common law came to believe that charges should be brought only by a group of disinterested citizens empanelled as a grand jury. Otherwise, there was a clear temptation for political authorities to injure rivals or detractors simply by accusing them.

Or, on what grounds should a person be held in custody? Should a sheriff, for example, be able to arrest someone on suspicion of some crime and then simply lock him away until a trial became convenient? Once again, the common law judges said no. They evolved the writ of habeas corpus as an instrument to secure the release of anyone for whom there was insufficient evidence to hold.

Who should decide guilt or innocence? There were obvious dangers in allowing the government to do it. But what about some neutral party, such as a judge, someone who could bring learning and sophistication to the task? While there were arguments in favor of this solution, the common law evolved away from it and toward the use of juries. The "jury of one's peers," as the phrase goes, consisted of ordinary citizens like the accused. If *they* could be persuaded that the accused was guilty, the evidence had to be pretty convincing.

The law of nature applied not only to the legal process but to the political process as well. Should a king, for example, be given a free hand in taxing his subjects? What king wouldn't take full and probably unfair advantage of such a blank check? The famous Magna Carta laid down the natural law principle that the taxpayers themselves ought to have a say in such matters, and Parliament traced its roots to that day in 1215 when King John reluctantly agreed.

Even so, the experience of the tumultuous seventeenth century demonstrated that the law could still be misused. For instance, those who made the law could still use it for political ends, as in the notorious bills of attainder. There was a case in which Parliament, in a desperate move against Charles I, passed a bill pronouncing the Earl of Strafford—one of the king's evil counselors—guilty of treason and prescribing his punishment. It was all perfectly legal, wasn't it? asked the authors of the bill. After all, Parliament *was* the voice of the people!

Actually, it wasn't perfectly legal, but it took a long time and much thoughtful reflection before anyone could explain why. The problem, in four words, was *the rule of law*—possibly the single most important concept evolved by the English legal system. The rule of law provided a way of distinguishing between cases in which the law supported freedom and cases in which it didn't. It was not a law itself. It was a set of metalegal principles which, if respected, ensured that the law would be a beacon of liberty.

The rule of law encompassed a number of principles. The following five were uppermost:

1. Generality

The laws must be general. They must apply to broad categories of people. They must not single out individuals or groups for special treatment. If there is any such desig-  nating, it should be done by people themselves *after* the laws are passed. That is, I place *myself* in the category of drivers when I climb into my car and start the engine.

We would sense something wrong with a law that singled out the drivers of red Toyotas, for such an ordinance could also target Mormons, Southerners, or liberals. Those who make the laws should never know in advance to whom they apply. Lamentably, the British Parliament lacked that sort of blindness when it singled out Americans and began laying special taxes on them.

In practice we, too, create exceptions. We address some laws specifically to children, for example, forbidding them to purchase alcohol or drive a car; by zoning certain neighborhoods, we deny specific landowners the right of commercial development. Our tax code discriminates between rich and poor. Some of these laws violate the principle of generality and ought to be viewed with mistrust. Others are a practical necessity. There is no hard and fast way to tell which is which.

However, a few categories of designation have become absolutely taboo. These involve ethnicity, gender, religion, political affiliation, and increasingly, sexual preference. Above all, we abominate separate laws for the rich and the poor. "Equality under the law" has become one of freedom's great banners.

2. Prospectivity

The laws must apply to future action, not past. The theory is, of course, that the potential violator must always be able to decide *in advance* whether or not to obey. We

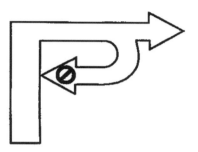

would see as unjust, for example, a law punishing those who failed to vote in the *past* election, because the opportunity for moral decision would be absent.

Tyrants and demagogues don't like this principle. The last thing a Hitler or Stalin would desire is for intended victims to evade sanctions by altering their behavior. *Ex post facto* laws—the term we give to violations of prospectivity—commonly single out an individual or group and in effect say, "We don't like what you did and you must be punished for it." Thus, most violations of generality also violate prospectivity, and vice versa. Together, these two abridgements of the rule of law account for much of the tyranny the world has known.

3. Publicity

The laws must be both known and certain. They must be well publicized so that everyone knows of their existence—the laws of tyrants are often kept secret—and their enforcement must be reasonably

reliable. Laws that are capriciously enforced, or else not enforced at all, do no favors for the rule of law. On the contrary, they sow public contempt.

But police apparatus is expensive, and so governments occasionally trim back by funding a mere token enforcement of the laws, hoping that the possibility of punishment, no matter how remote, will suffice to deter law-breakers. Some people will accept such gambles, betting they won't be caught. If government isn't serious about the laws, citizens won't be serious either.

Capricious enforcement was an aspect of British policy before the Revolution. It led to widespread smuggling on the part of colonials, and to customs racketeering on the part of the authorities. Later on, when the British sought to reform the system and enforce the Navigation Acts rigorously, Americans were outraged.

4. Consent

The laws must be generally acceptable to those who must live by them. Electing the lawmakers and upholding the constitutional system are examples of the way we give consent.

Yet not all lawmaking is subject to such formal approval. Natural law, customary law, and judge-made law are never submitted to the voters. What counts, however, is that the people, if they truly *dis*-like a certain law, have the means at their disposal to wipe it off the books. Theory holds that the people as a whole would never consent to injustice—because they themselves would be its victims. The theory only works, of course, when the laws are *also* general and prospective.

Consent becomes mandatory in the matter of taxation. Once the people themselves consent to the amount they will be taxed, the entire character of government is transformed. For if the lawmakers themselves have to pay taxes they approve, all incentives toward exploitation go out the window.

It was the absence of consent that brought on the American Revolution. Parliament was allowed to make laws for another group, the colonists, and was not accountable to those laws itself. There was nothing whatsoever to restrain it. Why *not* pass a Stamp Act? asked the members of Parliament. *They* didn't have to buy the stamps.

5. Due Process

The laws must be administered impartially. Justice, as the saying goes, must be blind, considering no questions other than guilt or

innocence. If the accused is black, or poor, or a communist, or a Christian Scientist, the law must say: So what? And there must be established procedures to insure that everyone is given a fair trial, an adequate defense, and, if guilty, a reasonable punishment.

Due process accounted for yet another sore spot in British-American relations. The British authorities had few qualms about revoking jury trial and other traditional rights in the interest of tighter law enforcement. If Americans were a bad risk, they said, then by all means let's close up those procedural loopholes. We often say the same thing about bad risks today.

Once the laws met all five of these tests, chances were that the rule of law was a working reality, and the result would be freedom. Under the rule of law, the laws of society become very much like the laws of nature—steady, evenhanded, predictable. We use the laws of nature to our advantage because we know in advance what they are and how they apply. Just as we don't have to step off a cliff in order to know whether gravity is working, so too we don't have to steal that shiny red Porsche in the parking lot in order to know if the laws against theft are in force. In societies without the rule of law, a person must in effect step off the cliff. He might steal the red Porsche and never get punished—because the laws were not working that day. Worse, he might decide *not* to steal the car and get punished all the same—because the laws were working in some unfathomable way. Under the rule of law, we alone determine what happens to us. That's how the law makes us free.

Virtue and Structure

After the Glorious Revolution, the Whigs became the essential rulers of England. Kings still sat on the English throne, but Parliament had to approve all of their royal commands. Yet Whig political thinkers continued to worry. Liberty had shown itself to be a fragile thing. If the power of the monarch was no longer a direct threat, other concerns were just as unsettling, and among these was the pattern of corruption that always seemed to appear in high places. There were some spectacular scandals in British politics, and they weren't just about money. Sometimes, the very governing body that checked the king's power mired itself in scandal.

The Whigs had a dark view of human nature, believing that those who gained power—even in their own Parliament—would probably misuse it. For answers to this difficulty, they turned once again to the ancient world. Their reading of Aristotle convinced them of the value of structure as one way of curtailing the misuse of power.

The idea was fairly simple. Aristotle, a careful student of constitutional forms, had noted that power in a relatively few hands always seemed to spell trouble. By contrast, if one mixed and balanced power among rival authorities in a constitutional system, chances were that no single one of them would amass enough power to do the others harm. The Whigs took some comfort in this, noting that in their own government the powers of the king were now shared with those of Parliament, that the House of Lords tugged and pulled against the House of Commons, and that all parties in government had to contend with the will of the judges. The phrase "checks and balances"—which would become crucial to the American Constitution—gained currency.

The British government became a model for Europe's premier political scientist, a Frenchman by the name of Charles-Louis de Secondat, Baron de la Brède et de Montesquieu. Living under an often corrupt and occasionally tyrannical monarchy, Montesquieu was filled with admiration for the British system. While it was unwise to say so too pointedly, he nonetheless made his preference clear. In his masterwork of

Baron de Montesquieu praised the English political system in *The Spirit of the Laws*, which was read by the American Founders.

comparative government, *The Spirit of the Laws* (1750), Montesquieu virtually argued for the genius of British institutions on every page. And the American Founders would comb through those pages with extreme care.

All the same, history afforded abundant examples of corruption leading to tyranny in governments that enjoyed mixed and balanced powers. Structure was important—but structure wasn't enough. In time, Whig writers developed an alternate approach to the problem of preserving liberty: the commonwealth ideology. The following is an outline of its main points.

Certain individuals will always be drawn to the center of political power, like moths to a flame. In Great Britain, the chief center of power was the royal court, consisting of the king and his favorites, some of whom also sat in Parliament and called themselves Tories. If unchecked, this "court party," as the Whigs called it, would draw more and more power to itself. If it couldn't openly challenge Parliament, it could resort to other means—the granting of honors, the bestowal of titles, the offering of bribes—for corrupting or subverting other authorities. A license here, a franchise there, political favors somewhere else could undermine the integrity of the body politic. And in the end, the court party would succeed in building up its own power—structure or no structure.

The court party, the Whigs concluded, could be held in check only by a political rival of equal weight and determination, "the country party." This group consisted of merchants, bankers, manufacturers, and especially landed gentlemen out in the shires. These "commonwealthmen" were economically and, consequently, morally independent; moreover, residing out in the country and close to the land kept their motives pure. They were the members of Parliament who really counted, the ones who must oppose the wiles and machinations of the court party at all cost.

Whig writers vested their heroes with a sense of ancient virtue. In ancient Greece, we recall, the quest for excellence was manifested in political life by the exercise of *aretē*, or virtue. Just as it was the *aretē* of the athlete to win contests, it was the *aretē* of the statesman to excel in such qualities as leadership, oratorical skill, and an uncompromising sense of honor. Plato had laid out four cardinal virtues, each of which was to count heavily with the English Whigs—wisdom, courage, temperance, and justice. In addition to these classical elements, the commonwealth writers factored in some Christian virtues as well, things like patience, humility, personal integrity, and brotherly love.

The virtuous patriot was supposed to behave in carefully prescribed ways. In circumstances where others might be hasty or foolish, he was supposed to be wise. In situations where others might lose heart, he was to be unflinchingly courageous. Above all, when others were being bought off and compromised, the virtuous patriot was the one who couldn't be corrupted—his independence shining like a beacon.

This was a lot to ask of the political world, which had never been known for sterling qualities, but the commonwealthmen were serious. They turned out dozens, even hundreds, of books and pamphlets arguing the commonwealth ideology and its importance for the preservation of liberty. One particularly noteworthy book, *Cato's Letters*, written by two Whig journalists named John Trenchard and Thomas Gordon, became a sort of bible of the country party. It circulated widely in Great Britain—and even more widely in the British colonies.

The Moral Basis of the Founding

In chapter 2 we pointed out that the American colonies began to gain political experience, and with this came a sense of political maturity. In large measure, these three inheritances from Great Britain provided the sum and substance of such maturity.

Americans read John Locke, along with other writers of the European Enlightenment, and they rejoiced in the triumph of the Glorious Revolution. They saw the victory of Parliament over the king and his cronies as the guarantee of American liberties. They resented any intimation that as "Americans" they were somehow stepchildren in the empire, and thus not fully qualified for the "rights" of Englishmen.

More important, perhaps, Americans had more or less come to live in a Lockean world. No one had planned it that way. Locke himself, who had played a role in colonizing the Carolinas, had not foreseen such a development. Yet here they were, these American colonists, living in a world where freedom seemed to emanate from the rocks and trees. The colonists were coming together, organizing their own governments, taking part in the political process, spelling out their rights in little documents that would soon be called bills of rights, asserting a kind of moral independence from the Old World. Out on the frontier, where social controls were particularly weak, Americans were living their lives in Locke's state of nature.

Americans such as John Adams studied English law and conducted their own investigations of constitutional theory. Adams became a strong advocate of the rule of law. Indeed, after the infamous Boston Massacre in 1770, Adams took on the courtroom defense of the British soldiers who stood accused of murdering Boston colonists, believing that the whole thing had been a political matter, not a criminal one, and that criminal charges in such a case would undermine the rule of law. Adams demonstrated in court that the soldiers had fired into the crowd only after being goaded beyond human endurance.

Later on, when they drafted the Constitution, Americans carefully inserted provisions for generality, prospectivity, publicity, consent, and due process. When it came to designing the structure of the federal government, they tried to think of structure as a way of promoting rule-of-law outcomes. The way they separated the judicial branch and insulated it against political interference, for example, spoke of their desire for keeping rule making and rule enforcement in separate hands, so that the law could not be used to "get" someone.

In the Constitution, Americans created more checks and balances than the British system had, and invented a whole new structural idea they called "separation of powers." So complex did the federal system become that skeptics doubted it could work.

As for the commonwealth ideology, Americans adopted it as their own. They, too, read their Plato and Aristotle—works such as *The Republic, The Politics,* and *The Nicomean Ethics* were found in hundreds of private libraries. Dog-eared copies of *Cato's Letters* were read and reread in the colonies, and hotly debated in village taverns. When Washington sought entertainment for his troops, it was not dancing girls or stand-up comics but the production of Joseph Addison's play titled *Cato,* the general's personal favorite, recounting a story of Roman *virtu* against overwhelming odds.

THE PATRIOTIC AMERICAN FARMER.
J-N D-K-NS——N Esq.ʳ BARRISTER at]
Who with civic Eloquence and Roman Spirit hath
The Liberties of the BRITISH *Colonies in America.*

The Granger Collection, New York

John Dickinson as "The Patriotic American Farmer" by James Smither, 1768. The American version of the commonwealthman, Dickinson (a signer of the Declaration of Independence) was influenced by classical and British philosophy and history.

Virtually all of the American Founders saw themselves as commonwealthmen, and they played that role well. After all, they were men of independent means, beholden to no one, and most of them lived out in their country estates. America itself was the country, of course, both in the sense of country living and country as *patria*—far removed from the nefarious dealings of the court. There was one single important exception. Every place in the colonies where there resided a royal governor there was to be found a rough facsimile of the British court, right down to the tea-drinking and hand-kissing that made many Americans uncomfortable. When royal governors like Benning Wentworth and Robert Dinwiddie indulged to excess, or took bribes, or placed their henchmen in high office, Americans knew in advance what that meant. *The court strikes again—the country must stand fast.*

American piety played an important role in this response. We saw in chapter 2 how influential the Puritans were. Think of their city upon a hill in terms of court versus country. Think how a Puritan would react to the fear that agents of corruption and tyranny were attempting to corrupt *them* in order to fasten a yoke upon their necks.

For Americans, the English legacy became all important. Its three components fit together into a single whole, and the meaning of the whole was this: America had been blessed by God as a land of freedom, and it must resist any and all who would imperil that birthright.

Chapter 4

A Conflict of Interests

The abundant land across the Atlantic presented an unsurpassed economic opportunity for Europeans, especially for ordinary people. The contrast between England, where every square foot of land was owned (most by the king and nobles), and America, where millions of acres lay unclaimed, could not have been more stark. From 1600 to 1770, hundreds of thousands of ordinary men and women endured the Atlantic crossing to make their homes in North America. This chapter discusses the colonial economy and the influence of Adam Smith on the Founders.

Labor in the Colonies

Migrating from Liverpool or London to Boston or Philadelphia was an economic investment that paid substantial dividends. Labor in the colonies was scarce, and therefore more valuable than labor in England. With higher wages, a migrant could live better and eventually own land and begin climbing the economic ladder. The scarcity of labor also changed social and political relationships in the colonies. A wagon maker in Connecticut had to treat his apprentice with respect and dignity or risk losing the apprentice to a wagon maker in New York. A man who aspired to the colonial legislature had to watch his manners with the lower classes, because many of them would soon own property and be voting in the next election. America was a fluid social environment. There was no nobility by birth. When newly arrived immigrants looked at the wealthy landowner or merchant,

The Granger Collection, New York

A colonial potter assisted by an indentured servant, eighteenth-century American engraving. Many immigrants agreed to work for several years in exchange for passage to America.

they saw someone who had arrived a few years before them, worked hard, and with good fortune, succeeded. They expected to follow the same path themselves.

Indentured servitude offered many Europeans the chance to come to America. Since large numbers of the would-be immigrants could not afford the expensive passage across the Atlantic, poor migrants agreed to be servants for a period of time, say seven years, in exchange for passage and a small amount of money to get started after their service. Unfortunately, indentured servitude and free immigration did not fill the demand for labor in the Americas.

European colonists found the work of growing the plantation crops of rice, sugar, and tobacco to be unfamiliar, difficult, and something to be avoided. The general shortage of labor prompted colonies, particularly the Southern ones, to look for new sources of labor. African slavery filled this demand, but it also provided a deep and divisive challenge to the values espoused by the colonists. Several hundred thousand slaves were imported from Africa to the American colonies. The typical slave had been captured and enslaved by other Africans and then taken to the west coast of Africa. There, European or American ship owners purchased the slaves and brought them to the Americas, stretching from what is now the United States to Brazil; the largest numbers went to the Caribbean and Brazil. All of the American colonies used slaves, but during colonial times they

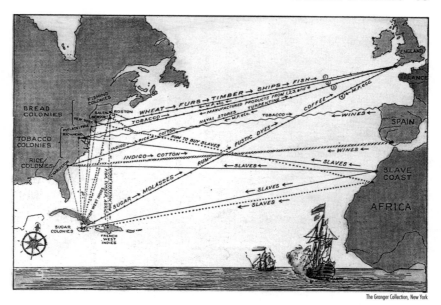

Seventeenth-century slave trade map. Slaves were imported to the colonies to help produce commodities that were sent to England.

were especially important for the production of tobacco in Virginia, naval stores (tar, turpentine, and pitch) in the Carolinas, and rice in South Carolina and Georgia. Slavery, along with indentured servitude and free immigration, partially satisfied the colonies' appetite for labor, though high wages and economic opportunities continued to attract migrants. By 1770 the colonial population had grown to about two and a half million people.

On the eve of the American Revolution, the colonists were rich by the standards of the day. They ate better and were taller than their British cousins. Though their homes were often rude huts or simple cabins, the colonists enjoyed plenty of space for growth. Their incomes were about the same as those in England, but they had much better economic opportunities. The colonists had developed new industries and crops, making them an integral part of the British Empire. Southern colonies exported tobacco, rice, indigo (a deep blue dye), naval stores, and timber. The middle colonies exported wheat and flour to the West Indies. Because of abundant wood and adequate iron ore, the colonies also exported iron bars to be made into iron manufactures in England and elsewhere. New England

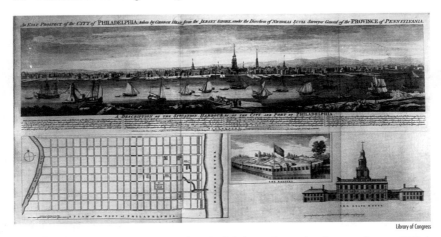

"An East Prospect of the City of Philadelphia" from the Jersey shore, 1754. Shipbuilding and trade became thriving industries in New England.

had to look to the sea for their exports. They sent good quality cod to Catholic Europe and the leftovers to the West Indies as food for slaves. They hunted whales for their oil and bone. With ample raw materials and high wages for skilled craftsmen, shipbuilding became a thriving industry from Boston to Baltimore. Ships and excellent harbors naturally led to a vigorous seafaring trade in the colonies, especially in New England. Yankee traders were soon pursuing profits throughout the world.

Economic prospects could not have been more rosy for the colonists. They had solved their labor problems through indentured servitude and slavery. They could already produce food at a lower cost than Britain. The colonists had excellent resources to exploit for profit. They would expand to the west if they could convince Britain to ignore the rights of the Native Americans occupying the land. Soon the colonies would become better at manufacturing goods as well. Unfortunately, the British king and Parliament had different ideas. For them, the colonies were an important cog in Britain's economic machine. Parliament and the king did not view their American colonies as an opportunity for ordinary Englishmen to get rich. For them, the empire existed to enrich the British treasury.

Mercantilism

From 1500 to 1800, mercantilism—the idea that the government should regulate the economy to strengthen national power—dominated English economic policy. What gave a nation power? For the mercantilists, the key to national power was large stockpiles of gold and silver to finance the army and navy necessary for an empire. But how could a nation build up its treasury of gold and silver? The primary way to bring gold and silver into a country was through a favorable balance of trade, where exports—goods sold to other countries—exceeded imports—goods purchased from other countries. Thus, the mercantilists wanted to encourage exports and discourage imports. If exports were greater than imports, other countries had to pay gold or silver to settle their accounts.

Consequently, mercantilists tried to manage the economy of the empire, including the economy of the colonies, in a way that would increase the quantity of gold and silver in the king's treasury. They encouraged domestic manufacturing to compete with imports. They prevented craftsmen and artisans from moving to other countries. They paid subsidies, or bounties, to encourage exports. In other words, the government managed the economy to further government interests.

As part of this overall effort, the British Parliament passed many economic regulations, referred to collectively as the Navigation Acts, and set up admiralty courts to enforce these trade regulations in the colonies. All trade had to go through British or colonial merchants and be shipped in British or colonial ships. Certain goods such as tobacco could only be shipped from the colonies to England, rather than directly to other countries. The end goal of all regulation was to generate large exports from England, with few imports, so that gold and silver would flow into the motherland.

The American colonists found the Navigation Acts and other British efforts to manage their economy frustrating and demeaning. Why couldn't the colonies sell tobacco or naval stores directly to the rich Dutch or to the French? Why were the colonists pushed to purchase everything from England and her other colonies? (Ninety-eight percent of imports to the colonies came from English lands.) George Washington found the regulations so irritating that he

The Granger Collection, New York

The Artisans of Boston, 1766. The artisans and craftsman of Boston felt burdened by British regulations and taxation.

stopped growing tobacco and tried to purchase domestic goods and become self-sufficient. The Navigation Acts were not an overwhelming burden to the colonists, but the acts were a nagging reminder to the colonists that they were subservient to the British Parliament and to British courts in matters of commercial policy. When King George, his ministers, and the Parliament decided to raise more revenue from the colonists with a series of taxes and fees, the colonists realized their position as dependents and second-class citizens of the empire. It was one thing to be subject to the same king as the people of England. It was quite another to have the English merchants and manufacturers collectively viewing the colonists as their subjects.

The Market Economy

As American colonial discontent was reaching its peak, a Scottish philosopher was writing a book that effectively attacked mercantilism and described the basic operation of what we today call capitalism, or a market economy. Adam Smith's *An Inquiry into the Nature*

The Author of the Wealth of Nations

Engraving of Adam Smith by John Kay, 1790. Smith wrote *The Wealth of Nations*, describing a free market economy.

and Causes of the Wealth of Nations, commonly referred to as *The Wealth of Nations*, was published in 1776. Smith was part of the remarkable Scottish Enlightenment. A professor of moral philosophy at the University of Glasgow, Smith was already famous for an earlier book, *The Theory of Moral Sentiments*, which gave a description of human nature that included both self-interest and benevolence. *The Wealth of Nations* pushed Smith into a brilliant level of intellectual accomplishment and made him the father of modern economics.

In the introduction to *The Wealth of Nations*, Adam Smith immediately broke with the mercantilists by stating that the wealth, or goal of a nation's economic activity, is not the stock of gold and silver, but instead what a nation can produce and consume in a year's time. His definition of a nation's wealth would be what we think of today as per capita income. In some ways, this view of a nation's economic goal was revolutionary, since Smith focused on the happiness or welfare of ordinary people, rather than on the condition of the king or the government. Later on, economists would refer to this emphasis on consumption as consumer sovereignty. Adam Smith put economic sovereignty in the hands of consumers, just as John Locke put political sovereignty in the hands of the people.

Smith's Description of a Market Economy

Smith began *The Wealth of Nations* by describing a market economy free from government regulation and intervention. Such an economy starts with simple, ordinary exchange, or trade, between two

MARKET SYSTEM

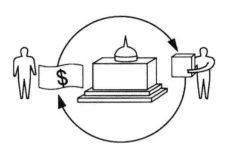

A market economic system is characterized by free and voluntary exchange. Government is limited to the role of maintaining an environment conducive to such exchanges.

individuals. A farmer trades some grain to the cobbler for a pair of shoes, or the weaver gives a bolt of cloth to a flour miller for a cask of flour. Smith noted very early in *The Wealth of Nations* that exchange was motivated by self-interest:

It is not from the benevolence of the butcher, the brewer, or the baker, that we expect our dinner, but from their regard to their own interest. We address ourselves, not to their humanity, but to their self-love, and never talk to them of our own necessities but of their advantages. Nobody but a beggar chooses to depend chiefly upon the benevolence of his fellow-citizens.

A simple, but very powerful, truth about exchange is that both parties involved feel the exchange benefits them. An exchange is a voluntary act between two parties motivated by their interests in improving their circumstances. Both parties can benefit from an exchange because they value the items traded differently. The hungry student exchanges $5 with the pizza maker for a pizza because he values the pizza more than the $5, while the pizza maker values money more than the pizza. By rearranging who has what through exchange, both parties benefit. This small miracle of exchange happens billions of times each day across the world.

Mercantilism ignored this fundamental characteristic of exchange. Government restricted exchange in ways that benefited the king by increasing his stock of gold and silver. But his benefit came at the expense of his citizens, who lost substantial benefits because they were restricted from trade that would have been beneficial. Smith used this simple fact to condemn mercantilism. And this fact of who benefits in trade remains a powerful criticism of government today. Whenever government restricts exchange, for whatever purpose, some people are going to be worse off, because they have been denied beneficial trade.

Role of Money

One of the oldest innovations of civilized societies plays a central role in the process of exchange. Money allows individuals to extend the benefits of exchange into a complex pattern of trade, often involving hundreds of individuals. Imagine a world without money. Each of the two parties considering an exchange would have to want the particular good possessed by the other party. The hungry student would

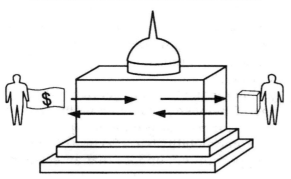

COMMAND OR PLANNING SYSTEM

A command economic system is characterized by exchange under government control. Mercantilism functioned in this way.

have to trade work, or something else of direct value, to the pizza maker for a pizza. If the two parties were fortunate, the pizza maker and the student might be able to work out an exchange that brought in a third party—the student worked for the flour miller, who gave flour to the pizza maker, who gave a pizza to the student. But these "coincidences of wants" are very awkward and sometimes rare. (How many auto mechanics are going to want to have a lecture from a humanities professor on Gothic architecture in exchange for a car tune-up?)

Money eliminates the need for a coincidence of wants and separates the exchange process into parts. The student exchanges money he earned as a groundskeeper for a pizza. The pizza maker combines the student's money with the money of others to buy a new oven. The oven maker uses that money to buy metal to make the oven. Money allows us to exchange over a much broader area, which makes the patterns of exchange much more complex. Money rivals the wheel in importance as an innovation of early civilization.

Anything may be used as money as long as everyone agrees on the commodity. Different cultures have used stones, shells, cows, cigarettes, beads, and animal skins as money. The most common forms

MONEY: THE MEDIUM OF EXCHANGE

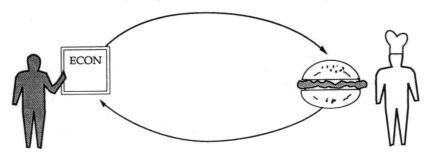

In an economy with no money, an economist who wanted a hamburger would have to search for a fast-food resauranteur who wanted to hear a lecture on economics in exchange for a hamburger. Such coincidence of wants is unlikely and greatly inhibits exchange.

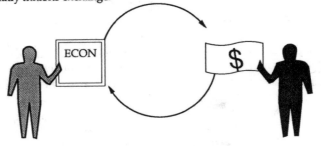

Money as the medium of exchange, splits the exchange process into two parts. First the economist exchanges an economic lecture for money (above). The economist then exchanges the money for a hamburger (below).

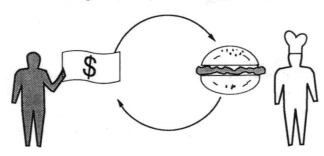

of money have been metals with high value for their weight and durability, like silver and gold. In modern times, we have added paper currency because it is lightweight, convenient, and easy to produce. Governments have often standardized money by minting coins or assuming control of paper money. Problems sometimes occur with government control of money because there is a temptation to cause inflation by increasing the amount of money in circulation.

Specialization

Once people use money, the patterns of exchange become very complex. The production of any single item could involve hundreds of different exchanges because money allows the separation of the different aspects of exchange. Adam Smith noticed this complex pattern of trade, and he began *The Wealth of Nations* with a discussion of the value of specialization. To illustrate, Smith took his reader on a visit to a pin factory. He noted that one person drew the wire, one straightened it, another cut it, one sharpened the point, another ground the top of the wire to receive the head, and so on. Smith calculated that ten workers could produce twelve pounds of pins in a day with 4,000 pins to a pound—over a million in one year's time. Smith was describing the great benefits that come from specialization. He referred to this complex pattern of work and trade as the "division of labor."

Specialization, or the division of labor, increases productivity tremendously. The pin makers became adept at their particular tasks. They also developed machines or tools that helped them with each specialized function. As a consequence, the pin makers produced the pins at a very low cost. Indeed, the cost was so low that even the most self-sufficient individuals would not want to make their own pins. They would find it preferable to spend a few pennies for the pins they want. Remember that this specialization is only possible because of the extensive patterns of exchange. The pin makers must be able to trade pins to people across a very wide area to be able to specialize in pin making with a process that produces a million pins.

Why could the pin makers trade with people far away? For one thing, pins were light and easy to carry. For another, transportation costs were declining. Oceangoing shipping was getting cheaper, in part because of all the fine timber and naval stores in the American colonies. This process of declining transportation costs would prove to be very important in improving the standard of living from Smith's time to the present. Declining transportation costs make it possible to trade with people farther and farther away and to trade heavier and heavier objects. More to the point, declining transportation costs meant that there could be more and more specialization, or division of labor.

Smith observed "that the division of labor is limited by the extent of the market." By this, he meant that specialization would be limited if the market were very small, but specialization could be very extensive as the market grew in size. In Smith's day, the market for most goods was confined to the British Isles, parts of continental Europe, the American colonies, and the Caribbean. Today we have a worldwide market in almost all but the heaviest of goods, such as gravel and cement. The invention of new forms of transportation has allowed the U.S. to trade with the whole world and to specialize evermore extensively.

In sum, voluntary exchange is the foundation of economic activity. We are motivated to trade or exchange because we value goods differently. We value goods differently because we may simply have different tastes or preferences, and because we have different production costs. (The pin makers make the pins much cheaper than others.) Money and declining transportation costs allow individuals to specialize and trade with others across a very wide area.

Economic Competition

All of this exchange and specialization is simply the pursuit of self-interest by individuals as they go about their daily lives. But what will regulate this self-interest? Will not the pin makers want to charge an exorbitant price for the pins that we can hardly make ourselves? Will not the butcher charge us all we could possibly pay for that Sunday roast? Isn't it better to be self-sufficient, and not at the mercy of others' self-interest? Smith's answer is that these are false worries. Economic competition will curb the excesses of self-interest, allowing each of us to specialize and trade. If one butcher tries to charge a high price, he will find the trade going to his competitor down the street.

Smith and economists since him have used the word "competition" to describe the actions of buyers and sellers in a market for a commonly traded good. They say a market is competitive if there are sufficient buyers and sellers, so that no single seller or buyer has a significant influence on price. In any market, say the market for bread, buyers want to pay a low price, and sellers want a high price. Clearly, their interests are in direct conflict with one another.

What then prevents exploitation or unfair advantage on one side or the other? The primary safeguards are competition and the interests of others. If there are many sellers and buyers, then an attempt by any single seller or buyer to manipulate or determine the price

COMPETITION

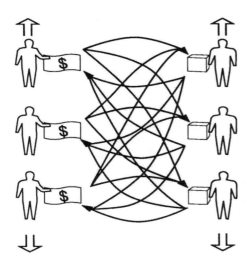

In the economic market there are hundreds or even thousands of different firms (right) and millions of consumers (left). Consequently, there is usually no single individual or business firm able to set the terms of exchange. Competition prevents the abuses of high prices and poor quality and distributes the gains from exchange widely.

will fail, because others will undercut the attempt. Suppose a bread maker asserts that he will not sell his bread for less than $5.00 a loaf. If others are willing to sell it for less, say $2.00 a loaf, the first baker sells no bread unless he lowers his price. If there are enough bread sellers, all of them will perceive that the price for bread is largely beyond their control. They compete with one another to sell their bread, but they accept the price as whatever bread is going for that day. Similarly, customers would like to pay nothing, or pennies, for the bread. But if other customers are willing to pay more, then the price of bread will be higher.

If there are many customers, then all of them believe the price of bread is beyond their control. As long as the bread sellers compete with one another to sell their product, and bread buyers compete with one another to buy bread, no one should have a particular advantage and the interests of all should be well served, yet controlled.

Smith, like economists today, worried about collusion by sellers or by buyers, or the unusual situation where there might be a single seller or buyer. Collusion implies that sellers are conspiring to maintain a high price and avoid competing with one another. In those circumstances, there would not be economic competition. Bread makers in collusion could set the price of bread high. As long as none of them cheated on their agreement, they could extract more money from buyers. Adam Smith knew that businesses would be attracted to collude:

> People of the same trade seldom meet together, even for merriment and diversion, but the conversation ends in a conspiracy against the public, or in some contrivance to raise prices. It is impossible indeed to prevent such meetings, by any law which either could be executed, or would be consistent with liberty and justice. But though the law cannot hinder people of the same trade from sometimes assembling together, it ought to do nothing to facilitate such assemblies, much less render them necessary.

But as this quote suggests, he also did not think collusion and monopoly would pose large problems for the economy unless government promoted conspiracies to fix prices or monopolize a market. By and large, Adam Smith expected competition to control economic interests and to generate reasonable prices. He saw that prices would generally be determined by the impersonal forces of supply and demand, with both buyers and sellers feeling that price was largely beyond their control.

Role of Prices and Profits

In a competitive market in which buyers and sellers see price as a given, what actually determines the market price? Why is bread $2.00 a loaf instead of $2.50 or $1.50? Adam Smith and the economists who followed him observed that markets tended toward an equilibrium price, one where everyone who wanted to buy or sell at that price was able to do so.

Suppose the equilibrium price of bread was $2.00 a loaf. If bread were being sold at a price below equilibrium, say $1.50 a loaf, more people would be willing to buy bread due to the lower price, but fewer people will supply bread given the lower price. A shortage would then develop because there would be buyers who want to buy bread but are unable to find bread to purchase. Whenever there is a shortage, price will rise.

Conversely, a price above equilibrium, such as $2.50 a loaf, creates a surplus because there would be fewer buyers who are willing to purchase bread at the higher price, and suppliers would want to supply more bread than they supplied at $2.00 a loaf. This surplus would cause the price of bread to fall. Leaving price to be determined by natural market forces causes a market to reach an equilibrium, where both buyers and sellers are satisfied with the price. In most cases, equilibrium in a market is easily attainable because demanders (purchasers) and suppliers (sellers) respond in opposite ways to changes in prices.

When the price of a good rises, buyers will demand less of that good; when the price falls, buyers will demand more. On the other hand, a rise in price induces sellers to sell, or supply, more of a good, just as a fall in price induces them to sell less. If the amount demanded has an inverse relationship to price while the amount supplied has a direct relationship, there must be some price where the amount demanded equals the amount supplied. That price is the equilibrium price. The simple, but profoundly important, feature of free markets is the ability to find an equilibrium price. No single individual knows in advance what the equilibrium price will be. But the actions of all the participants in the market will move the price to its equilibrium level.

There are many markets in any economy. There are markets for all goods and services, markets for labor including markets for each kind of skill, markets for land and natural resources, and markets for capital—tools, machinery, and buildings. These markets are all linked to one another by prices. These prices act as signals to indi-

MARKET EQUILIBRIUM

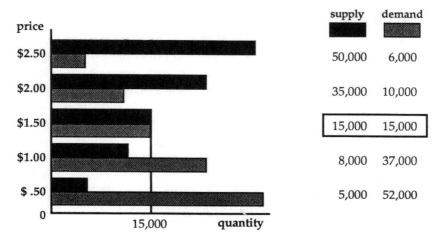

In a market, the price will move to an equilibrium ($1.50 in this chart), where quantity demanded equals quantity supplied.

viduals participating in the market. Suppose people start eating less bread, causing the price of bread to fall. The price change in bread will affect flour millers and the wheat market, causing farmers to grow less wheat and, perhaps, raise more livestock, causing the price of beef to change. The market for baking equipment will be affected. All of these markets are linked together and respond to one another without intervention by government or other institutions.

One other element besides prices links a market economy together. Profits, the excess of revenues over costs, perform an important function in Smith's market economy. Profits and losses represent an important signal to businesses as they allocate resources. When profits in a particular industry are high, it is a signal to invest more resources in that industry. New businesses enter production and old businesses expand production. When losses occur, it is a signal to leave a particular industry and pursue some other opportunity in the economy.

Thus it is that prices and profits act as signals for all of the participants in the market economy. Each individual observes the prices and profits generated by market forces and decides on the best course of action. As Adam Smith noted, when working properly, the free movement of market prices and profits, combined with the pursuit of self-interest by individuals, achieves the most efficient outcome for the economy as a whole. To capture this remarkable property of market economies, Smith coined the phrase "the invisible hand":

> As every individual, therefore, endeavours as much as he can both to employ his capital in the support of domestic industry, and so to direct that industry that its produce may be of the greatest value; every individual necessarily labours to render the annual revenue of the society as great as he can. He generally, indeed, neither intends to promote the public interest, nor knows how much he is promoting it. By preferring the support of domestic to that of foreign industry, he intends only his own security; and by directing that industry in such a manner as its produce may be of the greatest value, he intends only his own gain, and he is in this, as in many other cases, led by an invisible hand to promote an end which was no part of his intention. Nor is it always the worse for the society that it was no part of it. By pursuing his own interest he frequently promotes that of the society more effectually than when he really intends to promote it. I have never known much good done by those who

> affected to trade for the public good. It is an affectation, indeed, not very common among merchants, and very few words need be employed in dissuading them from it.

The invisible hand is the coupling of self-interest with efficiency-producing movements of prices and profits. Together they manage a market economy by allocating resources to the right ends, by inducing firms to produce the right constellation of goods and services, and by rationing scarce goods and services in the most beneficial way. Instead of an economy managed by the visible hands of the mercantilist bureaucrat signing decrees and approving actions by private business, the invisible hand of prices and profits manages the economy. Moreover, Smith argued this invisible hand does it more efficiently.

Smith used his description of a market economy and its ability to allocate resources efficiently to criticize the mercantilist wisdom of the day. Gold and silver were of little economic importance compared to the productive capacity of the economy. Mercantilists were concentrating on the wrong goals. Trade with other countries was good and should be fostered, just as trade among farmers and shopkeepers was of value. Government trade restrictions, subsidies or bounties to exports, and interference with the natural development of colonies were of no value. Mercantilism inevitably sacrificed the interests of consumers to the interests of producers—particularly to the interests of merchants and manufacturers. In general, Smith advocated a *laissez-faire* government policy; in other words, he wanted the government to leave the economy alone. Government should not interfere with exchange, trade, or market prices. The economy worked best when individuals were left free to pursue their own interests restrained by economic competition, but unrestrained by government regulations:

> Every man, as long as he does not violate the laws of justice, is left perfectly free into competition with those of any other man, or order of men. The sovereign is completely discharged from a duty, in the attempting to perform which he must always be exposed to innumerable delusions, and for the proper performance of which no human wisdom or knowledge could ever be sufficient; the duty of superintending the industry of private people, and of directing it towards the employments most suitable to the interest of the society.

Smith leaves individuals free to pursue their own interests within the laws of justice. Additionally, Smith excuses the sovereign from the duty of trying to regulate economic activity. Smith bluntly reminds the ruler that he does not have the wisdom or knowledge to undertake that task. Indeed, it is delusional for the king or sovereign to think himself capable of managing the economy.

Role of Government in a Market Economy

There are a few functions left for government, even in Adam Smith's market economy. A market economy requires a clear definition of property rights. Unrestrained trade requires that the ownership of property and the rights associated with property be clear. Otherwise exchange is difficult because the characteristics being traded are unclear. Suppose ownership of a piece of land does not entitle the owner to build on the land, only farm. The value of that property right would be different from a property right that allowed the owner to do anything with his land. Definition of property rights is usually left to government. The government also assumes the responsibility for preventing fraud or coercion. Voluntary exchanges are only beneficial if they are truly voluntary and are based on good information. The government has to develop a context for exchange. Courts are needed to resolve disputes about exchanges or the terms of exchanges. As noted earlier, the government usually provides money in a market economy. Finally, Adam Smith also suggests government should provide improvements in transportation.

In short, the government creates an environment to encourage exchange and the ordinary workings of a market economy. According to Smith, once the environment is in place, government does not interfere with the operation of the market economy.

Economic Basis of the Founding

Mercantilism and the market economy posed the two basic alternatives for economic organization facing the American colonies as they struggled with their role within the British Empire. Mercantilism represented an economy organized to serve higher social purposes defined by government. In a market economy there were no higher purposes of economic activity; individuals were simply left alone to pursue their own individual objectives.

ROLE OF GOVERNMENT IN A PURE MARKET SYSTEM

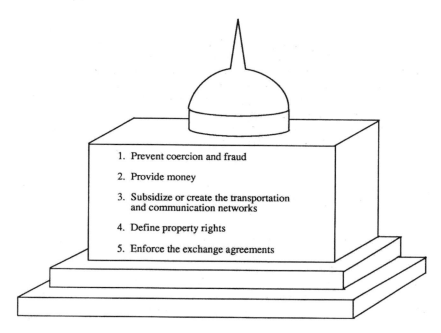

1. Prevent coercion and fraud

2. Provide money

3. Subsidize or create the transportation
   and communication networks

4. Define property rights

5. Enforce the exchange agreements

After the Revolution, Americans found a market economy consistent with their general values and approach to government. A
market economy promoted individual liberty and the pursuit of
happiness. It left the success or failure of individuals to their efforts.
Success did not depend on connections within the government or
the privileges garnered at court. This view was consistent with the
moral view that individual self-government was the foundation of a
moral society. Adam Smith's description of the workings of a market
economy also reassured the Founders that a market economy could
control the conflicting interests in economy through economic competition without the heavy, and perhaps tyrannical, hand of government. Smith's *The Wealth of Nations* made a powerful and persuasive
case that a market economy could be a key component in the creation of a free society. With a market economy, government could
be smaller and more narrowly focused, since economic matters were
not part of the government's tasks.

Mercantilism and the later more powerful philosophies requiring the government to control exchange and manage the economy
would remain an attractive alternative to the Founders and later

government leaders. It is always tempting to use the power of government to placate a constituency, or to pursue some larger goal of government. We will see this tension between free markets and government control of the economy played out over and over. Both the Founders and the United States started from the base of a free economy, but we have often succumbed to the attractive certainty of a hands-on government managing the economy. Of course, Adam Smith, a towering figure of the eighteenth century, would tell us that government management of a complex economy is a delusion.

Chapter 5

The American Revolution

We saw in chapter 1 that foundings typically occur after a political upheaval. The American Revolution certainly was that. The Revolution not only separated the American colonies from the British Empire, it also brought them together for the first time as a single *patria*. It forced Americans to think about what they shared in common, what distinguished them from their British cousins—indeed, from the rest of the world—and what principles they might stand on if they had to stand together. It gave them firsthand experience in creating their own government, and threw them together in that most extreme and demanding of human undertakings—war.

Apart from their English heritage, the colonies had little in common before the Revolution. They had been established

The Granger Collection, New York

Map of the thirteen colonies at the time of the Revolution.

by different groups and for different purposes. Some were ethnically and culturally diverse, while others were homogeneous. Their economies operated very differently, some closely tied to the empire, others independent from it. Their societies, even their political systems, were markedly dissimilar. To the extent that they identified with one another, it tended to be regional. New Englanders acknowledged their Puritan background, Southerners their plantation agriculture, the middle colonies their polyglot diversity, and so on. These regions were no more "American" in their sense of identity than we are "North American" today.

Before 1763 the colonies were bound to the British Empire by economic interdependency—as "hen and chicks," it was said—and by the fear of France and Spain, who were often poised to attack the fledgling chicks. When the French and Indian War ended in 1763, all of that changed. French Canada passed into British hands, and the situation in North America was suddenly and dramatically different.

This turn of events sparked a sequence of developments that would soon rend the proud British Empire to tatters. In the space of little more than a decade, chicks and hen would part company for good.

The Coming of the Revolution

The complex events that brought on the American Revolution lie largely beyond our scope of study. A few generalizations are in order, however, because certain aspects of the imperial controversy had a direct impact on the Founding.

To begin with, the administration of the Empire had often been lax, and the colonies had grown accustomed to a large measure of independence. Consequently, the colonies had developed political maturity. Additionally, most colonists ignored British economic regulations like the Navigation Acts—smuggling abounded. With the conclusion of the French and Indian War, however, the British government launched a determined effort to tighten colonial administration, close loopholes, throttle smuggling, and weld the empire into a single strong entity.

The difficulty growing out of this project was that the imperial authorities did not view the colonies the way the colonies viewed themselves. Instead of seeing them as mature political societies with

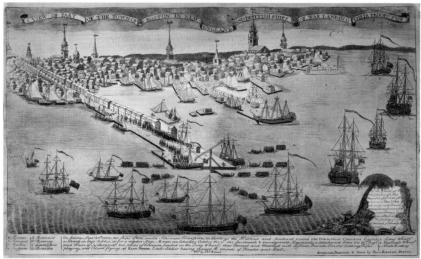

"A View of the town of Boston in New England and British Ships of War Landing their Troops!" Engraving by Paul Revere, 1770. The British tried to gain greater control over the colonies after the French and Indian War.

local self-rule and a common allegiance to the crown, the authorities saw the colonies as mere possessions that could be administered at will. Administration is very different from the rule of law. To administer someone is to order him around, giving instructions here, changing instructions there, allowing this, revoking that, and revising something else. It is anything but the general, prospective, public rules that approach nature in their predictability. Americans felt their rights as Englishmen were being violated. The lords of empire believed in no such rights, at least not for colonials.

This fundamental disparity gave rise to compounded misunderstandings and apprehensions of wrongdoing on both sides. A particular aggravation lay in the matter of taxation. Imperial authorities noted that the colonies had largely escaped taxation in the past, and they believed that the time had come to rectify this oversight—Americans at least ought to defray the cost of their own defense. Nor was there any hesitation in turning to Parliament for the necessary authority, for the principle of parliamentary supremacy in the funding of government was now firmly established. But the colonies took a completely different view. The whole point of parliamentary supremacy was representation, they argued. Parliament alone could levy taxes because Parliament alone represented the taxpayers. Since the colonies were not represented in Parliament, it had no authority whatsoever to lay a tax upon them—that could be done only by their own houses of assembly. This was, of course, a thoroughly English response; it just didn't make sense to the Parliament in England.

Repeated attempts to establish the principle of parliamentary taxation ended in violence, bloodshed, and deepseated suspicion of the colonists. American intransigence confirmed suspicions on the other side that the colonists just wanted a free ride. The Stamp Act became the most infamous of the tax squabbles. The colonists became so heated at the thought of purchasing government stamps that they took to the streets in violent protest. Parliament backed down, but only for the time being.

Die Americaner wiedersetzen sich der Stempel Acte, und verbrennen das aus England nach America gesandte Stempel Papier zu Boston. im August 1764.

A German engraving of the Anti-Stamp Act in Boston, 1765. Bostonians protested the Stamp Act by burning stamps in a bonfire.

Other quarrels merged into the tax issue and intensified its effects. The British government closed western settlement to the colonies—dramatically slamming the free land door in their faces. Parliament reinvigorated the Navigation Acts and dispatched a new regulatory bureaucracy to poke into private lives and multiply corruption. To stem smuggling, officials broadened the language of search warrants, allowing them to snoop anywhere for contraband. The officials then revoked the right of jury trial for accused smugglers, believing that local juries would never convict. They sent British soldiers to troublesome enclaves, notably Boston. Rumor had it that British officials would soon install an Anglican bishop in Virginia—with orders to stamp out religious freedom.

To all of these initiatives, American colonists responded emotionally, dramatically, and with exaggerated paranoia. After all, they had been primed by the English Whigs to expect just such nefarious dealings with the "court party." Instead of seeing a misguided attempt to reform imperial administration, colonists saw an insidious conspiracy to corrupt them and defraud them of their liberty.

Matters came to a head in 1774 with the famous Boston Tea Party. It began as the British government attempted to rescue a failing monopoly, the British East India Company, by granting it new privileges. The trouble was that the cheap tea to be dumped on the American market not only undercut other suppliers, it came shrink-wrapped with a parliamentary tax—one last effort to get the colonies to pay up. Bostonians took the law into their own hands, boarding the tea ships and dumping their cargo overboard.

The British concluded that any further appeasement of the Americans would only make a bad situation worse, and in last-ditch desperation, the British opted for a severe response—closing the port of Boston, imposing military rule, and resolving to starve the dissidents into surrender. Divide and conquer, they supposed: single out the chief offender, Boston, and make an example of it.

The American response was equally warlike. Colonists began preparing for armed resistance. In their preparations, we see not only

Library of Congress

The battle of Lexington, April 1775, the beginning of the Revolutionary War.

the first signs of open revolt, but also the first signals of American unification. Committees of correspondence launched frantic efforts to apprise one another of the situation in their respective colonies. Faraway Virginians, with no direct stake in the Boston controversy, rallied to the side of their besieged compatriots. "Give me liberty or give me death," cried Patrick Henry in the House of Burgesses, his speech treading perilously close to treason. More important, the colonies organized their own government forthwith. The Second Continental Congress represented an extralegal—indeed *il*legal—gathering of delegates from all the colonies, a Lockean coming together in the most literal sense.

Sooner or later, armed conflict was virtually inevitable. In April 1775, after thrusts and counterthrusts around the Boston area, the spark landed in the tinderbox at Lexington Green.

The Declaration of Independence

There are several ways that the rebellion might have ended short of independence. The quarrel behind it might simply have been mended. The British might have overwhelmed all resistance on the battlefield and crushed the separatist movement. A dominion status might have been worked out as a compromise, placing the United States on the same footing as Australia or Canada today. There were influential groups who favored each of these alternatives and forces were set in motion toward each one.

The story of the Declaration of Independence is thus a story of colonial unification. Colonists had to decide on their own that separation from Great Britain was a good idea, that a war of separation could actually be won, that the colonies could exist as viable entities, and that some sort of nationhood among them was possible. These were all uncertain propositions. Accordingly, political battles waged between the outbreak of hostilities in 1775 and cutting the final tie in 1776 were intense, complex, and highly emotional. Americans' entire world was at stake.

The battles were fought in the Continental Congress, without umpire or referee. This body represented one of the strangest innovations in the modern world—government created by the governed. It lacked much that we would expect from government today—careful organization, established rules—and with no king to impart a sense of legitimacy, it stood in danger of falling apart. Yet somehow it held together and pushed on, the voice of a disparate and divided people.

Of the many arguments in the case, most were narrow and particular, reflecting only local interests. As the delegates hammered away, an "American" interest began to emerge. It was vague in the beginning. (Remember, the colonies were still very different from one another, and their sense of identity almost wholly local.) They came to see that they shared something powerful, and that the word *liberty* had gained great importance for them. It meant more than escaping from British tyranny. There was something in it of John Locke and the English Whigs, something of Adam Smith and the nobility of the individual, and more than a little of John Winthrop's city upon a hill. More than anything else, though, there was that compelling connection between national autonomy and personal freedom. Free societies create free people, and vice versa.

As the military battles grew more intense, delegates were more concerned with the hard facts of separation—not to mention the war that was raging all around them—than with theories of nationhood. They were working politicians, not political philosophers. Yet for Americans to forge themselves into a single nation, nationhood was a theory that was most needed. A nation, after all, is a group of people united on some basis. For it to truly work as a nation, the people must know what that basis is and believe in its cogency. This is where the story of the Declaration of Independence takes on layers of meaning that were never originally intended.

Library of Congress

The Writing of the Declaration of Independence, by J. L. G. Ferris, ca. 1932. Thomas Jefferson, Benjamin Franklin, and John Adams met to review a draft of the Declaration of Independence.

As soon as independence seemed likely, members of the Continental Congress chose to make a formal declaration, a gracefully written document that would set forth the American case persuasively and curry the favor of neutrals and bystanders alike—especially the French. Young Thomas Jefferson of Virginia, only thirty-three years old, seemed the logical choice for its initial draftsmanship, for he was nothing if not facile with a pen. There were at least two others on the drafting committee, John Adams and Benjamin Franklin, and beyond them the whole of the Congress, which would fight over every word in the document and end up changing many of them.

Jefferson later claimed to have no particular source of inspiration, pulling ideas from the very air of wartime Philadelphia. Yet the crucial passages, in the first and second paragraphs, read like a page out of Locke's *Second Treatise*. There was more to the Declaration than those two memorable paragraphs—it was, after all, a bill of indictment against the British crown—but in that brief flight of poetic prose, Americans sensed an irresistible idea of nationhood.

The final debates were fierce; they included competing sectional interests, the power of local attachments, and the institution of

The Declaration of Independence by John Trumbull depicts the signing of that document on July 4, 1776.

slavery—issues that would live to haunt American history. By July 4, 1776, Congress was ready with a final, unanimous vote, followed by a signing ceremony. The United States of America was an accomplished fact.

It was only in the aftermath of this event that Americans began to reread the Declaration of Independence and find those deeper meanings in its text. For within its flowing cadences was to be found an outline of the agreement that Americans had made with one another as the basis of their social compact:

- All human beings were created equal—there was no ruling class among them.
- All were endowed with the same rights, granted by nature, not by government, and these rights could never be alienated or abridged.
- The purpose of government was to protect such rights.
- Government was legitimized only by the consent of the governed.

It was an argument fully intelligible to Americans, each point leading logically to the next, and one that gave full account of the American Founding. There was a way the world had been set up, it asserted, yet few if any of the world's nation-states appeared to grasp that fundamental truth. The United States, among all of them, would be the nation-state that was constructed on the *right* foundation—a city upon a hill indeed.

The Declaration of Independence foreshadowed both the Constitution and the Bill of Rights. It anticipated the emergence of political parties and the advent of a representative democracy. It implied the eventual triumph of the market system and pointed to the egalitarianism and individualism that would come to define the American soul. It even gave a hint of civil war. More than anything else, the Declaration provided a sense of what American nationhood would mean. The United States would not be a nation of rulers but of people. Governance would not be its main business—human life would. Of all political societies on earth, it would be the one dedicated, not to war and conquest, not to wealth or power, not to aristocratic brilliance, or cultural excellence, or the brave accomplishments of the few—but to life, liberty, and the pursuit of happiness.

The Revolutionary War

Just as the Declaration of Independence was the great unifying idea, the Revolutionary War was the great unifying event. For centuries afterward, Americans would come together on Independence Day and act out symbolic tableaus of the war era. Folklore would come to swirl around Paul Revere ("To arms, to arms!"), Nathan Hale ("I only regret that I have but one life to lose for my country!"), John Paul Jones ("I have not yet begun to fight!"), Betsy Ross, Molly Pitcher, Ethan Allen, Francis Marion, the Pennsylvania Riflemen, and those sturdy souls who turned out in the dead of night to answer the call of the Minutemen. It all rolled up into that heartwarming image of color-bearer, fifer, and drummer limping victoriously to the tune of "Yankee Doodle."

The unifying aspects of the war were several. To begin with, Americans came together from the length and breadth of the colonies to fight in the Continental army. It was a rabble army, to be sure, and it lost many battlefield victories, but it was indeed "continental" in scope, and its officers and men got to know one another as Americans rather than as Virginians or New Yorkers.

Americans also experienced common privation and suffering. The war was fought everywhere, north and south, east and west, in cities and towns, along rivers and inlets, up and down country roads, across farms, in open fields and dense forests. No one was safe from the war's ravages or immune from its sorrows. If the loss of life was modest by later standards, the war's physical destruction was catastrophic. It would take more than a generation for Americans to clean up the mess.

Americans took heart, however, from common sources of encouragement. Thomas Paine's little book titled *Common Sense* was a masterpiece of political propaganda, and its timely appearance in spring 1776 had much to do with swinging popular opinion in favor of independence. Paine also went to work on the sixteen *American Crisis* papers, whose notable beginning rang: "These are the times that try men's souls." Taken together, Paine's apologetics struck not one but a whole series of responsive chords in the American heart. Paine convinced Americans that monarchy truly was a thing of the past and that Britain's claims of sovereignty over them were more than a little absurd. Most of all, Paine succeeded in placing the American struggle for independence in the context of a human struggle for freedom. There was more at stake here, Americans concluded, than mere separation from the British Empire.

Thomas Paine by George Romney, 1793. Paine wrote *Common Sense* to help persuade colonists to support the movement for independence.

In facing the British Army, Americans knew they were challenging the best military force in the world. Symbolic victories, such as the battle of Bunker Hill near Boston, where a small contingent of determined colonials inflicted withering casualties on a command of British regulars, fired American self-confidence and turbocharged their sense of patriotism. However, the more numerous battlefield defeats, such as Brooklyn Heights, White Plains, Germantown, and Brandywine, showed Americans that their freedom would not be won easily. The Americans' determination to press on in the face of mounting catastrophe had its own effect on their feeling of nationhood.

The way the British handled the war may have had greater effect in unifying Americans than any other factor. British commanders enjoyed every kind of superiority—economic, military, and technological—but they lacked a clear, coherent policy for conducting operations, and worse yet, they failed to understand the character of their enemy. British commanders were never quite sure whether they wanted to conquer, pacify, or intimidate the American colonists. British commanders tried all three approaches at one time or another, making them seem weak and indecisive.

Almost every dilemma faced by the British commanders went unresolved. If they were lenient with rebel sympathizers, the British embittered the loyalists. If the British were harsh and vindictive, they angered the very people they were trying to win over. If the British dug in and fortified an area, the enemy would operate with impunity all around them. If they headed off in pursuit, their friends were abandoned to reprisals. And try as the British might, they couldn't seem to teach their own soldiers the difference between rebels and noncombatants—who were sadly treated alike. The cumulative effect was to isolate, offend, or betray the very people the British were trying to win over. Every mistake they made alienated Americans all the more—driving the undecided toward the patriot cause.

By contrast, the Americans got the politics of war making essentially right. In the beginning, opinion was evenly divided among three alternatives: support for the cause, opposition to the cause, and indifference to the cause. Most Americans did not understand the issues of the conflict very well, regarding it as a lawyers' quarrel. Moreover, Americans had little experience with, or interest in, politics itself, which many saw as a pursuit of the privileged classes. Most Americans just wanted to get on with their lives.

Yet events of the war kept pushing the undecided off the fence. There was horrific property damage, as we have seen, and most of it

The Granger Collection, New York

Minutemen: Heroes of '76. This lithograph by Currier & Ives celebrates the role of local militias in the Revolutionary War.

was sustained by civilians. Noncombatants were often targeted for reprisals, especially by loyalist commanders. Neutrals were harassed by both sides until it became more difficult to walk down the middle than to throw in with one group of partisans or the other. If the real war was a contest for the "hearts and minds" of the undecided, as John Adams maintained, indecision became increasingly difficult.

The single greatest factor in the war against apathy appears to have been the colonial militia. Every town had its militia company, which has been described as a combination fraternal lodge, drinking society, and political cadre. While they were often driven from the field in hot military engagements, militias played a useful role in many battles, especially as support and reinforcement. But their real value was political. Militias were instruments of political education. After a drill on the village green and a visit to the local pub, the company would often be instructed on fine points of natural law, the dark doings of the court party, and the importance of human liberty. While there may have been scant comprehension of the issues before Lexington and Concord, by the final battle at Yorktown there was a great deal of comprehension.

Indeed, by the war's end, there wasn't much support left for the British cause. Americans had gained a fairly clear understanding of those principles on which their founding as a nation was taking place.

George Washington

If the Declaration of Independence was a unifying idea and the war itself a unifying event, George Washington became a unifying symbol of nationhood. For fellow Americans, he became like the great founding heroes of antiquity—Lycurgus, Solon, Caesar—all rolled into one. Washington began as an aspiring young planter and would-be member of the gentry. He admired the aristocratic Fairfax family, whom he happened to know personally, and sought entry into their glittering world. Gentlemanly status meant more to him than land or wealth, but land and wealth were an integral part of the package. As a result, Washington became an aggressive entrepreneur, land speculator, canal promoter, and agricultural experimentalist—the complete American.

Washington believed that a gentleman must be first and foremost a person of character. Accordingly, he assiduously cultivated virtue—in the classical sense—while still very young. He made a list of desirable qualities and worked on developing them one at a time. He wanted to be the best at everything—the best farmer; the best husband; the best father to his two stepchildren; the best rider; the best poker player; the best military officer. In this last category he was shamefully outclassed by the scions of British families who had had the benefit of an old-school education. He would, he was told, amount to nothing but a provincial officer at best, and he could scarcely build a career on *that* footing. The bitter disappointment did not endear him to things British.

As he grew into maturity, Washington identified with the country party and saw himself as the quintessential commonwealthman. Accordingly, even as he continued to increase his acreage and augment the size of his house, he could never turn his back on public duty. He was elected to the Virginia House of Burgesses in 1759, where he contributed the classical virtue of temperance, or moderation, along with that of stolid wisdom. He was as different from the flashy and mercurial Patrick Henry as was possible.

Washington's military experience was not vast, nor was it the experience of victory. As a headstrong young officer, he actually touched off the French and Indian War in 1754 after being sent to investigate the building of a French fort on the Ohio frontier. Later, as commander of the Virginia Blues, he was caught in the disastrous ambush that spelled the defeat of British General Edward Braddock and the virtual annihilation of the army. That Washington's uniform was ripped and torn by no fewer than six bullets in that engagement may tell us something of interest about the role of providence in history.

Politics abounded in Congress' decision to appoint Washington, a Southerner, to take charge of an army up in the North. It was a gesture toward American unity, yet it was unpopular with the better trained and more experienced officers who aspired to general command, several of them New Englanders. The disappointed hopefuls did not argue Washington's southernness, of course; they argued his incompetence. What had he done, they asked, except start a war and take part in a debacle?

George Washington by Charles Wilson Peale, 1772. Washington was a unifying symbol of nationhood as a general during the Revolutionary War.

For all that, George Washington proved himself to be without peer in either army. He was high-minded and occasionally aloof, but never erratic, arbitrary, or unjust—the failings of his many rivals. He learned from his mistakes, acquired a sound sense of tactics, and knew how to deploy his inferior forces to good advantage. He gained a better sense of strategy even than his acclaimed British counterparts. He concluded early on that by holding his rag-tag army together, he might well force the British into a no-win situation. But how could he hold such an army together? After the British attack on New York in August 1776, the Continental army's numbers dropped from 20,000 to less than 4,000 by the following Christmas, and the remnant was perilously close to dissolving away. Challenging times, however, magnified Washington's deeper qualities.

He was absolutely beloved by those who served under him, his famous temper notwithstanding. It was one thing to be respected, but George Washington was adored. He was a man of stoical patience born of long-suffering and many battlefield reversals. Having been called by the people to serve a cause that was just, he was evidently willing to fight to the very last ditch; and he communicated that resolve to everyone around him. Finally, he was a canny politician, one who knew all the wiles and stratagems of infighting.

In addition to the superior forces that faced him on the battle-field, Washington had to deal with a host of other difficulties. Rival officers—Charles Lee, Horatio Gates, James Wilkinson, Thomas Mifflin—conspired to oust him as commander in chief. Congress played politics with the war effort, often shorting Washington's army in the process. American suppliers frequently sold to the highest bidder, which was always the British. There were logistical tangles, sagging spirits, intelligence leaks, and traitors in high places. Field guns blew apart. Powder became soggy. Allies had a mind—and of course an agenda—of their own. Militias melted away at the zip of enemy bullets. Regulars went AWOL by the hundreds.

Washington bore all of it and more, never flagging in his devotion. Where others blew hot and cold, switched sides, and jockeyed for personal advantage, he soldiered on, heeding only the call of duty, his patriotism flowing from some bottomless well. His vision of America as a nation was far in advance of his time.

A major British assault in summer 1776 drove Washington's army from its fortifications on the Hudson and pushed it deep into New Jersey. There he rallied his depleted forces and mounted bold counterstrokes at Trenton—the famous Christmas attack—and Princeton. These victories boosted a sagging American morale.

After this first year, the war settled into what might be called a dynamic equilibrium. The British continued to win important victories, but so on occasion did the colonists. One such colonial victory was the battle of Saratoga in October 1777, bringing British general John Burgoyne's Hudson River Campaign to a cataclysmic end. On the strength of this achievement, France decided to enter the war. Now an American victory truly *was* possible.

With France by his side, Washington was able to obtain more munitions, call upon superior experience, and more important, make use of a French naval squadron. At the same time, the British opted for yet another shift in strategy, heading south to pacify the lightly defended Carolinas. While this move proved effective, it also led to the entrapment of a large British force on the Yorktown Peninsula in Virginia in October 1781. With French and American armies before him and French ships blocking his escape, the British commander, Charles Cornwallis, decided upon the surrender that effectively ended the war.

Military historians have pointed out that with a few exceptions—and these largely symbolic—George Washington the general did not really participate in the war's key turning points. (Saratoga, for example, was credited to Horatio Gates.) Washington's role, rather, had been to engage the main thrust of British attention and keep an army on the field that proved worthy of such attention. While they faced Washington, the British were unable to sustain successful operations elsewhere.

The Granger Collection, New York

Ordinary Americans knew that Washington had contributed much more. They lovingly recalled a series of representations that embodied the revolutionary cause: crossing the Delaware on a snowy Christmas night to attack the Hessians in Trenton; mustering beleaguered forces at Monmouth Courthouse and pulling victory from the jaws of defeat; enduring the hardship of Valley Forge with his starved and freezing soldiers; and, finally facing down a mutiny of his officers by appealing to their

George Washington by Horatio Greenough, 1840.

dignity and pride. He had grown old in the service of his country, he told the mutineers, and so he had.

This was the man Americans came to revere as a demigod. They named cities, towns, and a state in his honor, wrote his name on bridges and highways, erected monuments to him, hung his portrait above their mantels, carved a statue of him clad in a Roman toga. It was not for his soldierly qualities per se but for his embodiment of virtue in all of its forms; for his willingness to forsake home and hearthside to answer the public call; for his patience and endurance in the face of daunting obstacles; for his ability to inspire others; and for his humble wisdom in the face of arrogance and pride.

Indeed, it was partly because they believed in George Washington that Americans came to believe in themselves.

Chapter 6

Designing Government

As the rebellion of the colonies morphed into the American Revolution, Americans turned their attention to the problem of governance. They had difficulty imagining a single American *government,* just as they had difficulty imagining a single American *nation.* As colonies, they had always been separate, and they assumed that would continue—they would vest sovereignty in the states *as* states, rather than in the nation.

Their model for this assumption was classical antiquity. Americans at first saw themselves in a situation somewhat like that of ancient Greece. The various republics would have amicable relations with one another and would bind themselves into a strong alliance against foreign attack. They would be a "nation" in the sense that ancient Greece had been a nation, a league with friendly rivalries, cultural exchange, and similar institutions. But the whole idea of a "republic" was to preserve a body politic that was small and cohesive.

State Governments

Republican theory became important to Americans as they considered the reality of their independence. The principal idea of a "republic"—from the Latin *res publica,* the "public thing"—was for citizens of the political state to govern themselves rather than submit to a despot or an oligarchy. In extreme forms of republicanism, the citizens literally handled the daily business of government, as in the

Athenian democracy. Most republics, however, operated by means of chosen representatives, which in practice was far more workable.

It was assumed that republics needed to be small in size—no larger than the Greek city-states—because citizens must remain close to the governing process and keep a watchful eye on it. Republics, however desirable in many ways, were known for their instability. Their histories in the ancient world were fraught with wars, revolutions, palace coups, and a pandemic factional turmoil the Greeks called *stasis*. Republics had their share of tyrants, but tyranny was often preferable to anarchy—where no one won and everyone lost.

Philosophers of the ancient world had spent a good deal of time and energy attempting to address what we might call the Republican Problem: how could the benefits of self-government be enjoyed without incurring the problems inherent in that self-government? Plato, in his famous work of political philosophy, *The Republic*, argued for *aretē* (virtue) as the answer. He laid out a system for recruiting and training the best and brightest in Greek society to hold the reins of government, and for educating them in the highest performance of virtuous conduct. Aristotle, by contrast, still believed in virtue, but he tended to emphasize structural solutions to the Republican Problem. By mixing and balancing elements of monarchy, aristocracy, and democracy in a government, Aristotle supposed that power could be fragmented and shared among various groups and interests, the result being stability.

All of this became relevant to American constitution makers, for they soon came to realize that the Republican Problem was their problem. In addition to reading about the ancients, the Americans had their own experience to draw upon. They thought of themselves as laboratories for the development of republican practice, each state sharing its experience with the others. John Adams became so excited about this prospect that he began writing a comparative analysis of American state constitutions. What worked well among them? he asked. What didn't work at all? What led toward disaster?

Because most of the states were used to operating from charters, they favored written constitutions, whose provisions could be spelled out clearly. Some states, in fact, merely revised their old charters and struck out all references to the king. Most of them, however, worked up their constitutions from scratch. Many of the framers were men of learning, well read in the European Enlightenment, and virtually all of them were schooled in the art of politics. Even so, Americans began to learn that there was a big difference between theory and practice when it came to designing government.

Sometimes, for example, the smallest details in a constitution could have large consequences. A given mechanism might have unanticipated side effects, defeating the very purpose for which it was included; or a bias might suddenly pop up in the constitutional structure; or a new opportunity for malpractice; or an unfair advantage. Human nature could also be a surprise. In political situations, people often behaved at variance to their professed ideals, even at variance to their normal

The Granger Collection, New York

The Virginia Constitution, 1776. Many states wrote their own constitutions during and after the Revolutionary War.

daily conduct—though angels in their ideals, men could be monsters in practice. Constitutional governance was a new experience.

While some state governments could be counted successful, others displayed conspicuous weakness and outright failure. Some became stained with corruption. Others proved to be unworkable. Still others became known for high-handedness. Particularly troublesome among them was the phenomenon of "constitutional drift," when power in the government did not remain where it was originally placed. Legislatures, for example, proved to be adept at stealing power from governors and state courts, so that in time only the legislature's power remained. In the worst cases, such as Pennsylvania and Rhode Island, state governments seemed to behave like Old World tyrannies as a particular group or interest would gain control and then use its power to thwart all rivals. As for the rule of law, it was nothing for a state government to violate generality or prospectivity, enacting legislation requiring creditors to accept worthless paper currency in payment of debt.

Reflecting upon the difficulties of the ancient republics, some Americans were moved to observe how little had really been learned. Was this, asked some, what they had fought and died for in the name of liberty?

The Confederation

Just as there was precedent in the ancient world for republican government in the states, there was precedent for a continental government. The term for it was *confederation*: a defensive alliance among sovereign equals. Confederations were never intended to be true governments, for they lacked the sovereignty that government requires.

Even so, those who drafted the Articles of Confederation (the "constitution" of the Confederation) in 1781 wanted the American Union to be more than just a circle of friends. For one thing, they believed that Americans had a great deal in common and enjoyed some sense of nationhood already. For another, they feared that rivalry among the American states might lead to an endless cycle of conflicts, alliances, and diplomatic intrigues. Ancient Greece had known just such sorrows.

The structure of the Confederation was based on its legislative body, an outgrowth of the old Continental Congress. After all, Congress hadn't done so badly. It had united the states against a common foe, conducted a war, and forged a peace. Why not just carry on that tradition?

As an alliance of sovereign equals, the Confederation wasn't particularly unsuccessful, but it had all the weaknesses and shortcomings of its type. There was no executive, and thus no voice of American leadership. There was no national court system either, and accordingly no way to resolve the growing number of disputes among the states. Conflicting land claims alone had already sent state militiamen reaching for their muskets.

There was no authority for trade regulation among the states. As a result, the states conducted economic warfare among themselves.

THE CONFEDERATION

The confederation was essentially a defensive alliance among sovereign states. Each state had an equal say regardless of population size.

They slapped tariffs on imports and duties on exports. States with port facilities gouged neighbors without them, and the neighbors found ways to retaliate. America was the largest potential market in the world, but under the Confederation its benefits went almost wholly unrealized.

There was no centralized authority to conduct diplomacy. In its absence, states sent out their own envoys to foreign capitals, often at odds with one another. They also commissioned their own military forces, which proved dangerous. The outcome was that the diplomacy of the American "nation" was often confused, contradictory, and self-defeating. Few foreign creditors thought the United States was worth much of a risk. Great Britain became so annoyed with the disarray that it began breaching terms of the peace accord.

The Confederation was particularly hobbled by the way power was apportioned in Congress. The fact that all states had equal representation regardless of size or population underscored state sovereignty. Many confederations had foundered on this very point. When small, weak members can outvote large and powerful ones, the former face a constant temptation to gang up and get their way, forcing the latter to depart.

Finally, the Articles of Confederation were virtually amendment-proof. A unanimous vote was required for any amendment, leaving scant hope of resolving its difficulties. A sense of impotence and futility pervaded the American psyche. The fact that the Confederation functioned almost without funds (having no power to lay taxes) simply underscored the pall of defeat that hung over the fragile Union.

The lessons of the Confederation experience resembled those of the state government experience. Small constitutional details could cast very long shadows on real-world politics—and the rule of law was often lost in the process. Whether the country was a careening state government in the hands of a faction or a feckless league of disorderly sovereignties, the problem was the same. By 1787, Americans came to realize that their city upon a hill would require better urban planning.

The New Constitutionalism

Thoughtful Americans analyzed this situation and discussed possible reforms in both state governments and the Confederation. If Americans were sobered by the failures of constitutional structure, they were appalled by the failures of virtue. Americans considered themselves a uniquely virtuous people before the Revolution, and the challenges of the war effort greatly enhanced that feeling. But recent developments had undermined their confidence. Why, they asked, would groups want to take over state governments? Why would individuals seek tyrannical power or unfair advantage? Why would corruption and jobbery pop up here as in some Old World capital? What had become of American innocence?

Strengthening State Government

John Adams, who was exceptionally well versed in political theory, hit upon the beginnings of an answer. As a grandchild of Puritans, he shared something of their dark view of human nature. He believed that people responded to situations, not exhortations, even though he exhorted his own children to the highest standards of virtuous conduct. Thus the answer to America's version of the Republican Problem would be found in structure. He was an Aristotelian.

In a pamphlet titled *Thoughts on Government*, Adams set forth a number of ideas on how state governments could be strengthened, stabilized, and made more responsive to public duty. For example, legislatures ought to be made bicameral, with two separate houses elected on different principles, one of them more democratic, the other more aristocratic, making it difficult for a single group to exercise

Library of Congress

John Adams by Gilbert Stuart. In the pamphlet *Thoughts on Government*, Adams proposed many changes to strengthen and stabilize the government.

tyranny of the majority. The judiciary ought to be isolated from political interference—which could often trim judges' salaries or shorten their tenure—so that court decisions reflected true justice.

Adams's most controversial suggestion applied to the executive branch of government, the office of governor. Governors were not in high favor at the time, after the abuses inflicted by the old crown appointees. But that, said Adams, was precisely the problem. Weak governors, like weak judges, were becoming lackeys of the legislature. A strong governor would add a dash of monarchy to the structural mix and operate as a check on the legislature. Specifically, Adams proposed to hand governors back the veto power so they could hold the legislatures in bounds. Republican governors would not misuse the veto, Adams predicted, especially if they had to stand for *annual* elections.

Adams's proposals could be understood in terms of the rule of law. His structural modifications were aimed at eliminating confusion and willfulness from the legislative process and securing laws that would be more general, more prospective, and more *blind*. Such laws could still reflect the will of the people, Adams believed, but they would do so as *law*, not as arbitrary whim.

In 1780, Massachusetts overhauled its original constitution, and when the new delegates sat down to their task, they had *Thoughts on Government* directly in mind. The new constitution implemented virtually all of Adams's suggestions. It worked so well that it became a model for other states—and an inspiration for those who would draft the U.S. Constitution in Philadelphia.

Strengthening the Confederation

Where Adams's attention had been focused on the failures of state governments, others focused on failures of the Confederation. Both Alexander Hamilton of New York and James Madison of Virginia were prominent in this movement. So, significantly, was George Washington, who had never lost his continental perspective or his sense of American patriotism. In a series of informal gatherings, these "nationalists," as we might call them, argued the case for a stronger American union, urged on by a vision of the United States as a sovereign nation. They believed such a polity would enhance freedom, expand opportunity, and strengthen the rule of law. They also believed it would be more likely than the state governments to reflect the influence of virtue. A government of real sovereignty, so the argument went, would enlist the participation of America's most virtuous citizens—the Jeffersons, Hamiltons, Adamses, and Washingtons. It would speak for the dignity of all Americans and the achievements of their Revolution. It would be a nation among nations, to be admired, respected, and feared.

With the blessing of Washington, the nationalists engineered an interstate conference at Mount Vernon in 1785. Its official purpose was to resolve difficulties in navigating the Chesapeake. Nationalist feeling was in abundance, and the participants wound up calling for a wider conference to be held the following year at Annapolis. While this second meeting was not a success, the nationalists used it as a platform from which to call for yet another assembly, a grand convention this time, to consider ways

The Granger Collection, New York

A 1786 engraving of Shays Rebellion. This event motivated the states to participate in the Grand Convention in 1787.

of improving and strengthening the Articles of Confederation. The host city would be Philadelphia.

The cause of the nationalists was immeasurably strengthened by events in Massachusetts the following winter of 1787. Debt-ridden farmers in the western part of the state rose in open rebellion and shut down the local courts in order to escape foreclosure. Shays Rebellion, as it was called, raised the specter of American anarchy—a dreadful jolt to those who had recently fought for freedom. "I feel infinitely more than I can express for the disorders which have arisen," wrote a dispirited George Washington. "Who besides a Tory could have foreseen, or a Briton predicted them?" The colonists had not yet resolved the Republican Problem.

Creating a Federal Government

The Grand Convention in Philadelphia might well have failed. For a number of reasons, however—Shays Rebellion large among them—the states took the call seriously and sent some of their ablest statesmen as delegates. The fifty-five delegates who arrived in April 1787 could be generally described in terms of Plato's cardinal virtues. The delegates were courageous—most had fought in the Revolution. They were wise—among the most learned in the Western Hemisphere. They were temperate—always searching out the moderate, the possible, and the doable. They were just—and the injustice of reckless or impotent governments bothered them a great deal. They were also practical men of affairs, with long political and administrative experience. While they have been called "aristocrats" and "a master class," they are better described simply as America's best and brightest.

An important chemistry soon coalesced among them. A handful of truly exceptional individuals sifted themselves out of the rank and file and assembled into an informal corps of "primary framers." These included James Wilson of Pennsylvania; Roger Sherman of Connecticut; Gouverneur Morris of New York; Charles Pinckney of South Carolina; William Paterson of New Jersey; and George Mason of Virginia. The most important of this group was another Virginian, James Madison, who had thought long and hard about the weaknesses of the Confederation—and the kind of government that ought to replace it. Some of the primary framers were visionaries, inspiring their colleagues with scope and possibility; others were innovators,

A 1799 engraving of George Washington presiding over the Constitutional Convention.

facilitators, manipulators, and more important, negotiators. Virtually everything in the new Constitution would be hammered out by compromise.

George Washington's leadership was imperative to the success of the Convention. The American people watched him carefully—they were likely to echo his feelings about the new government. Washington took little part in the convention's tedious deliberations, but he presided with great dignity. His very presence reminded fellow delegates that this was serious business.

Troubled Politics

James Madison, the most ardent of the nationalists, arrived in Philadelphia with a proposal for a national government that featured "proportional representation" (representation by population) in the congress. Such a plan, he pointed out, would represent people more than states, and hence would reflect a truly *American* sovereignty. (State governments in his plan would fade into subordinate administrative units, much like counties today.) The new government would be powerful, with authority to tax and spend, conduct foreign affairs, raise an army, and settle all internal disputes. Madison read widely in the areas of political theory and historical practice, and was thus able to persuade other members of the Virginia delegation to support his plan.

From the beginning, however, it became clear that there would be no easy victory for Madison and the nationalists. Many delegates had been sent expressly to amend the Articles of Confederation, not abolish them. What Madison was proposing was far beyond their mandate. Also, a few delegates liked the Confederation the way it was. All of them had been sent by sovereign states, none of which wanted to surrender its power to a national entity.

These difficulties had been more or less foreseen. The one that threatened to wreck the Convention, on the other hand, popped up by surprise. Madison's proportional representation would give large amounts of power in the national government to big states like Virginia, Pennsylvania, and Massachusetts, and little to no power to small states like Delaware or New Jersey. The smaller states, which were in the majority, already saw themselves as threatened by their outsized neighbors. Madison's plan, as they saw it, would render that threat into a working tyranny. Accordingly, the small states asked for time to regroup and come up with a plan of their own. In the so-called New Jersey Plan, presented by William Paterson, the small states proposed only minor changes in the existing Confederation.

Neither side would budge. For months of the exceptionally hot and sticky summer of 1787, the delegates slugged it out in the stifling confines of Independence Hall. There was no air conditioning, of course, and the windows had to be locked in the interest of tight security. Matters were made even worse by a plague of black flies that swarmed the conference rooms, stung the delegates, and frayed nerves to the breaking point.

The Great Compromise

Ultimately, Roger Sherman—Connecticut's master negotiator—proposed a compromise. Proportional representation, he suggested, would apply only to the *lower* house of the bicameral legislature. This would insure Madison's basic principle of popular sovereignty. Equal representation of states would apply to the *upper* house of the legislature, as it had in the Confederation. This would address the small states' concern for state sovereignty. Since every bill would have to pass *both* houses, both principles could exist side by side.

While Sherman's compromise may strike us as eminently reasonable today, it sounded bizarre in the extreme to most of his listeners. Nothing remotely like this had ever been tried before. It seemed impractical, unworkable, and a shortcut to disaster. However, because neither side would give an inch, it remained the only ground of accommodation.

While rhetoric heated and tempers flared, the wearying debates dragged on. On more than one occasion delegates had to be restrained from physically coming to blows. A pall of gloom settled over the proceedings, and a few of the delegates packed up and headed for home. The breakup of the Grand Convention seemed imminent. It was in this context that Benjamin Franklin pleaded for prayer. Though the delegates did not heed Franklin's advice—they lacked funds to pay a chaplain—Franklin's speech rang in their ears. He placed them at the judgment bar of history, with future generations praising or scorning the outcome. "And what is worse," he added, "mankind may hereafter from this unfortunate instance despair of establishing government by human wisdom and leave it to chance, war, and conquest."

Whether by divine intervention or otherwise, events took a sudden turn. In the last week of June there was a puzzling absence during one crucial vote, switched votes on two other occasions, and the invocation of an obscure rule that nullified the ballot of New York. The majority that Madison and the nationalists had nursed

BENJAMIN FRANKLIN

Library of Congress

Benjamin Franklin by Antoine Maurin, 1778. During the convention, Franklin made a plea for prayer and placed upon the "delegates the judgement bar of history."

THE GREAT COMPROMISE

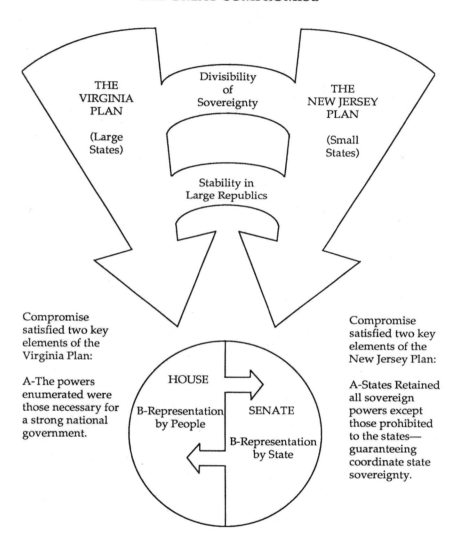

Compromise satisfied two key elements of the Virginia Plan:

A-The powers enumerated were those necessary for a strong national government.

Compromise satisfied two key elements of the New Jersey Plan:

A-States Retained all sovereign powers except those prohibited to the states—guaranteeing coordinate state sovereignty.

No political compromise would have been possible unless some intellectual bridges were made between the Virginia Plan and the New Jersey Plan. Since it was already accepted that legislatures shold be Bi (two) Cameral (chamber), everything fit together perfectly.

through thick and thin was suddenly reduced to a tie—leaving no other alternative but to embrace Sherman's compromise.

The delegates had no way of knowing it at the time, but "federalism," as it was ingeniously called, would turn out to be the Convention's single most brilliant achievement and one of history's great structural innovations. Federalism would actually *divide* sovereignty between the national government and the state governments. It would serve up all the advantages of Madison's unified national polity, while at the same time preserving the smaller units cherished by conservatives and sanctioned by republican theory. The genius of the Constitutional Convention lay precisely in such an outcome.

The Compromise on Slavery

The Great Compromise was not the only anxious moment for the Philadelphia Convention. The disagreement over slavery was almost as traumatic. Although the "peculiar institution," as it was called, had died out in most northern states by 1787, slavery survived in the South. All parties at the Convention recognized slaveholding as morally dubious, and most of them acknowledged its dissonance with founding principles. (All are born *free* and *equal*. . . .) Yet, the practice could be defended by similar, albeit twisted, principles. The people of the South, for complex social and economic reasons, chose to retain the peculiar institution as a matter of their own "popular sovereignty."

No one supposed that the Convention had a mandate to abolish slavery. (As well might it abolish marriage or private property.) Yet southern delegates knew that a federal government armed with commercial power might conceivably harm the peculiar institution, deciding, for example, to abolish the slave *trade*. The issue was further complicated by southern demands that slaves be counted in state populations for the purpose of representation in the lower house—and the northern belief that slaves shouldn't be counted at all. Conversely, should slaves be counted or not for the purpose of levying a given state's taxes?

Once again the voice of compromise prevailed. After much debate, the delegates decided upon the three-fifths rule, allowing three-fifths of a state's slave population to be counted both for representation *and* taxation. The slave trade would remain unmolested

Library of Congress

A Slave Auction in the South by Theodore Davis, 1861. The Constitutional Convention allowed slave trade to continue for twenty years.

for a period of twenty years, which gave the South a bit of breathing space. And authority would be included for fugitive slave legislation, without which slaves might flee from the South to freedom.

Major trouble would ensue from the slavery compromise. The protection of a morally doubtful enterprise was written into the nation's charter. The fugitive slave law would someday license kidnapping—after all, who could tell that a given African was *not* an escaped slave?—while the three-fifths rule would invite Southerners to expand their political power by importing more slaves. The twenty-year reprieve for the slave trade rolled out the welcome mat to slavers around the world, foreclosing any possibility of the peculiar institution dying out. Americans, on the record for human freedom, were now on the record for human bondage. Yet, as the delegates well knew, compromise on the slavery issue was *the* price of union, period.

Behind the Constitution

Whatever else it did, the Constitution had to confront the Republican Problem. The government it created must be given sufficient power to govern effectively, lest anarchy ensue. But the government must also be constrained from drifting into tyranny, as had the government of Great Britain.

James Madison, who became the Constitution's chief architect, agreed with Plato that the virtue of the people was the greatest single check against the abuse of power. He believed, however, that virtue would often fail. His view of human nature, shared by many other delegates and borne out by historical experience, was that power could and would corrupt. There would always be a "court party."

The framers turned attention to what Madison called "auxiliary precautions"—a backup system to virtue. The idea was to structure the government to make it more difficult for power to become concentrated in anyone's hands, especially those of a tyrannical majority. Here, of course, they were following Aristotle.

As a guide for their structural architecture, the framers read Adams's *Thoughts on Government*. They also read prominent writers of the European Enlightenment—Hobbes, Locke, Puffendorf, Rousseau—and of the more recent Scottish Enlightenment, especially David Hume, whose jaded view of human nature argued for virtue's fragility. More than anything else, they read Montesquieu's *Spirit of the Laws*. What elements of structure, they asked themselves repeatedly, were conducive to free government?

Three Structural Devices

One of the answers was the bicameral legislature. The lower house would represent the people as a whole and be responsive to their desires. Its members would serve short terms of a mere two years, and they would have to return to the people repeatedly to renew their mandate. The upper house, representing the states, would be far different. It would be distanced from the people, and its members would serve long terms of six years, with staggered elections. Where the lower house would be "hot" in its responsiveness to public opinion, the upper house would be "cool" with wisdom and reflection, and it was assumed by the framers that many a measure passed in democratic enthusiasm by the House of Representatives would fail in the more dispassionate Senate.

A second device was indirect election. Their reading of David Hume convinced them that the consent of the people could be filtered

HUME'S FILTER

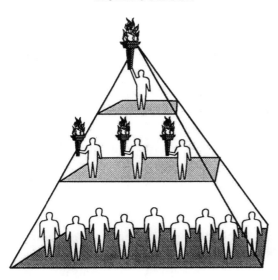

David Hume's idea of filtering the consent of the people through successive elections with representatives choosing representatives of their own, as if in an ascending pyramid. With each ascending tier of representation, there would be a refining process in the search of virtuous statesmen. Those few at the top of the pyramid would be far removed from popular passions and hopefully patriotic individuals of national reputation.

to good purpose in ascending tiers of representation. Voters, Hume argued, would always choose representatives from the wisest and most virtuous of their fellows, and if these representatives chose representatives of their own, the latter would be wiser and more virtuous still. The process would reflect the consent of the people, but it would be filtered through wisdom and virtue. Senators would be chosen not by the people directly but by their representatives in the various state legislatures. The president would be chosen by special electors in each of the several states. Federal judges would be chosen by presidents who themselves had been elected indirectly. It was a complicated system, and to some an unworkable one. But it did work.

A third structural device was called "enumeration." The powers of the federal government were enumerated—listed in black and white. Accordingly, unlike any government before it, the federal government's sovereignty lay only in certain areas. Congress was given the authority to lay and collect taxes, regulate commerce, coin money, set up a postal service and a patent office, declare war, raise and support a military establishment, and attend to certain other national concerns. All other powers of government remained with the equally sovereign states.

Separation of Powers

Beyond these elementary devices, the framers set about to fragment power and place its components in separate hands. The term for this unusual approach to structure was *separation of powers*. It had been discussed by Montesquieu, and provisions for it had been included in several state constitutions. But no one really knew how to make it work. How could the executive power actually be separated from the legislative power, while still allowing for their cooperation? How could the judicial power be separated from the other two? Toughest of all, how to make the separation actually work? The state experience had shown how easily an aggressive legislature could cross that parchment barrier and invade the other branches.

Yet there was a compelling theory behind the concept, having to do with the rule of law. If the rule-making power and the rule-enforcement power were placed in separate hands, then the rule maker would perforce have to operate blindly—he could never use his authority arbitrarily. The same went for the rule enforcer. If there really was a way to bring it off, the separation of powers promised laws that were more likely to be general, prospective, public, and so on.

The delegates in Philadelphia stumbled onto their method by accident while designing the presidency. They supposed at first that the executive should be chosen by Congress, that he should be a kind of servant to "execute" the congressional will. Yet they also wanted the executive to be a leader, like the British prime minister, capable of rallying public opinion and focusing common effort. The two requirements didn't fit together. Then James Wilson had a strange idea. What if it were possible for the executive to be elected by the people rather than by the Congress? This would take some doing, to be sure, in a world without rapid transit or mass communication. An indirect election would have to be utilized, but if it *could* be accomplished, think of the result. The executive could be made as strong and independent as Congress itself—yet be responsible to the people.

It required amazingly complex negotiations for the Committee on the Executive to put all the pieces together. We take the American presidency for granted, forgetting how improbable the office really is, and how deftly it combines enormous authority with humble submission to the popular will. That was precisely the point. With separation

The Granger Collection, New York

James Wilson by Albert Rosenthal, 1888. Wilson worked on the separation of powers in the Constitution and proposed that the president be elected by the people.

of powers, the president would be given powers *greater* than those of most monarchs. He would conduct foreign affairs. He would be commander in chief. He would appoint high officials. He would execute the will of Congress and implement the laws. He would run the federal establishment and wield awesome powers of patronage. He would be the country's foremost political figure. He would represent *all* of the people. As we scroll back through our history, the names of great presidents mark out eras and ages: Reagan, Kennedy, Franklin Roosevelt, Wilson, Teddy Roosevelt, Lincoln, Jackson, Jefferson, Washington. We build monuments to them, set up presidential libraries, and chisel their features on Mount Rushmore. Yet when their terms of office expire, they quietly step out of the limelight.

The framers managed this partly by giving the executive his own enumerated powers (and of course his own separate election) but also by giving him the conditional veto. Together these two devices made it possible for the president to be both strong *and* independent. John Adams had suggested as much in his *Thoughts on Government*. Congress could never push the executive around or usurp his authority as long as he could protect himself with the veto. Conversely, the executive could never terrorize or blackmail Congress as long as Congress could override the veto by a two-thirds vote.

Such was the genius of separated powers. Next to federalism, it was the Founding's most important contribution to political theory and constitutional practice: a strong executive and a strong legislature yoked, yet with independent wills—and *both* responsible to the people.

The founders also applied the separation of powers logic to the federal court system. Unlike those state courts where the legislature was constantly meddling, the federal courts were shielded. Once appointed and confirmed, justices of the Supreme Court (and later on, other federal courts as well) had tenure for life, barring bad behavior that could get them impeached. Their salaries could not be reduced, nor could their bureaucratic establishment be tinkered with, for they controlled it themselves. Those who enforced the rules were their own bosses. Accordingly, those who *made* the rules had to make them blindly.

Checks and Balances

Separation of powers created a tendency for each branch of government to go its own way. The framers did not want structural anarchy, of course, nor did they want gridlock. So they bridged their walls of separation with a system of *checks and balances*, which was a different kind of mechanism entirely.

The British government was replete with checks and balances, as we have seen. Each had a check upon the other, and the two must balance one another to consummate the action. Even if each eyed the other skeptically, they were motivated to cooperate.

In the U.S. Constitution, the bicameral legislature was a check and balance. Both halves of the Congress had to agree for a bill to become law. There were other examples of this mechanism. The appointment of many high-ranking officials—Supreme Court justices, ambassadors and ministers, Cabinet officers, and the like—was to be made by the chief executive but subject to the advice and consent of the Senate. Advice and consent altered the psychology of appointment considerably. The president would have a hard time installing mere cronies in high places if he must go before the Senate and explain each nomination.

The diplomatic and war-making powers both included checks and balances. Congress alone could declare war, but once that was done, it was up to the president (as commander in chief) to fight it. If Congress didn't like the way things were going, it could scotch any war effort simply by refusing to fund it. When it came to foreign affairs, the president was more or less given a free hand, but any treaty he negotiated had to be ratified by two-thirds of the Senate.

CHECKS AND BALANCES

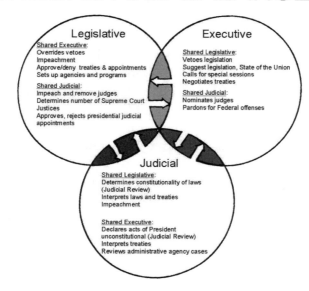

Legislative

Shared Executive:
Overrides vetoes
Impeachment
Approve/deny treaties & appointments
Sets up agencies and programs

Shared Judicial:
Impeach and remove judges
Determines number of Supreme Court
Justices
Approves, rejects presidential judicial
appointments

Executive

Shared Legislative:
Vetoes legislation
Suggest legislation, State of the Union
Calls for special sessions
Negotiates treaties

Shared Judicial:
Nominates judges
Pardons for Federal offenses

Judicial

Shared Legislative:
Determines constitutionality of laws
(Judicial Review)
Interprets laws and treaties
Impeachment

Shared Executive:
Declares acts of President
unconstitutional (Judicial Review)
Interprets treaties
Reviews administrative agency cases

Checks and balances in the Constitution.

Congress was given unspecified powers of investigation and impeachment—yet another element in the check-and-balance machinery. Congress could investigate virtually anything it chose to and bring corruption to light. For treason, bribery, or other high crimes and misdemeanors, Congress could impeach (by a majority of the House) and convict (by a two-thirds majority of the Senate) high officials in the federal establishment, including the president himself.

The framers, James Madison later explained, had tried to design their machinery in such a way as to give various authorities both the constitutional means and personal motives to seek justice, serve the public interest, and resist incursions into their respective domains.

The Extended Republic

Some of the Constitution's auxiliary precautions were extremely subtle. One of these deserves special mention. Like federalism itself—which created a whole new set of checks and balances by counterposing the sovereignty of the states against that of the federal government—the device in question was a happy accident. It derived from the size of the American Republic, which we recall to have been a major stumbling block going into the Philadelphia Convention.

Classical republican theory had held that republics must be compact in size and manageable in population, like the *poleis* of ancient Greece. The founders supposed that too large a nation-state would quickly succumb to factional infighting. In the ancient world, factions—groups organized around influential politicians or competitive interests—had been troublesome enough, creating endless turmoil and confusion. The Founders feared that in an extended republic such as the United States, factions might become so large and powerful that they could never be brought under control.

James Madison began to rethink this idea in the course of the constitutional deliberations, and by the end of the Grand Convention he had reached a surprising conclusion. Republican theorists had gotten it backward. In the extended republic, as Madison was soon to reason in *The Federalist*, there would be many factions, but for that very reason they would render the body politic not *less*, but *more*, stable. In a small *polis*, any given faction might be large enough or powerful enough to take over, as had been the case in tiny Rhode Island. In a sprawling, continental-sized republic, no single faction could come close to possessing such clout. In an extended republic the factions would contend with one another in an endless game of "king of the mountain," pulling each other from the pinnacle of power the moment any single contender threatened to succeed.

The United States Constitution was the product of nearly two centuries of historical development in which constitutions of various sorts played a role. It was inspired by the English experience and by that of the ancient world. It was designed for a free people and a virtuous people, as John Adams stoutly asserted, and many of its mechanisms were based on the idea that virtue, properly arranged, should play a decisive role in political outcomes. Yet it was also designed for self-interested human beings and even potentially corrupt ones, for its mechanisms depended on counterpoise, pitting interest against interest, ambition against ambition.

Perhaps the greatest achievement of the Constitution was its embodiment of the social compact. Americans had come together freely, analyzed their constitutional difficulties, and through wisdom and reflection worked out a plan of government that addressed the Republican Problem. At the signing ceremony in September 1787, emotions—which had been so ragged in the course of the long deliberations—ran high. Benjamin Franklin, who often cast amorphous feelings into memorable words, quipped about the sun carved into the back of the convention president's chair. He had long wondered, he said, whether it had been a rising or a setting sun, and was pleased now to conclude that it was a rising one. There was a chuckle or two and a light patter of applause. All the same, there were tears in the old man's eyes when he signed the historic document.

Corbis

The Sun Chair in Independence Hall.

Chapter 7

Starting the Engine of Government

The signing of the Constitution was an auspicious and poignant occasion, one often portrayed by American artists. Still, the drafted document was merely a proposal, not an accomplished fact. Just as few nation-states had ever worked up their own plan of government, few had ever faced the task of putting such a plan into action. It was a little like taking a rough sketch of some enormously complex machine and then figuring out how to build it.

The Signing of the Constitution by Howard Chandler Christy, 1940.

Ratification

The approval of the new Constitution was anything but a foregone conclusion. For one thing, the Grand Convention had vastly exceeded its mandated authority, which as we recall was only to modify the Articles of Confederation. Then, too, several of the Philadelphia delegates had left the proceedings in disgust and promised to fight any proposal that came forth. Even more embarrassing, three framers of the document—Edmund Randolph, George Mason, and Elbridge Gerry—had refused to sign it, believing that too much had been compromised.

A still greater difficulty was posed by the American people themselves. While most of them generally recognized the shortcomings of the Confederation, they accepted the basic premise of classical republicanism—local sovereignty. Their vision was of a loose federation of independent republics, like the *poleis* of ancient Greece. The idea of an American nation as such would strike them as radical and perhaps even dangerous.

As Locke imagined the social compact, it was the people themselves, not simply a few leaders, who must decide on their form of government. Americans took this injunction seriously. They understood, for example, that it would not be up to the Confederation to accept or reject the proposal made in Philadelphia. Additionally, Americans came to see that the state governments were irrelevant as well, so far as approval or disapproval went. The states as such could not create a constitution for the American people, only the people themselves could do that. They might ratify the draft document on a state-by-state basis for the sake of convenience; but the actual work of ratification, of debating the issue's pros and cons, needed to be accomplished in separate conventions, gatherings of the people *beyond* government.

At no time before or since have the American people been called upon to perform a more extraordinary feat. They were neither political scientists nor constitutional scholars—yet they had to perform the work of both. They had to decide for themselves if the mechanisms of the plan before them would really work, would truly deflect the danger of tyranny, and would actually hold a sweeping continental expanse together as a single *patria*. For this purpose, they needed to be mindful of Plato's cardinal virtues: wisdom, courage, temperance,

Library of Congress

Samuel Adams by John Singleton Copley. Adams was an opponent of the Constitution.

and justice. A great deal hung in the balance.

Opponents of the Constitution quickly emerged. Among them were some of the most accomplished and well-regarded statesmen in America: Samuel Adams in Boston, Patrick Henry in Virginia, Melancton Smith in New York. Nor were they lacking in substantive arguments, which came down to the following bill of indictment:

First, the Constitution proposed an "aristocratic" government, far removed from the people. The president would be as powerful as a king. The Senate would be like the British House of Lords. The Supreme Court justices, with their guaranteed salaries and lifetime tenure, would be politically untouchable. Didn't this all savor of that hated tyranny across the Atlantic from which we recently broke away?

Second, there could be no such thing as an "extended republic"—the term was an oxymoron. Republics were by definition "the public thing," as the term derived from Latin. They were small, local, particular, and run by the people themselves as friends and neighbors. What the Constitution proposed was no republic at all but an empire, like that of ancient Rome.

Third, the Constitution's carefully contrived mechanisms were all smoke and mirrors. Take the enumeration of powers in Article I, Section 8, for example. It looked impressive—laying out the boundaries of congressional power—but read the fine print. Congress could also make "all Laws which shall be necessary and proper for carrying into Execution the foregoing Powers"—a weasel clause if there ever was one. Who got to decide what was "necessary and proper" for building a navy or regulating commerce?

The most telling charge against the Constitution—and the one that packed the most weight—was that it lacked a bill of rights. Ratification would ultimately be decided on this issue. If the framers in Philadelphia had been so innocent behind their closed doors, why hadn't they included any guarantees of American rights and privileges?

The Anti-Federalists were more than just "anti." They had their own vision of America, and it was quite as compelling as the other side's. To begin with, it emphasized a healthy diversity. Anti-Federalist America would be a patchwork of local cultures, each of them vibrant and distinctive. The Anti-Federalists emphasized virtue. Americans would live a pastoral life close to the soil and close to the primary verities, a life of republican plainness and simplicity. Finally, the Anti-Federalists emphasized personal sovereignty. Americans would exercise power themselves, not pass it along to some distant capital. Theirs would be an energetic, town-meeting style of governance, under the guidance of decent, God-fearing citizens. If the Federalists' vision was of a city upon a hill, that of the Anti-Federalists was more like *Our Town*.

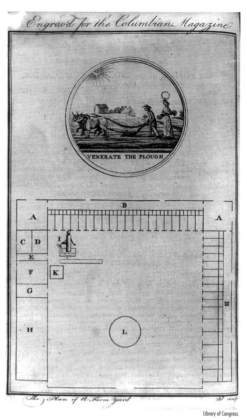

The Anti-Federalists emphasized a hardworking and virtuous life such as that depicted in this magazine illustration from 1786.

While the Constitution's opponents were more numerous and well entrenched, its advocates were on the whole younger, more energetic, and better organized. Moreover, they enjoyed stronger leadership, a factor that was to become crucial, sparked by many of the framers themselves. There were the Pinckneys down in Charleston, drawling softly as they outlined the Constitution's advantages to fellow planters. There was Hamilton in New York, intense, obsessive, fairly bursting with energy, anxious to face down his nemesis Melancton Smith.

That the Federalists could perform deft strategic maneuvers became evident by their appropriation of the word *federalism*. By calling themselves "Federalists," they made it seem as though they were advocating the very dispersal of power that their adversaries favored, which was not at all the case. At the same time, they forced the adversaries into the negative role of Anti-Federalists.

The Federalists soon hit upon a winning strategy. They would avoid rhetorical displays and empty bombast—the Anti-Federalists would become famous for both—and simply argue the merits of their case. On street corners, in ale houses, at public rostrums, the Federalists patiently answered their critics point by point, explaining how the Constitution not only created republican government but addressed the Republican Problem.

This 1793 cartoon ridicules the Anti-Federalists and depicts them as being in league with the devil.

When it came to the question of a bill of rights, the Federalists ran circles around their opponents. Anti-Federalists had hoped to use the bill of rights issue as a distraction. Their strategy was to call for another convention to insert the necessary clauses, knowing that any follow-up would surely fail. So instead of arguing that a bill of rights was unnecessary—which the Federalists truly believed—they promised voters that if the Constitution were ratified, a bill of rights would be the new government's first item of business, to be added by way of amendment.

Smaller states ratified the Constitution with less fuss, for once the Great Compromise had been forged, the small states saw themselves as benefiting from unification. The battlegrounds would be the three largest states—Virginia, Massachusetts, and Pennsylvania—plus New York. Without these four, no federal union could succeed.

Pennsylvania provided the Constitution's first real test. The state's politics was a free-for-all under the best of circumstances, with partisan bushwhacking, mass demonstrations, even the occasional riot. Friends of the Constitution had a majority in the Assembly, but foes thought they could block the call for a ratifying convention by keeping enough of their own members away to prevent the mustering of a quorum. No problem—in Pennsylvania. Federalist "bully boys" broke through a door, roughed up two of the truants and bodily carried them to the State House, where they were held in their seats for the roll call.

Nor was the convention itself much calmer. But James Wilson, one of the primary framers, delivered a masterful performance. Holding his head high to keep his glasses balanced on his nose, Wilson patiently answered objection after objection. The convention sat for a respectable five weeks and ratified the Constitution by a vote of 46 to 23. Wilson's reward was to be mugged—and nearly killed—by a band of ruffians while he was out celebrating.

The next test came with Massachusetts. This largest of the state conventions, some 355 delegates strong, gathered in Boston's Brattle Street Church, while controversy stormed in the press. As in Pennsylvania, local politics played a role in the proceeding, for backcountry farmers rattled into town to take on the seaboard merchants and their new-fangled government. One of these, a rough-hewn ploughman named Amos Singletry, discoursed at length:

These lawyers and men of learning, and moneyed men that talk so finely, and gloss over matters so smoothly, to make us poor illiterate people swallow down the pill, expect to get into Congress themselves. They expect to be the managers of this Constitution, and get all the power and all the money into their own hands. And then they will swallow up us little fellows.

Once again, though, the Federalists replied in kind. One of them also happened to be a farmer, similarly unlearned and similarly eloquent. "Mr. President," said Jonathan Smith,

My honorable old daddy there [referring to Singletry] won't think that I expect to be a Congress-man, and swallow up the liberties of the people. I never had any post, nor do I want one. But I don't think worse of the Constitution because lawyers, and men of learning, and moneyed men, are fond of it. . . . These lawyers, these moneyed men, these men of learning, are all embarked in the same cause with us, and we must all swim or sink together.

As happened in Pennsylvania, local politicos who had been among the framers in Philadelphia—Rufus King, Nathaniel Gorham, Josiah Strong—took to the floor in defense of their work, fielding question after question. On February 5, the opposition broke ranks and Massachusetts ratified 187 to 168. Had ten votes gone the other way, the American Union would have died.

If Massachusetts had been the largest of the state conventions, Virginia's was the ablest. The Assembly Hall of the House of Burgesses was packed with members of the tidewater elite. Madison was there of course, along with George Washington—but so were Patrick Henry and George Mason. Henry had boycotted the Philadelphia Convention when he "smelt a rat." Mason had sat through every hour of it and denounced the outcome.

Henry showcased the Anti-Federalist approach to constitutional debate. "Whither is the spirit of America gone?" he cried in rhetorical lamentation:

Whither is the genius of America fled? . . . We drew the spirit of liberty from our British ancestors. But now, Sir, the American spirit, assisted by the ropes and chains of consolidation, is about to convert this country into a powerful and mighty empire. . . . There will be no checks, no real balances, in this government. What can avail your specious, imaginary balances, your rope-dancing, chain-rattling, ridiculous ideal of checks and contrivances?

Against such a performance, James Madison must have felt puny indeed. He stood before the delegates, his hat in his hand (and his notes in his hat), his voice so frail that those in the rear had to strain to hear him. In the way of most Federalists, he simply plodded along with the dull, prosaic facts of the matter, answering questions, allaying concerns, parrying Henry's oratorical thrusts.

The real star of the show was Edmund Randolph. He too had been at the Philadelphia Convention and had refused to sign the Constitution. However, unlike his friend George Mason, who now hurled thunderbolts against the document, the stage-handsome governor had undergone a startling conversion and was in favor of ratification heart and soul. When Madison's strength finally gave out, Randolph rallied the flagging Federalists and took command—giving the political performance of his life.

Library of Congress

Edmund Randolph had initially opposed the Constitution, but later he helped it ratify in Virginia.

The Virginia convention made its decision on June 25. The Constitution won by a slender ten votes. When news of the victory reached Poughkeepsie on July 2, the New York delegates had been convened there for two weeks. As matters stood, Virginia was in the Union and the Constitution had sprung into life. The New York vote, taken on July 25, saw ratification squeak through 30 to 27.

It had been feared, early on, that New York might prove to be decisive—and its people were split down the middle. Three staunch Federalists, Alexander Hamilton, James Madison, and John Jay, decided to collaborate on a series of newspaper essays to enlighten the New York electorate. *The Federalist,* as they called their work, stands today as a monument of both political philosophy and political science. It provides us with one of the deepest and most penetrating inquiries ever into the nature of republican governance. It gives us some idea of the level on which the debate over ratification was carried on. We read it today with awe.

The Federalist answered all the charges leveled at the Constitution. It explained both the republican and democratic nature of the document, arguing that the framers had not set out to defeat popular government but to create an example of it that actually worked. The empire decried by the Anti-Federalists would be more stable, more free, and more just than any republic in the ancient world. As for the Constitution's intricate machinery, this, according to *The Federalist*, would purify consent so that public policy would truly reflect the public interest.

The essays were written in haste and were difficult to understand. But readers followed them, absorbed them, debated their fine points—as students continue to do today. For them it was not Political Science 101, of course, but a question that would shape lives and destinies. To their credit, the American people considered the merits of the case humbly and prayerfully. And in the end they ratified the Constitution.

First Captain of the Good Ship USA

No one was surprised by the election of George Washington as president in 1788. It was done by acclamation. Indeed, the ratification of the Constitution may well have turned on the assumption that Washington would be the first head of state. The framers had laid elaborate mechanisms in place to secure the president's election by the people as a whole, believing that the people—not Congress or some other body—would choose the wisest and most virtuous of all citizens as head of state. The system had worked, at least on the first go-around.

George Washington's classical virtues would be taxed to the limit by his calling as first president. For the *first* president, unlike his successors, would superintend the building of a new nation. Imagine for a moment what the job would entail.

Much of the constitutional text had intentionally been left vague. The framers believed that no plan of government should, or could, spell out details of institutional organization, much less describe how these would work in daily practice. In many cases, they had been

On April 30, 1789, George Washington was inaugurated as the first president of the United States.

unable to agree on important points and had left the text vague by way of compromise. In still other cases, the framers hadn't the slightest idea how a given concept would actually work. It was all left for Washington and his Cabinet to decide.

One thing the president could call upon was established tradition. Thus, some constitutional phrases could be taken as coded references to familiar practice. Moreover, because precedent was very powerful in the Anglo-American tradition, the president realized that whatever precedents he set might well be honored indefinitely. Small matters could assume large symbolic importance too. Consider the question of how to address the president: Your Excellency? Your Highness? Your Lordship? Your Majesty? Any of these might have set the presidency drifting toward monarchy—a danger much feared. Washington settled on the very republican "Mr. President."

If Washington happened not to like some feature of the Constitution, he needed only to ignore that feature or give it his own spin to banish it. When negotiating his first treaty, for example, he faithfully honored the wording of Article II, Section 2, that he should do so "with the Advice and Consent of the Senate." The first time he sought advice, however, he found members of the Senate to be so officious and meddlesome in proffering it that he never consulted them again. Nor have any of his successors.

Our impression of the federal government today is generally one of high organization and cool professionalism. It was not so in those early days. There was a hesitation and tentativeness in the national establishment that we would scarcely recognize—like actors on a stage in their first rehearsal, reading their lines mechanically and wondering where to stand. It was anything but certain, remember, that such a government could be made to work at all.

Had anyone but George Washington been the first president, we might still be arguing today about the shape, tone, and style of our governance. As it was, the United States was exceedingly fortunate to have a precedent maker in whom it could wholly trust.

The Bill of Rights

As the president and his Cabinet were reshaping the Constitution in one way, Congress was reshaping it in another. For, against all probability, the first Congress of the United States decided to press ahead on a bill of rights. The Federalists had promised to add this to the Constitution by way of amendment. However, there was nothing at all holding them to the promise, and since the whole issue had been trumped up in the first place, they might simply have forgotten about it. But this would be reckoning without Congressman James Madison of Virginia, a man who did not take campaign promises lightly. Madison volunteered to chair a committee to draft the amendments in question, and soon he was soliciting proposals from the states. These ten amendments were added to the U.S. Constitution in 1789.

The framers in Philadelphia had carefully considered the possible inclusion of a bill of rights—and had unanimously rejected it. There were important reasons for this. Bills of rights, which were very popular in the eighteenth century, had been affixed to several state constitutions and promulgated elsewhere as well. In rhetorical defiance, bills of rights challenged kings to remember the Lockean truth that the people had fundamental rights granted by nature, rights that government could not abrogate; indeed, rights which government was bound to protect. The framers accepted all this—it had justified their own Revolution—they simply didn't believe that it pertained to *republican* government. Why, they asked, would the people need to be protected against *themselves*? After all, the government's power lay with the people.

A second difficulty lay in enumerating the rights to be included in any bill. What were they, anyway, those "rights of man?" Some listings were short and concise, others lengthy and elaborate. Some included only a few basic items, such as Locke's "life, liberty, and property," while others delved into a luxuriant array, including the right to be taxed in proportion to one's means, and the right "to require of every public agent an account of his administration." The framers knew that any listing of rights would necessarily privilege the specific items named—at the expense of all others. Who knew what the future might bring? Could Madison have imagined, for example,

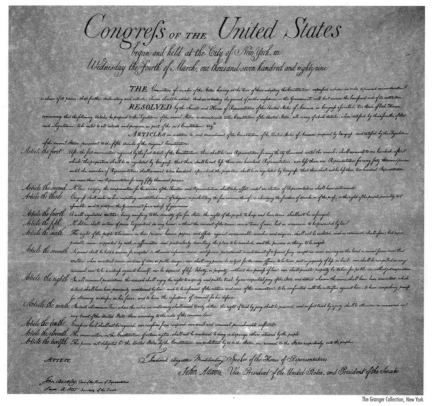

The Bill of Rights, 1789.

how twenty-first-century technology might undermine rights of privacy that in his time were taken for granted?

A third problem was enforceability. How was the vague language of natural rights ever to be applied to real-world situations? Affirming rights was one thing, actually protecting them quite another. Rights as such had never been respected, especially by Old World governments—rights had merely been *claimed*.

Finally, the American framers realized that the very notion of natural rights, however useful in a stand against tyranny, might also undermine legitimate governance. Should *all* people, for example, have an absolute and unqualified right to liberty? Or to privacy? Or to property? Or even to life itself? And if not, how do we deal with the various exceptions and qualifications? Put another way, the rights of the individual must always be seen in the context of society.

Madison the lawyer came to believe that these difficulties could be overcome. At the same time, Madison the political theorist came to believe that a bill of rights might indeed be necessary, even in a republican government. For, in spite of all the carefully contrived constitutional mechanisms, unpopular minorities still might be exposed and vulnerable. For example, what would stop a fear-driven Congress from, say, eliminating jury trial for accused spies, or denying aliens right of counsel?

Madison's strategy was to draft his document in careful legal language, trusting that judges of the land would see to its sane, moderate, and wise enforcement. He would create a bill of rights that could stand up in court.

Library of Congress

James Madison by W. H. Morgan, 1809. Madison wrote the Bill of Rights as a legal document that could stand up in court.

It was a tricky assignment. In drafting legal documents, one must make a fundamental choice in the kind of language to use. Broad, general, or abstract language might have rhetorical value, but it is difficult to apply to cases. Imagine, for instance, a court trying to interpret some general declaration such as: "All have a right to justice!" All who? Justice for whom? Justice from whom? Justice according to whom? What constitutes justice anyway? It might be a great battle cry, but it is awful legal language.

Fortunately there is another choice. Narrow, concrete language, full of specific terms and qualifiers, may have little rhetorical value—and usually sounds legalistic as well—but it is much easier to apply to cases. Instead of "all have a right to justice," think of drafting that general idea into a document that could stand up in to court:

> All members of the United Steelworkers, in good standing, with dues current, shall, in the case of a job dispute, have the right to an arbitration hearing in the presence of one company representative, one union representative, and one arbitrator agreeable to both.

It wouldn't make a great battle cry, to be sure, but if, say, a steelworker were to lose her job because of someone else's mistake, our long paragraph filled with specifics and qualifiers might at least get her a hearing.

Madison understood that natural rights had always been conceived the first way, which was the essence of the problem. Accordingly, he proposed to render them as civil rights wherever possible, toning them down and tightening them up, and thereby making them enforceable. Take the Third Amendment, for example:

> No soldier shall, in time of peace be quartered in any house, without the consent of the Owner, nor in time of war, but in a manner to be prescribed by law.

The wording is full of concrete terms such as *soldier*, *house*, and *quartered*, and with qualifiers like "in time of peace," "in time of war," and "without the consent of the Owner." Coded references are also used. While these may sound vague—"in a manner to be prescribed by law"—they actually refer to procedures that are well established.

Madison could have drafted the Third Amendment the other way, in which case it would go something like: "Government shall not

NATURAL RIGHTS
AND CIVIL RIGHTS

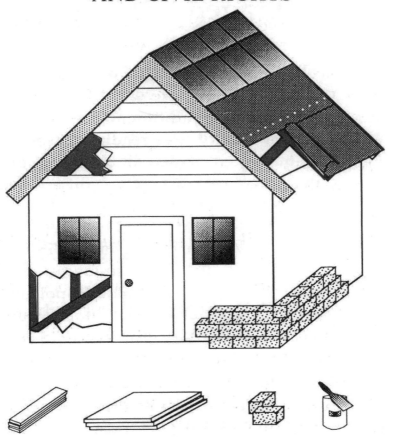

The framed, timbered house of natural rights provides very limited shelter
and privacy. Consequently, we use government to cover our framework of
natural rights with a variety of building materials, or civil rights, to make it a
more effective shelter for individuals.

interfere with private property." But think of the implications. Such
broad and abstract wording would prohibit quartering, all right—but
what else would it prohibit?

Madison's civil rights strategy explains why many of the rights
listed in the proposed amendments were drafted narrowly and concretely, and why the situations they addressed were not general woes

of mankind but specific difficulties that Americans had encountered before: the right to keep and bear arms, security from unreasonable searches and seizures, compensation for property taken by the state. In addition to these, Madison included a list of procedural guarantees, in the Fifth to Eighth Amendments, for those accused of crimes. Since most of these protections were found in the English common law, they, too, could be described by coded references. These amendments included everything from grand jury indictment, to trial by jury, to the right of counsel, to reasonable standards of punishment.

Three items in the Bill of Rights were not drafted narrowly and concretely. These are often regarded as the most important rights of all—the ones that come to mind when the Bill of Rights is mentioned. Clearly, Madison did not approach them in the way he approached the others, employing the language of natural rather than civil rights. They are:

- *Freedom of conscience.* Found in two separate clauses of the First Amendment.

- *Freedom of expression.* Found in four clauses of the First Amendment.

- *Right to privacy.* Implied by language of the First, Third, and Fourth Amendments.

The obvious question is Why, after Madison drafted most of the rights so narrowly, did he leave these three vague and general? Part of the answer is that there is simply no way to discuss religion, expression, or privacy in narrow and concrete terms—words fail. Beyond this, the topics themselves are of exceptional importance. Freedom of conscience, freedom of expression, and freedom to live one's own life may be considered the fundamental ends of republican government—the "happiness" that free people seek. Natural rights have been called "the Great Oughts," meaning that they don't proclaim an "is" so much as an "ought" about the world. People *ought* to be free. They *ought* to seek their own pleasure. And so on. Perhaps a good term for Madison's three exceptions to the will-it-stand-up-in-court rule is the Three Great Oughts.

Did Madison suspect that the inclusion of broad and abstract language in the Three Great Oughts might bring difficulties down the road? Possibly so. He must surely have known that courts would interpret and reinterpret terms like religion and speech, and courts might ultimately vest them with meanings that to him would seem bizarre. Satanism as religion? Nude dancers as free speech? This is not necessarily to say that Madison would have regretted his work. He felt strongly about republican government and the ends it served. Quite possibly he would allow his amendments to stand as they were written—protecting the flag burners along with those who stood to salute.

Judicial Review

The single greatest problem in putting the Constitution into practice lay in the question of how its text ought to be interpreted. Some of the blank spaces could be filled by common practice and others by executive decree. But in the early years of the constitutional experience, questions arose that could not be settled by either means.

During the administration of John Adams, for instance, France put the United States in a precarious situation. The French—who after all had helped out in the American Revolution—were seeking aid against their old foe, Great Britain. When such aid was not forthcoming, they took extraordinary measures to sway American opinion, including scalding denunciations of U.S. policy. Soon French privateers and American merchantmen were shooting it out on the high seas—and the new republic was drifting toward war.

In order to stifle the "seditious" writings of French propagandists, Congress passed a set of laws known as the Alien and Sedition Acts, prescribing heavy fines and jail terms for those who spoke out against the government. But wasn't this a clear violation of "free speech?" No one knew for sure, although opinion abounded on every side. Nor did anyone know whose opinion ought to prevail. The president's? Congress'? The courts'? Perhaps even the states', according to angry manifestos penned separately by Jefferson and Madison. With a written constitution, it was becoming clear, *someone* had to have the final say.

The framers in Philadelphia had discussed this problem, but they hadn't solved it. If a question of interpretation came up in colonial times, it was submitted to the Privy Council in London, which acted in the capacity of a law court. The framers may have assumed that the

Early chief justices of the U.S. Supreme Court, including John Marshall, by Kurz and Allison, ca. 1894. As chief justice of the Supreme Court, Marshall instituted the tradition of judicial review.

U.S. Supreme Court would play a similar role.

Such, at any rate, was the thinking of John Marshall, who was named chief justice of the Supreme Court in 1801. Marshall was about to pull off a stupendous filling in of constitutional blanks by unprescribed means—"writing" judicial review into the Constitution all by himself. Marshall believed that courts were the logical agency for resolving constitutional disputes. Having neither will nor energy of its own, the judicial branch was unlikely to exercise tyrannical authority, he reasoned. Therefore, when a question of interpretation arose, it was the judges who ought to answer it.

Marshall plotted his strategy with care. Sooner or later, he knew, a case would come along to provide the perfect pretext for judicial review, and when it did so he would be ready. Suddenly there it was. It emerged from the charged atmosphere in which the Alien and Sedition Acts had been passed, and in which John Adams had been defeated for a second term by Thomas Jefferson.

When it became clear that Adams and his party—who still called themselves Federalists—had lost the election of 1800, the outgoing president appointed a host of fellow Federalists to judgeships throughout the country. The triumphant Jeffersonians felt no great compulsion to deliver these midnight appointment documents. One of the new appointees, William Marbury, sued in court for the delivery of his commission. Specifically he requested a writ of mandamus, which was the traditional instrument used for such a purpose, to compel Jefferson's Secretary of State (James Madison) to convey the document in question.

Marshall instantly saw the beauty of the case. By deciding *against* Marbury, he would be thwarting the interests of his own party, and Jefferson would probably let the decision stand. Accordingly Marshall, in his written opinion, argued that there was no explicit grant of authority in the Constitution for the courts to issue writs of mandamus, and therefore that the Judiciary Act of 1789, which had set up the federal court system and specifically authorized writs of mandamus, had violated the Constitution.

It was a dubious argument. The Constitution had specified very few particulars pertaining to the federal court system, leaving Congress basically a free hand. The framers undoubtedly assumed that Congress would give the federal courts all powers that courts generally held—including that of mandamus. (Other such powers granted by the Judiciary Act went unchallenged.) However, finding no mention of mandamus in the constitutional text, the chief justice declared that clause of the Judiciary Act of 1789 null and void— unconstitutional.

Marshall went on to lay out four separate arguments justifying what he had done. None of the four was entirely convincing, perhaps, but judicial review did make constitutional sense. For one thing, it conclusively (and not unreasonably) answered the question posed above—*who decides*? For another, it added a whole new dimension of checks and balances to the federal system, very much in keeping with the framers' strategy. The judicial branch was now in a position to check both the legislative and executive, and they had to take that possibility into account.

Wisely, Marshall used the power of judicial review sparingly. What was important for him was to establish the precedent. Later, however, Supreme Court justices would have no such qualms. Like the Bill of Rights, judicial review would become something of a Pandora's box, especially when all those loose phrases found in the one came up for adjudication by the other. In due course, the U.S. Supreme Court would become an active player in the American political game.

By 1803, the year that *Marbury v. Madison* was handed down, it was clear that the American Constitution could indeed be put into action, and that constitutional government truly worked. Americans gained confidence in their new system—which they now spoke of as having been divinely inspired. At the same time, they increasingly thought of themselves *as* Americans rather than Virginians or New Yorkers. Proof of the Constitution's success galvanized a feeling of nationhood.

Chapter 8

From Unity to Political Parties

For most Americans, George Washington was the only acceptable choice as the first president of the United States. The citizens had much more confidence in him than they did in the new Constitution. Each of the electors selected for the Electoral College was to vote for two candidates. Every elector voting listed George Washington on his ballot. John Adams received the next most votes, and was selected as vice president. Washington's status and prestige was unrivaled, and no other political figure would dare directly challenge him. He assembled an extraordinary Cabinet with Thomas Jefferson as Secretary of State, Alexander Hamilton as Secretary of Treasury, Henry Knox as Secretary of War, and Edmund Randolph as Attorney General. Those four, along with Adams, brought great talent to the new government.

The Granger Collection, New York

A nineteenth-century engraving of the first Cabinet: U.S. President George Washington, Henry Knox, Thomas Jefferson, Edmund Randolph, and Alexander Hamilton.

George Washington hoped for unity within his administration. Indeed, the Founders did not really understand or accept the notion of a loyal opposition. They had been called traitors by the loyalists committed to the king of England, and the Founders saw those same loyalists, or Tories, as disloyal to the Revolutionary cause. Political parties were seen as factions to be lamented—and then controlled. The Founders held the hope that the new government with popular sovereignty and filtered consent would avoid political parties and the worst of factional behavior. Their hopes for the absence of political parties were soon shredded by the realities of political life.

Two towering figures dominated government in Washington's first administration: Alexander Hamilton and Thomas Jefferson. Thomas Jefferson, Secretary of State, was devoted to the ideal of a society composed of free, self-reliant individuals with a small government to protect their rights. He used the term "yeoman farmers" to describe the people who would dominate his ideal society. In Jefferson's utopian dreams, self-governing farmers tilled the soil by day and read science and political philosophy by candlelight in the evening. They were virtuous people in little need of government. Should tyranny arise, they would support another revolution and put things aright. Kings, with all their elegant trappings, held no philosophical attraction for Jefferson. He supported the revolution under way in France with an enthusiasm and hope not shared by many other Americans. Jefferson pretended to be uninterested in political power and intrigue. He claimed that he just wanted to retreat to his beloved Monticello to study, read, and farm. But he was always drawn back to politics and the challenges and intrigues of government.

The Granger Collection, New York

Thomas Jefferson by Rembrant Peale, 1800. Jefferson, as Secretary of State under President Washington, envisioned a virtuous society with a small government.

At the other side of the personality spectrum, Alexander Hamilton, Secretary of the Treasury, did not disguise his ambition. His view of the common people was marked by distrust and disdain. There must always be the rulers and the ruled, and he intended to be the one who ruled. For him, the task before the new government was the creation of a great empire that would dominate the Western Hemisphere and compete with the established powers of Europe. It was only a question of how best to create a great and powerful nation or empire. It was inevitable that Hamilton and Jefferson, two strong-willed and talented men with very different political ideologies, would clash. Indeed, the two men dominated the political scene most of the time until 1804 when Vice President Aaron Burr fatally shot Hamilton in a duel on a ledge above the Hudson River.

Library of Congress

Alexander Hamilton by Prud'homme. As Secretary of the Treasury under President Washington, Hamilton wanted a strong government to create an economic empire.

As Secretary of Treasury, Hamilton proposed an ambitious economic program to begin to build a nation, if not an empire. He argued with skill and, for the most part, success that the government should:

1. Assume the Revolutionary War debt of the states.

2. Pay off in full all the debt of the federal government, thereby establishing the financial reputation of the new nation.

3. Establish a Bank of the United States, patterned after the Bank of England, to manage the financial affairs of the country and to discipline and control private banks.

4. Negotiate a trade agreement with Great Britain.

5. Impose tariffs (taxes on imported goods) to encourage and protect domestic manufactures.

Hamilton's program was a U.S. version of the mercantilism of the British empire. He wanted to use the power of government to direct the economy in the path he thought best. He was certainly not committed to a free market economy that would follow its own course.

Jefferson was appalled by Hamilton's economic proposals. Paying off the government debt in full would enrich Hamilton's speculator friends, who had bought up much of the debt for pennies on the dollar. A Bank of the United States would put too much power in a few hands. Tariffs would hurt the yeoman farmers and create a merchant and manufacturing class that would be much like nobility. Jefferson believed in minimal government, not active management of the economy. He accepted Adam Smith's critique of mercantilism as well as Smith's advocacy of an unregulated market economy. Jefferson argued that the Constitution narrowly limited the powers of government. To Jefferson, Hamilton's program assumed powers that the Constitution had not granted to the government. Moreover, Jefferson saw revolutionary France as the young country's natural ally, rather than Great Britain, its former master.

Out of this clash of personalities and ideologies, America's first two political parties were born. On one side were those who wanted a relatively powerful federal government, capable of managing the economy and putting down any impulses of anarchy that might pop up among the common people. This government should align itself in Europe with the forces of stability (Great Britain) not the forces of revolution (France). This faction came to be known as the Federalist Party. The Federalists were led by John Adams and Alexander Hamilton, with the reluctant blessing of George Washington.

On the other side were those who wanted a narrow, strict interpretation of the Constitution. The Constitution said nothing about creating a bank or encouraging manufactures with tariffs. Government was best that governed least. This group was led by Jefferson and James Madison, but they had a problem. They couldn't be known as the Anti-Federalists, the name reserved for opponents to the Constitution. So they adopted the awkward name of Democratic-Republicans.

By 1796, Washington had served two terms as president and was ready to retire to Mount Vernon. Adams, with Hamilton's influence behind the scenes, became the Federalist candidate, while Jefferson was the candidate of the Democratic-Republicans. A hard-fought campaign ended with Adams narrowly winning, with 71 electoral votes to 68 votes for Jefferson. Because of the nature of the Electoral College, Adams became president and Jefferson, vice president. While Adams was occupied with the presidency, Jefferson and Madison were free to build a Democratic-Republican Party that would dominate national politics for the next thirty years. While Jefferson, with the aid of Madison, unified the Democratic-Republican Party, the Federalist Party was soon split between Adams and Alexander Hamilton. Only a few years after the adoption of the Constitution, these two distinct political parties emerged to contest the elections for president and Congress as defined in the Constitution. In his Farewell Address, a somewhat dispirited George Washington took the opportunity to "warn you in the most solemn manner against the baneful effects of the spirit of party generally." That warning went in vain.

From 1800 to 1828, the Democratic-Republican Party held the presidency, although Federalist opposition was active in the House of Representatives and the Senate. But by 1824, it was clear that the Federalists were out of step with the emerging nation. The presidential election of 1824 was a contest between several candidates representing wings of the Democratic-Republican Party. There was not a clear winner in the Electoral College, although Andrew Jackson received the most electoral votes as well as 41 percent of the popular vote. Without anyone receiving a majority of the electoral vote, the choice of president was left to the House of Representatives, where John Adams's son, John Quincy Adams, was selected as president. Jackson and his supporters were furious, feeling that the election had been stolen. They proceeded to build the Democratic Party, while their opposition coalesced into the Whig Party.

Jackson had achieved fame in the battle of New Orleans at the close of the War of 1812. He was a politician of the frontier, representing Tennessee in the House of Representatives and the Senate. He appealed to the common man and the democratic impulses in America. With his elections in 1828 and 1832, campaigns and voting took a large step down the path of increased democratization—a trend the United States has continued to follow.

These two parties dominated politics until the 1850s, when the Republican Party eventually supplanted the Whig Party. Since 1860,

Andrew Jackson by Howard Pyle. Jackson's election as president in 1828 was viewed as a triumph for the common man.

every president and virtually all representatives to the national government have been members of either the Democratic Party or the Republican Party. Strange as it may seem, neither the Constitution nor any election laws require that our politics be dominated by two parties. Yet, such has always been the case. The reasons for two-party politics in the U.S. may be found in the Constitution and our election laws following the Constitution.

The Constitution and Politics

The Constitution makes no mention of political parties, but it does outline a structure for selection of members of the House of Representatives, the Senate, and the Supreme Court, as well as the selection of the president. This structure exerts powerful influences on the nature of American politics and campaigns. It is important to understand the links between the constitutional structure and politics. This linkage between the Constitution and politics is the fundamental principle of a representative democracy and the rule of law—consent. The people gave original consent when the Constitution was ratified and first implemented. With each election, they renew their consent or give periodic consent for the government to function. The Constitution demands these elections in order to give the government legitimate authority from the people.

The Founders rejected the idea of "direct democracy," where the people vote directly on laws and directly manage the affairs of government. They knew that direct democracy could only be implemented in a very small country or a city. They had some experience with direct democracy at the town or county level. But, even in a small country or state, direct democracy was easily corrupted by a mob mentality, or by demagogues who led the people astray. The Founders were confronted with the fundamental problem of democracy. How do they give the power of consent to the people without exposing the country to the manifest dangers of mob rule?

The Founders chose "filtered consent," in which the people selected representatives, who then selected other representatives in the government. This process of election of representatives was to filter out the temporary feelings and mistakes of judgment that might dominate the direct vote of the people on matters of government. The more removed a decision was from the people, the more filtered the consent of the people. Of course, government too removed from the people loses consent, and its legitimacy becomes more susceptible to tyranny.

The technical problem was to pick the right set of filters for consent that preserved democratic control while preventing the problems associated with the temporary passions of the people. Consent becomes more filtered:

- If elections are further apart in time.
- If a larger population is represented by each representative.
- If the selection process is more indirect (that is, the people pick representatives who select the government officials).

Constitutional Structure of Politics

The House of Representatives

The Constitution specified direct election of members of the House of Representatives every two years in districts of more or less equal population. A census is taken every ten years to determine the changes in population and re-draw the boundaries of the House districts to

FILTERS OF CONSENT

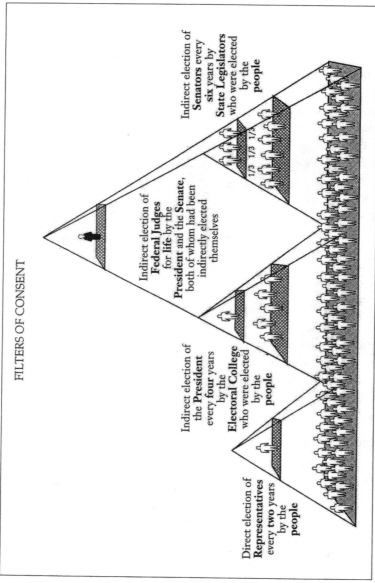

Indirect election of **Senators** every six years by **State Legislators** who were elected by the **people**

Indirect election of **Federal Judges** for life by the **President** and the **Senate**, both of whom had been indirectly elected themselves

1/3   1/3   1/3

Indirect election of the **President** every **four** years by the **Electoral College** who were elected by the **people**

Direct election of **Representatives** every **two** years by the **people**

To maintain a popular government while insuring against a democratic one, the Founders designed a complex system which would process the consent of the people through a set of filters. There were direct and indirect elections, staggered elections (in which one-third of the Senate would be up for election every two years) and overlapping terms of office (two, four, six, life).

Those with few filters between them and the people would necessarily be closer and more accountable to the often capricious passions of the people. Those with more filters between them and the people would be farther removed from the people, with greater opportunity for more cautious, reflective response to popular will.

reflect population change. Originally each representative represented no more than 30,000 people (with the odd provision of a slave being counted as three-fifths of a person). As the population grew, more representatives were added, with each representing more and more people. After the apportionment based on the 2000 census, districts for the House of Representatives were composed of roughly 650,000 people, except in the states with only one representative. By using direct election every two years, the Founders designed the House of Representatives as the part of government closest to the people. All other parts of the federal government are more removed from the people because of more filters of consent.

The Senate

The Senate represented more filtered consent. The two senators from each state were originally selected by the legislatures of each state and were to serve for terms of six years. The Seventeenth Amendment (1913) required that senators be elected directly by the people, but the term of office was left at six years. Thus, senators were more removed from the people than members of the House of Representatives because they represented a larger group of people and were selected for a longer period of time.

The President

The Constitution set up an elaborate and somewhat confusing mechanism for the selection of the president. Each state selected a number of electors, equal to the number of senators and representatives from that state, to vote for the president of the United States. This group of electors came to be known as the Electoral College. The Constitution gave the state legislatures the power to determine how members of the Electoral College were selected with the restriction that no representatives, senators, or federal officials serve as electors. In practice, most electors have been chosen directly by the people. That is, each party or presidential candidate chooses a slate of presidential electors. As the people cast their vote for the presidency, they are, in reality, voting for that candidate's slate of electors. The electors committed to the presidential candidate receiving the highest popular vote are chosen.

THE ELECTORAL COLLEGE

Original Practice

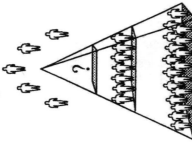

Originally, presidential electors were chosen by the people, solely on the basis of individual merit and voted according to their own discretion (above). Without changing a word in the Constitution, however, actual practice of the electoral college has changed significantly. The people essentially bypass the filter of the electoral college and vote directly for the presidential candidate of a given party. It is the political parties which now choose the electors, not so much on the basis of merit, but rather on the basis of loyalty to the party. For example, if a state has, say, seven electoral votes, each party chooses seven individuals committed to vote as a block for the respective presidential candidate of the party (below). The winning party candidate of the state's popular vote (Democrat) takes all the electoral votes, while the losing party candidate (Republican) takes nothing, despite receiving a substantial portion of the state's popular vote.

Originally, electors voted for two individuals for the presidency. This flaw in the Constitution created a deadlock in the election of 1800, when Thomas Jefferson and Aaron Burr, both Democratic-Republicans, received the same electoral votes even though Jefferson was the presumed presidential candidate, and Burr the vice presidential candidate. The Twelfth Amendment corrected this flaw so that electors now cast their votes for president and vice president. If a candidate receives a majority of the electoral vote, he or she becomes president of the United States. If no candidate receives a majority of the electoral vote, the selection of the president moves to the House of Representatives, with a complex procedure specified in the Constitution. Fortunately, that method has only been used twice, in 1800 and 1824. Like the Senate, consent for the president is more filtered than the consent for the House of Representatives because the president represents the whole nation, serves for four years, and is not directly chosen by popular vote.

The Supreme Court

The part of government most removed from the people is clearly the Supreme Court and the federal judiciary. Justices for the Supreme Court and other necessary judges are nominated by the president and confirmed by the Senate. They serve as judges for life or until they choose to retire. Consequently, consent of the people for the judiciary flows through the consent given to the president and senators.

Each branch of Congress is the judge of the qualifications of its members and may refuse to admit or remove a member deemed unworthy to be a representative or senator. The House of Representatives also has the power to impeach the president or any federal judge. Impeachment is similar to an indictment in a criminal case. Once impeached, the person is judged by a trial with all senators acting as jurors. If convicted, the official is removed from office. Two presidents, Andrew Johnson and William Clinton, have been impeached, but neither was convicted by the Senate.

Elections

We can see that the Constitution sets out an elaborate system of elections to implement the principle of popular consent required for the

Filters of Consent in the United States Government

Governmental Unit	Scope of Representation	Method of Selection	Time in Office
House of Representatives	Districts proportional to population	Plurality* winner in the district	Two years
Senate	State	Originally selected by state legislatures. Now plurality winner in the state.	Six years
President	U.S.	Majority* of the electoral vote. If no candidate has a majority, determined by state votes in the House of Representatives.	Four years with maximum of two terms
Supreme Court	U.S.	Nominated by the president with consent of the Senate	For life or voluntary retirement

*"Plurality" means the winner received more votes than any other candidate, while "majority" means the winner received more than 50 percent of the votes.

rule of law. This constitutional and legal structure reduces to four main characteristics:

1. Separate election of the president.
2. Single representative districts.
3. Plurality of votes is sufficient for election except in the Electoral College.
4. Fixed intervals for elections.

Separate Election of the President

In many democracies, the chief executive officer of the government (prime minister in most countries) is selected by the legislature. The party with the most representatives in the legislature, or a coalition of parties, forms a government and selects government officials. This power to select the prime minister and other executives of government is the most important legislative function in countries using this method. Because no single political party may have a majority in the legislature, a coalition of parties may be required to form a government. If a coalition is needed, small parties may play a role in forming the government and choosing the prime minister. This possibility may give small parties power beyond their few representatives in the legislature.

For example, four parties formed a government in Israel in 1993 with representatives of each party in the executive branch of Israel's government. Recently in Germany, the Social Democratic Party and the Green Party formed a coalition to govern. The Green Party, which received only 9 percent of the vote nationally for the legislature, was able to appoint several influential government officials because it was willing to form a coalition with the Social Democratic Party. Whenever a prime minister is selected by parliament, political parties exert discipline over their elected representatives because the government requires the support of the members of the ruling coalition to stay in power. If the coalition fails, the government fails, requiring new elections.

In the United States, the president is elected separately and independently from the legislature. Many times one party will capture the presidency in an election, and another party will hold majorities in one or both houses of Congress. Small parties cannot wield this disproportionate power by supporting another party's presidential candidate because the president is elected independently. This independent election of the president also weakens ties between the president and Congress. In a parliamentary system where the chief executive is chosen by the legislature, parties maintain tighter control over the voting behavior of members of the legislature. In contrast, members of the U.S. Congress are all elected independently and, consequently, behave more independently. There is less party discipline in the U.S. Congress compared to the legislatures of most other democracies because party control of the executive branch is not directly tied to legislative action. Winning votes in Congress often draw almost equally from both parties, just as the opposition may contain numerous Republicans and Democrats.

Single Representative Districts

Like the independent election of the president, the use of separate and distinct districts or states to elect each representative and senator has a major influence on American politics. In many democracies, representatives in the legislature are proportional to the national vote for each political party. A vote of 20 percent for the labor party translates into more or less 20 percent of the representation in the parliament or legislature. Consequently, a party with some strength or popularity throughout the country will gain representation in the legislature, even though it may not receive the most votes in any part of the country. In the United States as well as most countries with an Anglo-Saxon heritage, a candidate must have more votes than anyone in a particular district in order for the party to be represented in Congress.

This structural device of single representative districts in contrast to proportional representation is a significant impediment to smaller or new political parties. A party with 20 percent of the vote in many districts will still not be represented in Congress. A party must sponsor a candidate who is a plurality winner in a particular district to achieve representation. This particular characteristic of single representative districts is not written directly into the Constitution. The Constitution simply requires that representatives be apportioned among the states by the census. But, election by districts was the common practice among the colonies at the time of the Revolution and has been the practice followed by virtually all of the states since that time.

Plurality Votes

Ordinarily, U.S. elections do not require a candidate to receive a majority of votes, only a plurality. The requirement of a majority typically implies that there must be some sort of runoff where parties whose candidates did not make the runoff throw their support behind one party or another. Generally each party holds a primary election if more than one person wishes to be the party's candidate for a particular office. In contrast to other countries, where party leaders often directly choose party candidates, anyone with a little money and time is able to enter the election process. The use of primaries with open entry of candidates contributes to the lack of cohesion in the party, because party leaders do not control access to candidacy for office.

Fixed Intervals

Finally, U.S. elections are at fixed intervals—every two years for the House of Representatives, every six years for the Senate, which means about one-third of the Senate is chosen every two years, and every four years for the presidency. Many parliamentary systems of government do not have fixed intervals for elections. Instead, elections are called by the legislative body within certain time limits.

PLURALITY
The largest block of votes cast.

Plurality

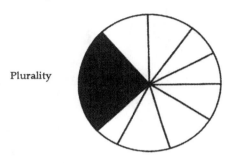

MAJORITY
More than half of all votes cast.

Majority

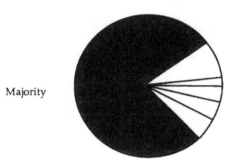

Electoral Changes in the Constitution since the Founding

The primary changes in elections have been increases in suffrage (those eligible to vote). The Fifteenth Amendment (1870) prohibited racial restrictions of the right to vote although that amendment was often circumvented until the Voting Rights Act of 1965. The Seventeenth Amendment (1913) required direct election of senators rather than choice by the state legislature. The Nineteenth Amendment (1920) extended voting to women, though women had been voting in various local and state elections for some time. The Twenty-fourth Amendment (1964) prohibited the use of poll taxes (a payment to vote) in federal elections. The Twenty-sixth Amendment (1971) reduced the voting age to eighteen.

Several other constitutional amendments deal with changes in the presidency. The Twelfth Amendment (1804) required presidential electors to vote once for president and once for vice president in order to avoid the problem encountered in the election of 1800. The

Library of Congress

A photograph of women surrounding Missouri Governor Frederick Garner as he signs a resolution ratifying the Nineteenth Amendment in 1920.

Twentieth Amendment (1933) changed the starting date of the term of office from March 4 to January 20 following the election and clarified the line of succession to the presidency under various scenarios. The Twenty-second Amendment (1951) restricted a president to two terms (or one term for a vice president who served more than two years in the presidency). Finally, the Twenty-fifth Amendment (1967) clarified the process to be followed if a president became incapacitated and unable to discharge his duties.

The Effects of This Structure on Elections

As we have seen in earlier discussions, the structure, or rules of the game, strongly influences outcomes. The constitutional structure of elections has profound effects on the nature of American politics. Overall, the result of this structure is to create politics characterized by large, relatively weak political parties, with politicians who try to appeal to the middle-of-the-road, centrist part of their electorate while keeping the support of their more extreme party supporters. This tendency for centrist politics is a direct result of the dominance of two parties in American elections.

The American political structure contains very strong incentives for two political parties sharing the power of government to the exclusion of all smaller parties. For 150 years, the Republican and Democratic Parties have shared political power and have been successful at either blocking or co-opting all third-party movements. From 1796 until 1860, a series of political parties were formed, but there were usually two dominant parties—first, Federalists and Democratic-Republicans, then Democrats and Whigs. This dominance by two parties does not mean that other parties do not exist or are not able to enter elections. There have been many small parties throughout U.S. history, representing a variety of points of view.

The colorful list of parties that have attracted some support over the years include Anti-Masonic, Free Soil, Greenback, Prohibition, Union-Labor, Populist, Socialist, Progressive, Farmer-Labor, Communist, States' Rights, American-Independent, Libertarian, Independent, Green, and Reform to name only the most prominent. But none of these parties was able to share directly in government power.

Why has American politics been characterized by two large political parties, competing for political power, while most other democracies have more than two parties represented in their legislature and other offices? The incentives run consistently against small parties. The separate election of the president deals a severe blow to the influence of third parties. Selection of the chief executive of the government by the legislature creates the real possibility that small parties may become power brokers in the selection process. Because the American president is elected independently, third-party candidates could affect only presidential elections by capturing electoral votes and then throwing that support to one of the major candidates. Unfortunately, they would have to win one or more states to have electoral votes. Even if a third party did capture a significant number of electoral votes, the selection of president would probably be determined by the House of Representatives, which is controlled by the two major parties. The U.S. method of presidential selection militates against third parties.

A third party can act as a spoiler by siphoning enough votes away from one candidate to elect the other major candidate. One of the most successful third-party candidates in recent history was H. Ross Perot, who ran in the 1992 and 1996 presidential elections. In 1992,

Perot received no electoral votes but won 19 percent of the popular vote. Election experts theorize that Perot acted as a spoiler because he garnered many votes that most likely would have been cast for George H. W. Bush. As a result, William Clinton became president with less than a majority of votes. For the 1996 election, Perot garnered only 8 percent of the popular vote, but even that was a respectable amount for a third-party candidate. Similarly, many observers believe that Ralph Nader and the Green Party were spoilers in the election of 2000 by costing Vice President Al Gore the electoral votes of Florida.

An election must be very close for a third party to have this effect on a presidential election, and the third party must be willing to see the candidate less congenial to their policies win the election. For most presidential elections, the effect of third-party candidates on the electoral vote and presidential elections has been negligible.

What about third-party representation in Congress? In the U.S., it is very difficult for a third party to elect even a few representatives. To do so, that party must gain a plurality in one or more congressional districts—a real challenge. Note again that it is much easier for smaller parties to gain representation in a legislature if there is representation based on national or regional voter percentages instead of single representative districts. Even if a third party were to prevail in one or two congressional districts, the two major parties would exclude the third-party representatives from influential congressional committee assignments, where legislation and government budgets are formulated. Voters would soon realize that their representatives were ineffective in the day-to-day business of Congress. In the past 150 years, there have only been a handful of congressional representatives not affiliated with the two major parties.

Third parties do affect the political positions and campaign efforts of the two major parties. If a third party becomes significant at all, one or both of the major parties will try to co-opt the third party by supporting issues important to the third party and inducing leaders of the third party to join their ranks. Through this effort, third parties or their members are usually absorbed into the two major parties. Suppose a "Green Party" were to become a significant third party in American politics. One of the two major parties would probably become more pro-environment in order to attract voters and candidates away from the Green Party. Thus, American politics is almost completely dominated by two large political parties running candidates in elections at various levels.

Competition between two parties for political power changes the nature of elections and campaigns. There is a simple strategy to win an election with only two candidates. Candidates will try to position themselves in the middle of voter sentiment and to portray their opponent as extreme in some way. Figure 1 illustrates this strategy for an election involving one issue—the size and power of the federal government. To win the election, a candidate will take position A in the middle of the distribution of voter sentiment and will portray the opponent at either position B or position C. In a two-candidate race, the politician who successfully occupies the middle of the political terrain wins the election.

In the election of 1800 discussed above, Thomas Jefferson and his supporters tried to take the middle ground and convince voters that John Adams and the Federalists wanted too much government power and too much control over the people (position C). John Adams and his supporters tried to paint Jefferson as a lover of the French Revolution and disorder (position B). Both wanted the coveted middle ground in American elections (position A). If neither candidate is successful at convincing the voters that the opponent is an extremist, the election is usually close, as it was in 1800 when Jefferson and Burr prevailed with 53 percent of the electoral vote to Adams's 47 percent.

If one candidate is successful at portraying the other candidate as "out of the mainstream," the election may turn into a landslide for the middle-of-the-road candidate. This general pattern of "I'm in the

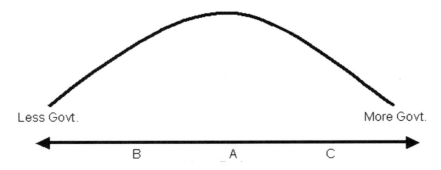

Figure 1. Voter Preferences

middle, my opponent is extreme" campaigning holds for presidential campaigns as well as campaigns for the Senate and the House of Representatives. It is important to note, however, that the distribution of voter preferences will change for each office. For president, the national distribution of voters is relevant. More accurately, presidential campaigns revolve around the distribution of voter sentiment in each of the fifty states since electoral votes are by state. For a Senate campaign in Arizona, only voter sentiment in that state is important, while a campaign to represent the Sixth Congressional district of Arizona involves primarily the voters of the Phoenix suburbs of Mesa and Gilbert. Politicians concentrate on the distribution of voters relative to their campaign. Note also that it is the distribution of voters that matters. If politicians know that one group, say the elderly, votes at a higher rate than another group, say young voters, they will tailor their appeal to the elderly and ignore the young, or try to mobilize a group of non-voters to participate in the election.

If both candidates are portraying themselves as middle of the road and have little chance of characterizing their opponent as extreme, campaigns are likely to be reduced to superficial issues and to personalities. Charisma, personal traits, campaign ads, and small differences in debates are likely to determine victory. (Election folklore has it that Richard Nixon lost the 1960 election to John Kennedy because he did not use make-up to hide the five o'clock shadow on his face. Similarly, John Dewey, the Republican candidate in 1944 and 1948, supposedly lost votes because of his mustache. Hair or lack of hair can be an issue in a close election.) In modern elections, campaign consultants and pollsters try to measure voter sentiment and position their candidate accordingly. They also fashion attack ads to portray the opponent as unethical or extreme. Campaigns are somewhat superficial and dirty when no big issues separate the two candidates. Personality and personal failings will receive undue emphasis.

Party affiliation may also play an independent role in a campaign. If a national party is viewed as extreme by the voters of a particular state or district, candidates from that party will have a difficult time trying to separate their own views from the views of the national party. In terms of Figure 1, a candidate may affiliate himself at position A, but his or her national political party is perceived by voters at position B or C. Such a candidate will probably lose the election,

The Granger Collection, New York

A photograph of John F. Kennedy and Richard M. Nixon during their 1960 televised debate. Did Kennedy win because of his charisma and Nixon's menacing five o'clock shadow?

because voters believe the national party will have some influence on their representative.

Influence of Elections and Campaigns on Government

Many Americans are dissatisfied with elections and campaigns. They complain that elections are too long, too dirty, too expensive, and have too little discussion of important issues. But the more important question might be how elections affect government. Because U.S. politics is centrist, government policy changes little in response to victory by either party. Government budgets tend to grow at about the same rate, regardless of the party in power. Legislation passed by one regime is rarely repealed when the other party comes to power. Just as campaigns concentrate on the middle of voter sentiment, government concentrates on middle-of-the-road policies. Only on rare occasions are there a wide policy difference between the major parties. Only rarely does American government shift dramatically from one policy position to another. Instead, changes are small and sporadic.

Many voters, especially voters without strong attachment to either party, respond to the times. If they believe the economy and society are going in the right direction, they tend to vote for incumbents (people in office) and reward the party in power. If they believe the direction is wrong, they tend to vote for a change in party. Historically, voters often punish officeholders for corruption or what they perceive to be personal failings by turning them out of office. Hence, U.S. elections tend to punish poor performance by political parties or individual politicians and reward positive performance.

Finally, because both parties tend to centrism, either party can successfully mobilize the government and the people in times of crisis. If there is truly a need for unity, such as during World War II or after the attacks of September 11, 2001, the government is able to command widespread support as long as the public perceives the need for unity.

Why Do Voters Vote?

Between 50 percent and 65 percent of the population over age eighteen vote in presidential elections. Less than half of potential voters cast ballots in congressional elections when the presidency is not at stake. Newspaper editorials and public officials urge people to vote and express wonder that so many people do not exercise their right to vote. To many social scientists, especially those who believe individuals are self-interested and rational, the question is the reverse: why do voters vote at all? The voter must find out where to vote, go to the polls, often stand in line, cast a ballot and travel home. Furthermore, to cast an informed vote, a voter must study some of the issues and the candidates' positions. This effort takes time that could be devoted to some other worthwhile activity. Why do voters incur the costs in time and effort to vote? The motive does not appear to be one of self-interest in the usual narrow sense of that term.

A rational voter realizes that it is very unlikely that his or her particular vote will determine the outcome of an election. The presidential election of 2000 was an exception in Florida. In that election, a shift of 269 votes in the official and disputed count would have tipped the electoral votes of Florida to Vice President Gore, making him the forty-second president of the United States. Even in this election, which was closer than any election in history, one had to live in Florida, and 268 other people had to vote differently, in order for one person's vote to determine the election. So it is unlikely that people vote because they think their vote will tip the balance. A rational voter also realizes that his or her vote is unlikely to have an economic effect on them and their family. One would find it difficult to identify a link between personal economic conditions and voting.

Voting appears to be motivated by personal, non-economic considerations. Some may vote because they enjoy the process of studying the issues and going to the polls. Others may vote out of a sense of obligation, or duty as a citizen. But it is hard to see how a rational person would vote out of self-interest. Following the philosophical underpinnings of the Founding, voting represents the act of consent of the voters. By participating in the voting process, voters are empowering the selected representatives with their consent to be governed by the laws and actions of their chosen representatives. This relationship between voting and consent may be the strongest reason for participation in elections and voting.

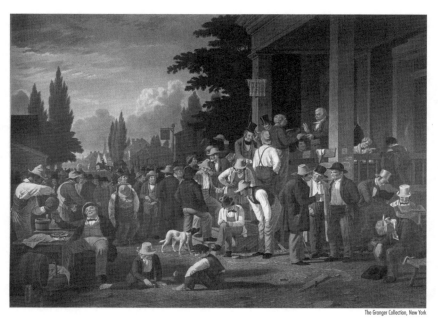

The Granger Collection, New York

The County Election by George Caleb Bingham. Voting represents the act of consent by the voters.

Chapter 9

Finishing the Founding

The bloodiest day in American history was in September—not September 11, 2001, but September 17, 1862. Fresh from victory at the second battle at Manassas, Virginia, General Robert E. Lee decided to take the Confederate army of Northern Virginia, 40,000 strong, north into Maryland to force U.S. President Abraham Lincoln to seek peace with the Confederacy. Confederate troops crossed the Potomac to Frederick, Maryland. Lee sent Stonewall Jackson to take the armory and garrison at Harper's Ferry, while Lee took the rest of his troops west to prepare for an attack in Pennsylvania. Near Sharpsburg, Maryland, Lee's group encountered the Army of the Potomac under Union General George McClellan, with some 60,000 troops; many of them newly recruited and untested in battle. Lee's troops dug in on high ground near a small church.

At dawn on September 17, Union artillery opened fire to soften Confederate positions for infantry attacks. The first large-scale battle was in Daniel Miller's twenty-acre cornfield. Confederate troops, positioned in the corn, waited for the Union troops to begin climbing over a small rail fence. Confederate soldiers then opened murderous fire; Union forces returned fire. The battle line surged from one side of the cornfield to the other. By 10:00 AM, about 8,000 men had been killed or wounded in that cornfield.

Later in the morning and during the noon hour, the battle shifted to a nearby lane used to haul farmers' produce. Through years of use, the lane had sunken down below the level of the fields, making it an ideal place for the Confederate troops to set up a defensive position. Time and again, Union troops, with battle flags flying, marched against the troops in the lane, but the Confederate troops held what appeared to be an ideal position to repel any attack. Eventually, that ideal defensive position was turned into a death trap. Two New York regiments captured the eastern end of the sunken lane and began to fire straight down, killing hundreds of soldiers and putting the Confederate army in retreat.

Elsewhere, a Union army of 12,000 attempted to cross a bridge over Antietam Creek to cut off the means of retreat for Lee's Confederate troops. A few Confederate sharpshooters, positioned in rocks and trees above the bridge, held off the Union troops until about 1:00 PM, when the Union army finally gained control of the bridge. With Union troops now nearing Sharpsburg, the Confederate army was in great peril. However, new Confederate troops arrived from Harper's Ferry about 3:00 PM, stopping the Union advance. General Longstreet, Lee's chief commander of infantry, later claimed that 10,000 fresh troops could have captured the whole Army of Northern Virginia, thereby defeating the South. But General McClellan, not one to take risks, had kept 20,000 troops in reserve, losing a precious opportunity to end the war. By 5:30 PM, the worst single-day battle in American history was over. The Army of Northern Virginia made its retreat back to Virginia, giving up the plan to attack Pennsylvania. Of course, they would come back to Pennsylvania the next summer and meet Union forces again at another small town—Gettysburg. Again, they would be driven back. And again, the Union army would fail to press its advantage.

September 17, 1862, was known as the battle of Antietam in the North and the battle of Sharpsburg in the South. Neither side really won that day, but Lincoln felt good enough about the result to issue his Emancipation Proclamation, freeing slaves in the areas of insurrection. Other battles fought over several days have had more casualties, but no battle in American history fought on a single day has ever concluded with such devastating results—an estimated 3,650 dead and over 17,000 wounded, many to die later of these wounds. For comparison, there were only 2,510 dead and wounded at Omaha and Utah beaches on D-day during World War II. Antietam was but one battle in a war stretching over four years and costing over

Library of Congress

A photograph of dead soldiers in front of Dunker Church at the battle of Antietam. This battle on September 17, 1862, was the bloodiest day in American history. Artillery damage appears on the side of the church.

600,000 lives. In every city, town, and village, there were men with an arm, a leg, or an eye missing. This was the worst kind of war—a civil war with horrific losses. It still seizes America's imagination and raises significant questions. What caused this bloody conflict? How could it have come to this just seventy-five years after a Founding with so much promise?

Unfinished Business—Slavery and Federalism

Every political act in a democracy involves compromise, and the Constitution was a political act. In an effort to reach agreement, issues were left unresolved, so each interest could read its own comforting interpretation into the document. The Founders left two vexing issues to be resolved by future generations, slavery and federalism. Between 1787 and 1860, many attempts were made to grapple with these tough problems. But these attempts failed, and the nation faced the bloody conflict called the Civil War in the North, and the War Between the States in the South.

First, the Founders did not confront the issue of slavery and its clear conflict with the ideals embodied in the Declaration of Independence and the new government. The issue was simply too volatile and too difficult to solve. Any direct attack on slavery would have been a "deal breaker" for the proposed Constitution. Instead, most of the Founders hoped that slavery would just fade away. The hope that time would solve this challenging problem shriveled as production of cotton in the South made slavery even more profitable. As Southerners moved west to new land in the Mississippi delta, they found the rich river-bottom land ideally suited to the plantation crops of sugar and cotton. Instead of fading away, slavery became more entrenched and economically important than ever in the early decades of the nineteenth century.

Second, the Founders kept the shared sovereignty between the national government and state governments studiously ambiguous. Federalism, this brilliant compromise between state sovereignty and national power, was at the heart of the movement from the Articles of Confederation to the Constitution. A precise definition of the relationship of the states to the national government was not conducive to ratification and acceptance of the new Constitution. In particular, a clear statement that either the states or the national government held ultimate sovereignty would have provoked intense opposition to the Constitution. Better to get it ratified, and leave it ambiguous and confused.

These two issues—slavery and the precise nature of federalism—were at the heart of the conflict ending in the Civil War. In some ways, the Civil War and its immediate aftermath may be viewed as the last chapter of the Founding, because both issues had to be resolved to make the Founding and the Constitution complete. In this chapter, we focus on the failure of the Founders' Constitution and political system to solve the immense problem of slavery and its related political expression of shared sovereignty, or states' rights. It is a story of the graphic failure of some of our most respected institutions. Ultimately the nation was saved and refounded through the virtue of ordinary people and the profound contribution of a revered president—Abraham Lincoln.

Slavery

The institution of slavery predates recorded history. Slavery was common throughout the ancient world. As Europeans colonized the Western Hemisphere and looked for ways to exploit the unsettled land, slavery was one ready solution to the demand for labor to work the land. Sugar cane, brought to the West Indies by Columbus, thrived in the mild, moist climate of the Caribbean. Europe's appetite for sweets and the decimation of the native population of the Caribbean caused Europeans to look to Africa for slaves to do the tough work of growing and processing sugar cane. About nine million Africans were forcibly brought to the Western Hemisphere as slaves. Most were sent to the Caribbean or Brazil, but over one-half million slaves were eventually brought to the area that would become the United States. All of the colonies had slaves, but slaves proved to be especially productive in growing four crops—tobacco (grown primarily in Virginia and North Carolina), rice (grown in South Carolina), cotton (grown in the Deep South from Georgia to Texas), and sugar (grown in Louisiana). These four plantation crops absorbed the productive efforts of most slaves, though slaves could be found in a variety of occupations, including domestic servants for the wealthy.

Slaves proved to be particularly productive on the large plantations that grew rice, sugar, and cotton. Because slaves did not have a choice about their working conditions, they could be organized to work in slave "gangs" that would move through, say, a cotton field like a giant machine performing the necessary tasks of planting, maintaining, and harvesting crops. Older slaves directed

PICKING COTTON.

The Granger Collection, New York

Nineteenth-century engraving of slaves picking cotton in the South. The expanded production of cotton increased the demand for slave labor.

young children and teenagers in caring for animals or gardening, while still other slaves were craftsmen or skilled workers. Economists studying slavery have concluded that slavery was a highly productive form of labor. Owners of slaves could expect a profitable return on their investment and a substantial income from the work of slaves.

The living conditions of slaves, though not at all good by modern standards, were somewhat similar to the living conditions of unskilled nonslave laborers. Slaves usually lived as families in cabins, were issued clothing by the plantation owner, and were often allowed to keep a small garden. Their diet, based on cornmeal, pork, and sweet potatoes, was relatively nutritious. The life expectancy of slaves in the United States was not quite as high as that of whites in the U.S., but they had a higher life expectancy compared to most Europeans and people living in cities of the time. Because of favorable living conditions, the slave population grew rapidly even though slave importation had been outlawed in 1808. By 1860 continued importation of slaves along with natural increase swelled the slave population in the United States to nearly four million.

The burdens of slavery were more psychological than material for most slaves. Slaves were subject to the arbitrary, and at times, unpredictable will of their masters. The threat of separation and family breakup always hung over slaves since the master could sell slaves at will. Whipping was a common form of punishment on most plantations. Very few slaves were literate, given that there were often laws against teaching them to read and write. Slaves could look forward to a life where the basics of food, clothing, and shelter were provided, but they could not aspire to progress or to better themselves very much. Even the most talented slave could not move above a position as a skilled craftsman, servant, or foreman of a slave gang.

Slavery had been an accepted part of society throughout most of human history. Even John Locke had defended the institution of slavery. By the time of the American Revolution, however, society was beginning to question the morality of this familiar institution. In 1776 the Society of Friends, or Quakers, passed a resolution condemning slavery and requiring its members to free their slaves. John Wesley, one of the founders of the Methodist Church, condemned the slave trade and preached against slavery. Other religious leaders took up the antislavery cause. By the 1830s the movement against slavery

Library of Congress

A photograph of abolitionist Frederick Douglass, ca. late 1800s.

had grown into an abolitionist crusade. At first, abolitionists concentrated on the immorality of slavery and urged Southern slave owners to repent and free their slaves. Failing at this effort, some abolitionist leaders considered dissolving the union of states to be free of the stain of slavery.

The abolitionists did not attract wide support until the 1850s, when they succeeded in attaching the antislavery cause to the concerns of laborers fearful of slave competition and farmers interested in keeping the land to the west free from slavery. Moreover, abolitionists were convincing many Northerners that slavery was also a poor economic choice, reinforcing their moral position with an economic argument. Southerners viewed these developments with increasing alarm, since about a third of their income derived from slavery. They saw slavery as being gradually strangled by the elimination of the slave trade and the prohibition of slavery in some western territories. Southerners saw their "peculiar institution," the basis of their romanticized view of Southern life, in great peril. The confrontation between slavery and its critics represented the greatest crisis the United States had faced to that time.

The political expression of this conflict centered on interpretation of the rights of states and the rights of slaveholders. Southerners had long held the view that the states, predating the Constitution, held sway over the federal government. South Carolina had passed a law in 1832 declaring the national tariff law of 1828 null and void within that state. Even more radical measures were considered—secession or withdrawal from the Union. Secession rested on the belief that the states held sovereignty over the union they had formed. Because the delegates from the states wrote the Constitution and because the states had ratified it, states could unratify and withdrawl from the Union. Though slavery was the root cause of the conflict and the impetus for secession, this political dispute about the sovereignty of the states in relation to the sovereignty of the national government precipitated the Civil War.

Constitutional Structure and the Slavery Crisis

The Founders had sought to appease the interests of slave owners in three direct ways. First, slaves were counted as three-fifths of a person, even though they were entitled to none of the privileges of citizenship. This provision gave Southern states increased representation in the House of Representatives. Second, the Constitution explicitly prevented Congress from passing any law prohibiting importation of slaves before 1808. Third, the Constitution explicitly required states to return slaves or indentured servants who had run away from their owners to another state. These requirements as well as the deference given states in the Constitution caused some abolitionists to condemn the Constitution as a proslavery bulwark. More moderate Northerners saw these three clauses as the price supporters of the new Constitution had to pay to secure Southern support for ratification. With good fortune, slavery would disappear when the slave trade was abolished. If not, later generations could solve this problem.

But did the Constitution provide the avenues and processes to resolve the slavery crisis?

Madison's large-republic argument is a good place to begin to see why the Constitution was not effective in the slavery crisis. Madison assumed that a large republic would have many different interests scattered among the various states. If power were kept at the state or local level, one interest or faction might become dominant. If power were transferred to the national level, many interests or factions would compete with one another for the attention and favor of the Congress and the presidency. In the period before the Civil War, a different pattern of interests emerged. Interests became concentrated regionally rather than being dispersed nationally. Manufacturing and commerce dominated New England, New York City, and

Lowell, Massachusetts, 1851, was a typical New England mill town dominated by industry and commerce.

This Currier & Ives lithograph "A Cotton Plantation on the Mississippi" depicts the South's dependence on agriculture and slavery.

Philadelphia; family farms and their support dominated the Midwest; and slavery and plantation agriculture dominated the South.

This regionalization of interests created sectional or regional politics. Many political battles pitted one or two regions against the other. For example, the Northeast wanted tariffs to protect their growing manufacturing, while the South strongly opposed tariffs because they felt their cotton exports would be economically damaged by tariffs. The West and Northeast wanted the government to subsidize internal improvements, such as railroads and canals, to tie their markets together. The South, blessed with an effective river system, opposed government involvement in transportation. Powerful factions dominated each section of the country and often frustrated each other's wishes.

On no issue was this sectional/factional rivalry more apparent than in the possible expansion of slavery to the West. The explosive issue of slavery in the territories was first manifest when Missouri sought statehood status in 1819. The Missouri Territory, with a large number of slaves, was to be admitted to the Union as a slave state, upsetting the balance of eleven slave states and eleven free states. The House of Representatives, with a Northern majority, approved a bill that would gradually turn Missouri into a free state by prohibiting further migration of slaves to Missouri after statehood, as well as freeing young slaves at age twenty-five. The Senate rejected the bill from the House and passed a bill admitting Missouri as a state without restriction on slavery.

The idea of Missouri as a slave state was very disconcerting to the North. Parts of Missouri were as far north as Illinois, Indiana, and Ohio. To the South, the thought of prohibiting the introduction of new slaves to Missouri and freeing young slaves was terrifying. If these alarming actions could be taken in Missouri, why not in other states? The issue appeared beyond compromise. An aging Thomas Jefferson, fearing for the Union, pronounced, "This momentous question, like a fire bell in the night, awakened and filled me with dread." The most ominous aspect of the Missouri crisis was the sectional nature of the vote in the House and Senate. Finally, a compromise was fashioned in 1820 that admitted Missouri as a slave state but restricted further expansion of slavery to the territory that is now Arkansas and Oklahoma. The Missouri Compromise did little to solve the long-term problem. It simply set the stage for the next regional crisis. Politics became increasingly regionalized. Madison's hopes for the benefits of controlling factions through a large republic simply did not apply.

The mechanical devices of the Constitution were intended to promote compromise and cooperation among the branches of government and between the two parts of Congress. With block voting by regions, however, the system produced gridlock rather than compromise. The North tended to control the House, while the South held at least equal power in the Senate. Presidential candidates in the two-party race between the Whig Party and the Democratic Party had to appeal to the South, or at least to the border states, to win elections. In short, candidates had to commit to avoid creating any solutions to the core issue of slavery and its expansion. Many other countries in the Western Hemisphere had successfully resolved the problem of slavery through "gradual emancipation," a process that freed slaves at some date in the future and prohibited additions to slavery. Gradual emancipation could not even be considered seriously in the United States due to the carefully constructed balance of power between North and South.

The potential for slavery's westward expansion reached its final crisis in the 1850s with the possible inclusion of Kansas and states from the large Nebraska Territory. In 1854, Stephen Douglas, a senator from Illinois with presidential ambitions, engineered passage of a bill that repealed the Missouri Compromise under cover of a requirement that each territory would vote on the issue of slavery. This requirement, known as "popular sovereignty," was an incentive for proslavery and antislavery factions to subvert the voting process by every known method in order to get their way. Proslavery Missourians temporarily moved to Kansas to get their way. John Brown, an abolitionist of dubious background, led his sons and others on a search for proslavery settlers, which ended in the killing of five people at Pottawatomie Creek. Popular sovereignty was leading to anarchy on the western frontier. Successive presidents in the 1850s tried to appease the South by pushing Kansas into the slavery column, with two results. First, Kansas settlers, tired of being pushed around by national politics, rejected statehood altogether. Second, political parties realigned with sentiments about slavery and its

The Kansas-Nebraska Act, 1854. Before the Civil War, each territory could vote on whether to allow slavery.

John Brown by John Steuart Curry. As an abolitionist, Brown led a raid on a proslavery settlement in Kansas.

expansion westward leading the way. Out of that realignment came the Republican Party, committed to future territories and states free from slavery. Here was a regional political party that was completely unacceptable to the South.

The conflict of slavery foreshadowed important conflicts today. Douglas's concept of popular sovereignty was attractive to many national politicians because they hoped it would remove pressure from them to solve a deeply troubling, passionately felt moral issue. Notice that politicians are quick to gravitate toward popular sovereignty when they do not want to deal with the issue in front of them. Social conservatives, having lost the battle on abortion in a Supreme Court decision, argue that abortion should be left up to the states. Liberals, caught between support for gay rights and concerns of their more traditional supporters, argue that the issue of gay marriage should also be left to the states. On the other hand, those who see a particular issue in stark moral terms do not usually accept voting as an appropriate resolution.

If Congress and the presidency could not even approach a long-term solution to the problem of slavery, perhaps the Supreme Court could step in and resolve the issue. Dred Scott, a slave owned by an army surgeon, had lived a number of years in Illinois and the Wisconsin Territory. Illinois was a free state, and the Missouri Compromise had made Wisconsin a free territory. In 1847, Scott sued for his freedom. The case finally came to the Supreme Court in 1856. All of the justices issued opinions about the case, but the opinion of Chief Justice Roger B. Taney, with which seven of the justices concurred, carried the

Library of Congress

In 1846, Dred Scott, a slave who lived with his master in a free state, sued for his freedom.

most weight. Taney tried to end the controversy over slavery and the territories by declaring that the Missouri Compromise, which had prohibited slavery from some territories, was unconstitutional. Taney argued that Congress did not have the power to prohibit slavery in a territory or state. Taney's decision was a victory for the South, but it infuriated the North.

A series of compromises delayed the confrontation, yet did nothing to solve the basic problem. By the 1850s, many Northerners were committed to a "free-soil" position, that there should be no slavery in western settlements, a position intolerable to the South. Madison's brilliant and generally correct analysis of factions summarized in *Federalist* 10 proved to be inappropriate for the pre–Civil War period. The power of sectional factions controlled politics and pitted regions against one another.

Politics and the Civil War

Under the extreme conditions of the 1850s, with strong regional factions and moral views of slavery that were directly opposed, compromise was impossible. Instead, the mechanical devices of the Constitution produced gridlock, with each group checking the other, making movement toward a solution impossible. In effect, each region held a veto, preventing a real solution to the problem of slavery—a solution that would have to be the emancipation of the slaves with minimal economic and cultural damage imposed on the South. Just as the mechanical devices of the Constitution were to promote compromise, the political structure of the Founding was to promote middle-of-the-road politics, helping the country find a solution acceptable to both North and South. Following the turmoil and conflict in Kansas, the election of 1860 provided an opportunity for the political structure to use the will of the people to solve the most serious crisis facing the nation since the Revolutionary War.

The political system proved unable to solve the slavery crisis by compromise. The election of 1860 was the most divided and least centrist election in American history. Instead of two candidates with middle-of-the-road positions, the election brought forward four viable candidates representing markedly different points of view about slavery and its expansion westward. Abraham Lincoln was the nominee of the growing Republican Party. In debate against Stephen Douglas, Lincoln said that he did not believe the nation could exist half slave and half free. While that statement was undoubtedly true, it was also a statement that was repugnant to Southern slaveholders. The Democratic Party could not agree on a national candidate. Southern Democrats supported John Breckinridge of Kentucky, running on an extreme proslavery platform. Northern Democrats ran on a platform of popular sovereignty, with Stephen Douglas as their candidate.

Dissatisfied with the Democratic Party and the Republican Party, some former Whigs formed the Constitutional Union Party, with a platform of moderation on slavery and John Bell of Tennessee as their candidate. Figure 2 illustrates the basic positions of the candidates on the fundamental issue of slavery and its extension to the western territories. Though most people today would strongly support the position of Lincoln, his position and the position of Breckinridge represented the extremes of the day. Bell and Douglas represented centrist positions. Note that the voting public was also divided between ardent supporters of slavery and equally ardent abolitionists, vowing to destroy slavery.

The election reflected the diversity of opinion among the voters, as well as the effect of four viable candidates rather than two. Lincoln received about 40 percent of the popular vote, but almost no votes for him came from the South and less than 5 percent of the popular vote from the border states. Even though Lincoln received only 40 percent of the popular vote, he received 59 percent of the electoral vote because his votes were concentrated in the populous North.

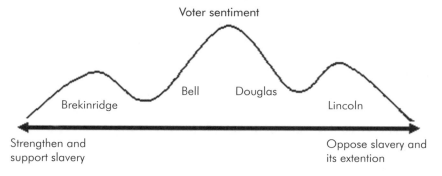

Figure 2.

ABRAHAM LINCOLN,
SIXTEENTH PRESIDENT OF THE UNITED STATES

Library of Congress

With four candidates in the 1860 election, Abraham Lincoln won with only 40 percent of the popular vote.

John Breckinridge received only 18 percent of the popular vote, but 24 percent of the electoral vote because his votes were concentrated in the South. Stephen Douglas received nearly 30 percent of the popular vote, but only 4 percent of the electoral votes. He came in second in most states, but a strong second translates to no electoral votes. John Bell took the border states, winning nearly 13 percent of both the popular vote and the electoral vote. Because votes were so regionalized, the candidates at the ends of the spectrum garnered the most electoral votes. Since Lincoln was the regional candidate of the more populous North, he became president.

Can States Withdraw from the Union?

Since adoption of the Constitution, various states, both in the North and the South, had considered withdrawing from the Union. No state had actually taken that step. With the election of Lincoln, Southern states were ready to test the nature of federalism and the nature of the Union created by the Constitution. In December 1860, South Carolina held a special convention and repealed that state's ratification of the Constitution. By February 1861, six other states—Alabama, Florida, Georgia, Louisiana, Mississippi, and Texas—had also seceded. Efforts at compromise failed. Lincoln, desiring to limit the secession to as few states as possible, tried to keep Virginia, Maryland, Delaware, and Kentucky in the Union. To do that, he needed

A newspaper engraving depicting Confederate troops firing on Fort Sumter on April 12, 1861.

the seceding states to appear extreme and anxious for war. Consequently, he was intent on making the Confederacy fire the first shots. He chose to send food and supplies to the most threatened federal facility—Fort Sumter in Charleston Harbor, South Carolina. The resupplying caused the Confederacy to fire on the fort. Lincoln issued a call for troops. The border states now had to choose a side. Virginia, at least the eastern two-thirds of it, eventually seceded, as did Arkansas, Tennessee, and North Carolina. Delaware, Maryland, Kentucky, and Missouri chose to stay with the Union.

What was the nature of the Union formed by the Constitution? Did the states, many of which had existed before the Constitution, have the right to dissolve their relationship with the Union? Or did the people, by ratifying the Constitution in state conventions, transfer sovereign power from the states to the national government? Shared sovereignty, which had seemed such an ingenious invention eighty years earlier, now seemed a political mirage. Shared sovereignty was serviceable when the nation dealt with ordinary issues and superficial problems. In the end, however, only one entity—either the states *or* the national government—could have the final say. Unfortunately, the Constitution was completely silent about the issue of state versus federal sovereignty or the right of secession. Each side was free to interpret federalism and the relationships between states and the national government as it wished. The states of the Confederacy asserted the right to secede from the Union. Lincoln, as president of the United States, rejected the right of the states to dissolve the bonds that brought them together under the Constitution. In his first inaugural address, he said:

> I hold that, in contemplation of universal law and of the Constitution, the Union of these States is perpetual. Perpetuity is implied, if not expressed, in the fundamental law of all national governments. It is safe to assert that no government proper ever had a provision in its organic law for its own termination. Continue to execute all the express provisions of our National Constitution, and the Union will endure forever—it being impossible to destroy it except by some action not provided for in the instrument itself.

Library of Congress

A photograph of the inauguration of Abraham Lincoln, March 4, 1861. In his speech he rejected the right of states to secede from the United States.

If neither side acquiesced, then war was inevitable. Both sides under-estimated the resolve of the other, and neither saw the unimaginable conflict in front of them.

Saving the Union

The structures and devices so brilliantly crafted in the Founding failed the country in the reluctant march to the Civil War. Checks and balances made the gradual elimination of slavery impossible. No proposal for gradual emancipation of slaves was ever seriously considered in the U.S. Congress, in spite of the example of many other countries that had struggled with it. Supreme Court pronouncements were unenforceable and ineffective. Politics produced no will toward compromise. The Constitution left open the legitimacy of secession. What then saved the Union? At the core, the Union was saved by the virtue of a few leaders and by the virtue of countless ordinary citizens.

Lincoln was the most extraordinary man to assume the presidency since George Washington. Lincoln overcame widespread opposition to war, generals unwilling to fight, foreign support for the South, and pervasive northern racism to prosecute a terrible war, free the slaves, and maintain the Union. It is difficult to measure the importance of a single individual on history, but it is not difficult to imagine the breakup of the Union without Lincoln as president. Lincoln's perseverance in the face of so many challenges was miraculous.

Beyond the saving graces of a most extraordinary president, the virtue of the ordinary soldiers who volunteered to fight was also key to overcoming the crisis of secession. For whatever motives, millions left home and family to help save the Union with the corollary of freeing the slaves. Why did they volunteer? There were bounties paid to appeal to their self-interest. But by 1862 it was clear to all that this was a dangerous war, where loss of life was a significant possibility. Yet they continued to come to fight. Eventually, a draft was instituted, but most of the soldiers were volunteers who fought in part because the Union and freedom meant something to them.

Finally, there was virtue in the aftermath of the war. Southern leaders, defeated on the battlefield, could have conducted a protracted guerrilla war in which bands of southern soldiers harassed and impeded the lawful government. There were isolated incidents

A photograph of black freedmen beside a canal in Richmond, Virginia, 1865.

of this kind, but almost all Confederate leaders counseled cooperation with the federal government. The South had lost. It was time to move on and put the country back together. Without some good will on both sides, a guerrilla war or widespread resistance could have gone on for years and made reconciliation of North and South impossible.

Rebuilding the South without slavery was very difficult, especially following the assassination of Lincoln just five days after the end of the war. Freed slaves needed to be housed and employed. The challenges of race relations and racism needed to be addressed. Political institutions needed to be remodeled to include freed slaves. In practice, Reconstruction ended without a solution to these problems. When state control was given back to southern whites, they enacted state laws to maintain segregation and to disfranchise freed slaves. There was occasional violence in the form of beatings and lynching to maintain race control. The Civil War had ended slavery—but not racial antipathy and discrimination.

Structural Changes after the Civil War

The victory of the North ended the ambiguity surrounding federalism. Four years of war had resolved the question of sovereignty in favor of the national government. States did not have the right to secede from the Union. Federal law and the federal government were supreme over state law. The war changed the character of federal/state relationships. States still handled important governmental functions, such as supervising the police and providing education, but the federal government now had a different character and a different level of power.

Three amendments were adopted to eliminate slavery and to clarify the relationships between the national government and the states. The Thirteenth Amendment (1865) abolished slavery immediately throughout the country. The Fourteenth Amendment (1868) eliminated the constitutional clause counting slaves as three-fifths of a person for the purposes of representation, repudiated the debts of the Confederacy, and prohibited individuals active in the Confederacy from holding office. The Fourteenth Amendment also applied the Bill of Rights and other rights mandated in the federal Constitution to freed slaves. Furthermore, this amendment guaranteed *all* individuals equal protection under the law, including state law. Finally, the Fifteenth Amendment (1870) guaranteed the right to vote regardless of race, color, or previous condition of servitude. Unfortunately, states later found ways around this amendment by applying literacy requirements unequally.

The Civil War was both tragic and heroic. It inflicted suffering and hardship on the whole country, yet it renewed the dedication of the United States to the ideals of the Declaration of Independence. To Lincoln and like-minded people, the war initiated a "new birth of freedom," which reaffirmed the fundamental propositions of equality before the law and government by the people. Inconsistencies between the ideals of the Founding and the practice of government would continue to beset the country, but racial slavery, the greatest gap between ideals and reality, had finally been eliminated.

Just as the Founders had left issues to be resolved by the Civil War generation, the leaders of the Civil War and Reconstruction left to others the challenge of bringing race relationships into conformity with the ideals of the Founding. Neither North nor South was ready to accept African Americans as full and equal participants in the American enterprise. The problem of inequality among races would not be addressed until the civil rights movement in the twentieth century.

Chapter 10

The Challenge of Change

When the American Founding took place, it reflected the optimism of the Enlightenment. There was a sense in the Western World that mankind had been in darkness for centuries, but now—with the rebirth of learning, the progress of science, the exorcising of superstition—the light had dawned at last. Much in line with such thinking, the Founders saw themselves as paring away the bad things of the past: monarchy, aristocracy, compulsory religion, restricted speech and assembly, and so on. In a word, they were modernizing.

Yet the American Founders did their modernizing in a moderate way. French revolutionaries were radicals who junked the past and opted for extreme modernization, using only human reason for a guide. In contrast, Americans consciously retained much from the past, and looked backward to their English rights and freedoms as much as they looked forward to a brave new world.

Given these assumptions, the American Founders did not really expect radical social change in the future. Why would they? Their attitude was: *We've finally got things right. Let's stay with what we have.* They expected change, of course, and in America they expected such change to amount to Progress—with a capital "P." Yet the Founders did not expect change to be revolutionary, only evolutionary, more of the same but steadily improving. To this end, they included an amending process in the Constitution, one that truly worked, and they left certain passages of their founding document purposely vague, so that it would be flexible and adaptable to a limited degree.

But we should underscore *limited*. Too much flexibility would mean no Constitution at all.

What the Founders did not expect to change were fundamentals of human nature, human problems, and the human condition. What we have called the problem of government, for example, they never expected to vary from one century to another.

Change Anyway

We have seen already how the Founding was overtaken with important and unanticipated political developments, such as:

- The emergence of political parties.
- Judicial review.
- The democratization of U.S. politics.
- The advent of virulent sectionalism.
- Questions about the fundamental nature of the Union.

These changes exerted enormous strains on the Founding, leading eventually to the Civil War—and still further change. The Constitution that emerged from this crucible is recognizably similar to what we have today, shaped and honed by historical experience, reconfigured by war, and significantly altered by amendment.

Change overtook the market system too. As good as it was—and good in as many ways as it was—the market system had a number of weaknesses that gave rise to historical innovations and adjustments as important, if not always as dramatic, as those in the realm of politics. These weaknesses are discussed in the chapters that follow, but it might be helpful to quickly summarize them here.

Imperfect Information

The market system assumes that buyers and sellers have access to good information. Otherwise exchanges may not necessarily benefit both parties. Throughout the past two centuries, the economy grew in size and complexity in post–Civil War America. Expanding markets required consumers to acquire more information and sophistication to make beneficial transactions. Exchanges were no longer necessarily face to face. The opportunities to mislead and deceive grew along with the economy.

Externalities

While market exchange benefited both parties (call them A and B) directly involved in exchange, it sometimes affected third parties (C) in helpful or harmful ways. If A exchanged money with B for alcohol and then drove his car in such a way as to demolish C's house, C might have reason to believe that the market system had not served her well. Through time, these third-party effects became more apparent.

Public Goods

Some kinds of goods in the marketplace were susceptible to what economists call the "free rider" problem. If someone builds a lighthouse, for example, it serves not only the person paying the bills but everyone else who enters the shipping lane. The owner of the lighthouse has no way of excluding "free riders" who do not pay for the navigation services. Hence, there will not be a market for public goods such as a lighthouse. With public goods, there are no market signals to help us determine the proper amount of production and consumption. Since national defense, the most important public good, grew in importance, this problem presented increasing challenges to the economy.

Monopoly Power

In the market system there is a certain temptation for producers to collude with one another to limit production and raise prices. "Cartels," the technical term for such collusion, often self-destructed because members of the cartel were constantly tempted to cheat on the others by selling more than their allotted share. Other forms of monopoly were more aggressive—*and* effective. If by fair means or foul a single producer could find ways to become the only seller in a market, he had a monopoly

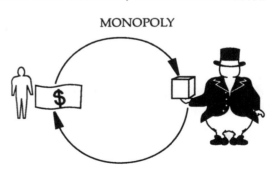

MONOPOLY

A monopolist, being the only seller of a good or service, has significant control over the terms of exchange and will try to capture all of the gains from exchange.

and gained economic power to wield over consumers. As business firms grew in size and scope, concerns about economic power grew.

Economic Instability

Market systems are often afflicted by two kinds of economic instability: inflation and recession. Economists believe that inflation is basically political in nature, the result of deliberately creating an expanding money supply. But periodic recession is clearly a side effect of market mechanisms. Recession can be grim indeed, as we will see, and when severe enough, it can be catastrophic.

Economic Injustice

Market systems always create haves and have-nots in society, and tension between the two groups often leads to charges of injustice. Is it right, we ask, that the rich should be so very much richer than the poor—that corporate CEOs should earn hundreds of times more than their own employees? There are no easy answers. Still, questions persist. For many, the unequal distributions of income and wealth represent the most serious weakness of a market economy.

Each time one of these market weaknesses surfaces in a new way, it creates political demands for *intervention*—that is, using the power of government to intervene in the market economy. Intervention always complicates economic life and may bring forth a host of unintended consequences. Indeed, government intervention may prove worse than the market weakness it was designed to fix. Yet the appeal of government as an antidote to market weakness persists. Economics and politics come together in issues surrounding intervention and provide some of the enduring themes in American life in the nineteenth and twentieth centuries.

Deep Change

Beyond the political and economic developments sketched out here, American history has been characterized by *deep change*, which we might define as change in the structure and operation of society. Deep change tends to occur slowly within society, so slowly that politics and public debate focus on symptoms of this change while ignoring the fundamental change. Deep change has affected the way both constitutional and economic mechanisms work, for, as the term implies, changes may run to the very marrow of society. Change may impose such severe strains and stresses on the political and economic structure that the society is unable to survive. To appreciate how the American Founding has fared in its two-hundred-plus years of experience, we need to have a rough idea what some of those deep changes were. The following list is by no means exhaustive, but it represents some of the most important and powerful areas of change.

Demographic Change

The word *demography* has to do with people, especially in the aggregate. The United States underwent revolutionary demographic changes in the course of the nineteenth and twentieth centuries. These profound demographic changes included:

- Continued international immigration.
- Persistent westward migration.
- Increasing life expectancy.
- Falling fertility and declining family size.
- Rising rates of divorce and illegitimate births.
- Urbanization.

Immigration and Migration

At the close of the Revolution, there was a surge of movement toward the west. Americans pushed through the Appalachian barrier and into the Mississippi and Ohio Valleys. By the 1830s Americans were crossing the "Great American Desert," as the Mountain West was then called, and into Oregon and California. Jefferson's Louisiana Purchase would nearly double the land mass of the United States, and the Mexican Cession, at the close of the Mexican War in 1848, would add another sizable chunk, including coveted California.

A sprawling nation, sparsely populated, undergoing significant economic growth, cried out for new inhabitants. Natural increase could never have met the demand, nor could immigration from, say, northern Europe or the British Isles, America's traditional sources. Gradually, Americans decided to open their gates to peoples who were unlike themselves in significant ways.

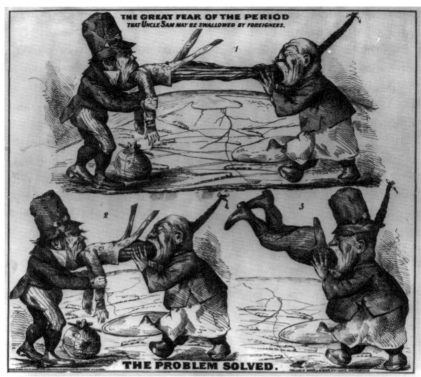

Lithograph, San Francisco: White and Bauer, [between 1860 and 1869]. A cartoon expressing the fear that America would be swallowed by foreigners; then depicts a Chinaman swallowing the Irishman to solve the problem.

Beginning in the 1820s and 1830s Palatine Germans and ordinary Irish (as opposed to the Scots-Irish of earlier times) began arriving in large numbers. Both groups were Catholic. The Germans headed for the upper reaches of the Mississippi Valley, where they were joined by Scandinavians, and most of them took up the farming life. The Irish preferred the big cities, such as Boston and New York, where they substantially changed the tenor of life.

The growth of American industry after the Civil War attracted a so-called "new immigration" of workers for the burgeoning mills and packing plants. The new immigrants came from southern Europe (Greece, Portugal, Italy), and from eastern Europe (Poland, Hungary, Ukraine, the Balkans, Russia). Many of the new immigrants were also Catholic, but others were Greek and Russian Orthodox, as well as Jewish. Almost all of them crowded into the booming industrial cities of the Midwest.

Both Chinese and Japanese were drawn toward the Pacific Coast. The Chinese came first with the California Gold Rush, then later to build the transcontinental railroad. Many Japanese took up farming.

Around the turn of the twentieth century, there began a sizable influx of Hispanics, mostly from Mexico but from Central America as well, spreading northward across the borders of Texas, New Mexico, Arizona, and California. As these areas developed labor-intensive agriculture, the demand for such immigrants steadily increased. Hispanics also arrived in Florida from Cuba and the Caribbean. After the Spanish-American War in 1898, Puerto Ricans and Filipinos also began immigrating.

In the twentieth century, African Americans left the South in large numbers, attracted by industrial jobs in the North. And during the Great Depression, many impoverished farmers left the "dust bowl" (Oklahoma, Kansas, Arkansas) for California and the West, competing with Hispanics for agricultural work.

All these movements created individual opportunity, but they also created stress. The American sense of oneness, which was never very strong, was severely strained by the "swarming horde of foreigners," many of them with marked religious and cultural differences. Periodic waves of "nativism" broke out, subjecting the new arrivals to various forms of persecution and proclaiming that America was for Americans. The situation eventually resulted in legislation to radically restrict immigration.

While some of the difficulty was merely cultural, some was also racial and ethnic, and could never be melted away in the American "melting pot." Racism, which was destined to be America's particular bane, grew up side by side with the partial accommodation of foreign immigrants.

Fertility and Mortality

At the same time America became a land of immigrants, it became a land of radically altered social characteristics. Demography was at work here as well. At the time of the Founding, life expectancy hovered around forty years for most of the world, including advanced and enlightened Europe. While this number is skewed by extremely high rates of infant mortality, it nonetheless illustrates a fairly bleak picture of the quality—not to mention the duration—of human life. Life expectancy was a bit higher in the American colonies, where living conditions were better and diet was markedly improved, but even there most families witnessed the deaths in infancy or childhood of nearly a quarter of their children. To insure heirs for family holdings (and care-takers for the elderly), it was prudent to have six or seven children. The average family gave birth to eight children.

Beginning in the late nineteenth century, a steady progression of improvements led to a decline in mortality rates. The discovery and acceptance of the germ theory of disease and related advances in biochemistry and the understanding of anatomy and physiology put the training of medical professionals on a scientific basis. Public sanitation, based on the germ theory of disease, cleaned up water and

The Granger Collection, New York

Margaret Sanger and her two children. Sanger founded the birth-control movement in early twentieth-century America, which led to a decrease in family size.

milk supplies, improved sanitation, and greatly reduced the spread of infectious diseases such as cholera and yellow fever. At the same time, economic growth promoted similar improvements in diet, housing, and private sanitation. Infant mortality shrank dramatically. During the twentieth century, life expectancy increased from forty-four years to seventy-four years—an unparalleled improvement.

While life expectancy increased, family size or fertility steadily decreased. The latter trend was accentuated by the increased use of family planning techniques after 1900, and later by oral contraceptives and abortion. By the 1980s, the average American family had only two children.

The increase in life expectancy and the decline in family size had revolutionary impacts on American life. To begin with, the entire nature and meaning of the family began to change. Once a large organization cemented by social instincts or economic necessity, the family became a small organization often held together solely by affection. Children who once grew up in a world of hard work and common sacrifice began growing up in a world of affluence and self-indulgence—under compulsion to "do better" than their parents. Increases in life expectancy combined with falling fertility created many older couples, widows, or widowers with the choice of living alone or with married children.

Post–World War II saw a major shift in the nature of families. Divorce rates spiraled upward leaving many children to be raised primarily by one parent, usually the mother, with only sporadic visits by the father. Besides the disruption of the family, divorce created economic stress, often throwing families into poverty. In addition to the challenges that divorce placed on families and children, births to unwed mothers became increasingly common. By 2000, 33 percent of U.S. births were to unmarried women. The social and economic costs of increasing rates of divorce and out-of-wedlock births are still being counted.

Longevity and decreasing family size created another set of difficulties among the aged. Because Americans lived much longer now, society faced skyrocketing health-care costs, an impaired elderly population, and painful dilemmas about medical intervention versus the "right to die." In the twenty-first century, Social Security burdens continue to grow with the elderly living longer and fewer workers to support them.

Urbanization

America's farthest reaching demographic shift has been from an essentially rural to a predominantly urban population. This dramatic change had a number of causes, most of them economic. The primary engine of urbanization was growing income. As incomes grew, consumers naturally spent a smaller and smaller fraction of their income on food, shifting purchases toward manufactured goods and especially toward services. In addition, improvements in agricultural technology made it possible for a smaller and smaller segment of the population to feed everyone else. And while jobs in agriculture were declining, those in the industrial sector multiplied exponentially. Factory jobs meant factory towns and then factory cities. Improvements in transportation—such as the electric trolley—made such cities possible. By 1915, a majority of Americans lived in urban areas.

Urban life was very different from the rural life they had known. It was cramped and crowded, with little in the way of amenities, for everything had to be within trolley distance of the job. City life was often squalid, too, especially for newly arrived immigrants, with

The Granger Collection, New York

The Ghetto, New York City, around 1900. City life around the turn of the century was crowded, impersonal, and dangerous.

jumbled tenements and cold-water flats by the square mile, coupled with few standards of health or safety. It also was impersonal. Various ethnic and cultural groups were thrown together, dependent upon institutions from the old country for a sense of belonging. At times city life was dangerous. Gangs ruled many neighborhoods, battling one another for turf. All manner of thugs and "bully boys" walked the streets, which also teemed with flimflam artists, swindlers, and racketeers. Runaway vehicles, electrical hazards, open sewers, dogs running in semi-wild packs added to the sense of menace.

Yet urban life was also exciting. Bustling streets filled people with a sense of motion and purpose. The city became the cutting edge of American culture, with new fashions, new music and art, new idiomatic expressions, new developments in lifestyle exported to the hinterland. That which would be called "cool" emanated from places like Harlem in New York and from Chicago's South Side.

At the same time, cities offered attractions unavailable to those living on the farm. There were saloons and taverns, cafes, restaurants, delis, brothels, melodeons, burlesque and vaudeville theaters, penny arcades, midways, drugstores, ball parks, beer gardens, skating rinks, prize-fight arenas, gyms, playgrounds, and after the turn of the twentieth century, movie palaces. For the upper classes there were luxury hotels, exclusive clubs, resorts, theaters, opera houses, race courses, museums and galleries, libraries, and educational establishments of one kind or another.

Shops and stores lined the streets, beckoning to the throng jamming the sidewalks. One could purchase anything from the most exotic and particular items to the most general sort of merchandise. In time, huge department stores—Marshall Field's, Wanamakers, Macy's—brought a factory-like efficiency to retail commerce, with live music, fashion shows, giftwrapping, and free delivery.

The atmosphere of the city played to American individualism. At the same time, it produced alienation and anomie, loosening the ties of family and community. Groups sought to reclaim what was lost through defensive—and sometimes offensive—displays of chauvinism. Irish taunted Italians. Germans jeered at Poles. In time, however, the city gave rise to *pluralism*, where groups tacitly agreed to tolerate one another, each within its own sphere of meaning.

Developments in the twentieth century made it possible for the white middle class to escape the city's hubbub and move into the suburbs, which bore some marks of the small town that many Americans had left behind. Suburbs, mushrooming after World War II, featured free-standing houses, tree-shaded streets, and a lifestyle shaped by the latest conveniences. The city's thronging streets became stylized into the suburban shopping mall. Even in suburbia, there was a longing for the simpler life that Americans had once known. Books and movies often celebrated the lost innocence of Grover's Corners or Bedford Falls.

With the flight of the middle classes, the city became entirely different. Abandoned to the poorest of the poor, it became a place of festering slums, of pandemic vice and crime, of gang-infested streets. Gone were the bustling shops and stores, along with the street life of urban communities. Office buildings took on the appearance of fortresses by day, while they towered by night over a netherworld.

Education

Many of the Founders believed that education was the key to republican happiness. The "aristocracy of talent and virtue" that Jefferson spoke of with enthusiasm must be first and foremost a product of the school, they supposed. Plans for a national university were seriously discussed at the Constitutional Convention and were strongly supported by George Washington.

Yet in reality, education in early America was anything but a given. Outside of New England, where local schools flourished, children were taught to read and write, along with elementary math skills, on a catch-as-catch-can basis. Reformers in the Age of Jackson made "the common school," what we think of as a public elementary school today, a top priority. The public school system that we enjoy in modern times has its roots in the common school. Still, the system taught only basics, and certainly not to everyone.

The demands of industrial society transformed American education in the early twentieth century. Factories and corporations needed skilled craftsmen with some knowledge of science, along with clerical staff for lower-level management. In short, companies needed a workforce with a high school education. In the early twentieth century, high school attendance and graduation exploded. In 1890, only 4 percent of seventeen-year-olds graduated from high school. By 1940, over 50 percent were graduating from high school. The high school revolution was followed by a smaller increase in college attendance and graduation.

Public education became the great leveler. Poor kids read the same text-books as rich ones and were given similar opportunities to excel. Immigrant children, while learning to read and write, also absorbed American speech, American manners, American values. This aspect of the educational process did not escape political notice. It was no accident, for example, that Asian children were segregated from their Caucasian cousins early in the twenti-

Library of Congress

Italian-American children (1943) learning the Pledge of Allegiance in a New York public school.

eth century, or that "separate but equal" schooling became a hard and fast rule throughout the South. *Some* barriers, said those resisting change, were too useful to tear down.

Public education altered the nature and meaning of childhood. In Jefferson's America, children were often regarded as adults in training until they could assume fully adult roles, usually by their mid-teens. Now there was an accepted category called childhood with specific temporal boundaries, and a world in which childhood was acted out according to settled expectations. Kids taught one another precisely how to be ten, thirteen, or eighteen, as the case may be. As schooling grew ever longer, so in a way did childhood. Marriage and child-rearing were put off further and further.

In the world of the public school, peer influences largely replaced, or at least strongly competed with, those of the family. Sociologist David Riesman described what he called the "lonely crowd" of American teenagers in the 1950s, anxiously looking to one another—not to traditional values or ingrained beliefs—to know how they felt about life. Pressures toward conformity at school were mirrored by similar pressures in the work place—what another sociologist called "the organization man"—and in suburbia itself, where it was well to "keep up with the Joneses."

Children with better learning and skill development made much more productive workers in the steel plants or on the assembly lines. Yet they were also the first to find such work unfulfilling. Beginning in the 1920s, an ever greater fraction of them wanted to go on to college, or to trade or technical schools after high school, where they could study engineering, accounting, business management, agricultural science, medicine, and law. Unconsciously, they were laying the foundations of a technocratic society that was to emerge after the world wars.

Yet, ironically, advanced education undermined technocracy as well. Students who specialized in humanities and the social sciences, for example, came to have their own view of the world and the way it worked, especially after World War II. They took a harder look at American ideas, assumptions, and values than any generation before them and found fault in much of what they saw. At the University of California at Berkeley in 1964, students pitted themselves against the "multiversity" as an institution of technocratic education and began raising fundamental questions about racism, poverty, discrimination, and America's changing role in the world. What followed was a decade or so of campus turmoil.

Science and Technology

Americans, observed Alexis de Tocqueville, took to science and technology like ducks to water. It was the applied sciences that Tocqueville had in mind, not the theoretical (that is, "useless") sciences that had been so conspicuously advanced by Europeans. Americans wanted science to deliver more efficient machinery and higher crop yields.

Americans proved themselves adept at technological development. In the early years of the republic, they made astonishing breakthroughs in the design of textile machinery, woodworking machinery, steamboats, sailing vessels, locomotives, firearms, and a host of other equipment. Of particular note were innovations that speeded up the production process, the most important of these being the use of interchangeable parts. When the various components of, say, a rifle no longer had to be hand-fitted to one another, it was possible to break the manufacturing process into discreet segments and arrange them in an orderly fashion. It was only a short step from this to the moving assembly line.

Some inventions literally changed the world. Eli Whitney's cotton gin helped entrench slavery and enhance Southern power in textiles.

Morse's telegraph, Colt's six-shooter, Glidden's barbed wire all had a revolutionary impact on economic development. Later on, the electric light, the telephone, the radio, and the motion-picture camera had a similar influence on domestic life. By the turn of the twentieth century, the horseless carriage was being perfected into the automobile, and later on nothing short of computers would have a more transforming effect. In the 1930s and 1940s, development of hybrid seeds increased agricultural yields dramatically, shifting even more people off the farm.

Library of Congress

Samuel F. B. Morse, ca. 1855–65. Morse's telegraph was one American invention that changed the world.

Yet it was those steady, anonymous improvements in production and transportation that would ultimately bring the greatest consequence. For with ever-increasing automation in the manufacturing process, opportunity costs were pushed lower and lower, and with ever greater efficiency in the movement of goods, the area of profitable exchange grew larger and larger. At the time of the Founding, most profitable exchange was limited to an area about the size of a county. Every improvement in transportation—canals, steamboats, railroads, internal combustion engines, airplanes—expanded the area of exchange. By the end of World War II, the area of exchange was approaching the entire globe.

These developments manifested themselves as higher and higher wages and lower prices. Where a worker in, say, an automobile plant in 1908 would have to work nearly two years to purchase one of the plant's own products, with the introduction of the continuous assembly line in 1910, a manufacturing worker could buy a much better car in 1929 for about four months' salary. Americans, who traditionally saw themselves as producers, began to think of themselves as consumers, too.

If technology brought blessings, it also brought curses. The most conspicuous of these were improvements in the art and science of warfare. Spurred by the Civil War, inventors began perfecting such weapons as the machine gun, the self-propelled torpedo, the long-range howitzer, the diesel-powered tank. By the mid-1920s, military aircraft were proving that they could not only scout enemy trenches, they also could sink battleships. The aircraft carrier followed upon this discovery—and was itself eclipsed by missiles that could be fired from submarines. The ultimate military breakthrough, of course, occurred when a nuclear blast lit up the desert sky at Alamogordo, New Mexico, on a summer's dawn in 1945. Nothing before or since more convincingly illustrated the problem of change.

New Ideas

After the Civil War, however, American interest in science broadened. At a time when colleges began renaming themselves universities and adding graduate programs, the study of science divided into the study of physics, chemistry, astronomy, botany, zoology, sociology, psychology, anthropology, and hundreds of smaller subfields. By the turn of the twentieth century, college graduates were supposed to know at least a smattering about all the fields of study.

B 26

'PHOTOGRAPH'
SERIES   DARWIN

Library of Congress

Charles Darwin.

Thus fortified, America provided fertile ground for three intellectual developments from Europe that would revolutionize human understanding.

Darwinism. Biologist Charles Darwin (1809–82) examined the world of supposedly fixed and unchanging species, and concluded that it was but a myth. Biology was all about struggle and survival, he said, and only the fittest were able to fend off their enemies and reproduce. As species became extinct, they were replaced by mutated versions better able to adapt and survive, thus evolving higher and higher forms.

Darwin's argument had several corollaries. One, arguably, was that the biblical account of creation simply didn't wash, and from this it was but a short step to scientific skepticism. Another was the application of Darwin's ideas to society. Instead of living in a world of fixed and permanent truths, as the Founders had supposed, Americans found themselves living with change and adaptation, where everything was in a process of evolution. Social institutions, governments, human nature itself were all moving forward, growing, developing, and replacing older forms with newer, more successful ones. The issue, claimed "Social Darwinists," was whether our continued evolution would be random and planless or controlled and guided.

Freudian Psychology. In the world before Sigmund Freud (1856–1939) psychology was understood largely in terms of stimulus and response, meaning that the ideas in our heads were put there by our concrete experiences. In his investigations of hysteria, Freud glimpsed an entirely different world, in which ideas arose from the mysterious dark realm of the subconscious mind and were governed by forces beyond human control. As Freud and others explored that world, they encountered symbols and images tracing back to earlier stages of human evolution and reflecting primal impulses. There was little here of the calm and rational approach of the American Founders, who assumed that problems had discoverable solutions.

Library of Congress

Sigmund Freud, 1938.

Freudians offered their own analyses of human behavior, of politics and war, of entertainment, humor, social conventions, and much else. While it is too much to say that they related all of this to sex, they clearly did relate it to urges that were far below the surface. For example, the ancient tale of Oedipus, destined by the gods to kill his father and marry his mother, made perfect sense in a Freudian world. Much of Freud's explanation of human behavior has been discredited or replaced by other theories. But Freud and his successors set in motion a view of human behavior that replaced individual responsibility and accountability with explanations grounded in the subconscious and biology.

Einstein's Physics. The American Founders had revered Isaac Newton for making the universe intelligible. Indeed, the U.S. Constitution has been called "Newtonian" in the sense that it utilized self-interest in the

Library of Congress

Albert Einstein, ca. 1931.

political realm more or less in the way that Newton's universe utilized gravitation to maintain order and balance. The physics of Albert Einstein (1879–1955) changed all that. In the strange world that emerged from Einstein's advanced mathematics, a straight line was no longer the shortest distance between two points, objects gained mass as they gained acceleration, and time and space became interchangeable. Einstein's famous formula, $E=mc^2$, would make nuclear weapons possible, and thus would radically alter the rules of the world power game. Equally revolutionary would be everyday notions of reality, dissolving into mass-energy and space-time. As with Freud and Darwin, Einstein's world belied the commonsense notion that things were as they seemed.

Socialism. Less widely accepted, but equally revolutionary were the ideas of Karl Marx (1818–83), whose theories of economics dominated much of the twentieth century. Marx believed that history followed a predetermined course, much as the Social Darwinists supposed, whose trajectory was explained by class conflict. As class struggled against class for domination, the human world shaped itself according to the ideology of the victors at any given moment. The "truths" of Adam Smith, Marx argued, were only capitalist truths in a capital-dominated world, and the ideas would pass away in the next stage of the struggle, when workers of the world would rise up and cast off their chains.

All these ideas had revolutionary implications, especially in a world where science had become a kind of religion. They militated against the Judeo-Christian understanding of the world that had existed at the time of the Founding. They undercut the concept of universal moral truth that the Founders had taken for granted. And they suggested ways of understanding human nature that were radically different from those of the Founders. Viewed from the perspective of the late twentieth century, the world of the American Founding began to seem quaint.

Scale

As technology drove down the costs of transportation and communication, the scale of cities, businesses, governments, and education expanded. At the time of the Revolution, Philadelphia was the largest American city with a population of 50,000. The five boroughs of New York City—Manhattan, Brooklyn, Bronx, Queens, and Staten Island—were separate communities in 1790 and had a total population of 49,000. By 1880, the five boroughs had become a city with a population of nearly two million people. By 1900, three cities had populations of more than a million people, and three others had populations over half a million. By 2000, metropolitan areas spilled beyond city boundaries to large metro areas such as New York with 18 million and Los Angeles with 12 million.

Just as city sizes increased, the scale of businesses increased over time. After the Revolutionary War, each business employed just a few workers. Before the Civil War, a few larger scale enterprises developed in textiles, railroads, sugar, and cotton production. After the war, the trend toward bigness continued with corporations in steel, petroleum, and eventually automobiles reaching mammoth sizes. In the 1920s, Henry Ford's plant at River Rouge could produce a Model T Ford every 45 seconds. In the 1940s, the plant reached its maximum number of employees at about 100,000 workers. As businesses grew to an unprecedented scale, other institutions such as universities, government, and non-profit organizations also grew in size.

The Consumer Society

The scale of American business helped make widespread access to basic consumer goods widely available. For an increasing number of Americans, there was the proverbial chicken in every pot and car in every garage. By 1900, roughly a third of American households lived in free-standing houses with their own separate yards. This fraction would steadily increase. During the economic boom of the 1920s, over half of American households also acquired an automobile—recently regarded as a plaything of the rich. Radios, phonographs, indoor bathroom facilities, and frequent attendance at the movies were more or less taken for granted.

While the Great Depression brought a jolting setback, World War II and the peace that followed ushered in a long season of unprecedented prosperity. Millions of additional American families moved to the suburbs for the first time, acquired one and even two automobiles, and began collecting an array of washers, driers, mixers, blenders, toasters, ranges, refrigerators, vacuums, televisions, stereos, cameras, projectors, and backyard barbecue pits.

Consumption had always had special meanings in America, and in the postwar years these

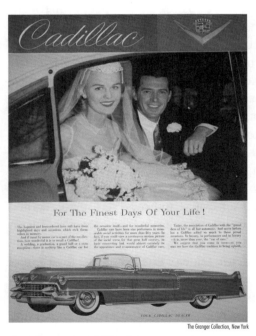

Cadillac ad, 1955. Advertising became a powerful force toward increasing American consumption.

meanings were enhanced for the new middle classes. Goods and services were regarded as badges of social worth, not just useful possessions. The advertising industry took it upon itself to explain taste and style to the American public, and to discourse on the dreamworld significance of various products. Lipstick became a ticket to paradise, beer a sign of the good life, automobiles Aladdin's magic carpet. On a roll, advertising urged consumers to buy products they didn't need, didn't want, and couldn't afford—and to pay for them on installment credit.

Not all Americans enjoyed the consumption bonanza. Ethnic minorities and recently arrived immigrants were among those groups still living in comparative poverty, and certain areas of the country lagged appreciably behind the norm. Even so, Americans as a society had become far and away the world's leading consumers.

Perhaps the single most striking phenomenon of the consumer society was leisure time. For thousands of years, only lords and ladies had known anything of the kind. Now, with the work week steadily declining and vacations steadily expanding, ordinary Americans found themselves with time for sports, hobbies, travel, entertainment, advanced education, and other leisure-time activities.

Some of these activities involved the entertainment media, made possible by the great technology bonanza. Edison's phonograph gave rise to the popular music industry. Motion pictures were also made possible by an Edison invention, the kinetescope. The "flickers," as they were called, came into the world as working-class entertainment, their language of pantomime being intelligible to the immigrant population. By World War I motion pictures were aspiring to the status of art. Radio developed dramatic forms, in addition to music, and these proliferated into variety shows, serious plays, and soap operas. Television was developed during the 1920s and 1930s, and became commercially viable after World War II. Borrowing from radio, vaudeville, and the movies, television became the medium of the century.

All the entertainment media mushroomed into big business, and most became permeated by advertising. As the art of persuasion, advertising grew adept at creating images of almost hypnotic appeal and packaging them in ever glossier formats. Advertising professionals learned much about what made their audience tick. They did not stress rational thought, as a Thomas Jefferson might do, but irrational, even compulsive, behavior. Their sources of inspiration were people like Sigmund Freud.

On the whole, consumption failed to deliver the promises implied in advertising—that it would bring people adventure, romance, fulfillment, and a meaningful life. But the promises remained and were amplified by other forms of media. Americans were told over and over again, in a thousand different ways, that they would be happy if only they possessed. . . .

The Growth of Government

All the change chronicled in this chapter was accompanied by a remarkable increase in the size of government. On the eve of the Civil War, the federal government employed just under 37,000 civilians. By 2000, the federal government employed about 2.9 million people. Actual government employment understates the full extent of government involvement in the economy because many individuals work for the government through sub-contracts and grants. By the year 2000, all levels of government (federal, state, and local) employed over 17 million people and controlled about one-third of national output. Even so, measures of government spending or government employees understate the overall influence of government in modern society. In addition to direct government spending and transfers, the government regulation of society and the economy has also increased dramatically. The IRS code and related court decisions consist of thousands of pages. The federal register of new laws and new regulations adds about 400 pages per day. It is fair to speculate that the founding fathers would be stunned to see that the limited government they set up had grown to such a size.

What caused this increase in the role of government through time? Were not the Founding and the Constitution designed to prevent this very thing from happening? The next few chapters will chronicle some of the periods and events that increased political pressures for more government. As you consider these chapters, keep this growth of government in mind. Ask yourself whether or not you believe the growth is the result of popular will. That is, does this growth simply reflect the will of the people? Or are there structural defects or problems that cause government to grow in spite of the will of the people for less government? Such questions are obviously not easily resolved, but they are at the heart of our evaluation of the Constitution and the Founding.

The Problem of Heritage

We have seen here only a few of the deep changes that transformed American life in a little more than two centuries after the Founding. There were many others, and the sum of them had revolutionary import.

It might be useful for us to imagine what the Founders themselves would make of these developments. They would obviously be impressed, even astonished, by some of them, though others they might not greet with approval. The question is, how would they measure deep change against what they took to be the Founding's primary aims? Did the Founding, in other words, produce a heritage worthy of the name?

In the remaining chapters, we want to focus on specific aspects of this general question. To do so, we must keep the Founding's central principles squarely in view. The Founders sought to:

- Create some approximation of the classical Good Society—a nation-state that benefits all groups, not just a favored few.
- Implement the ideals of the Declaration of Independence, in which all are equal before the law, all enjoy the same rights and privileges, and all consent to their own governance.
- Create a specific design of government that maximizes individual freedom and minimizes tyranny and anarchy.
- Develop a political-economy that provides individual opportunity and general prosperity.
- Establish justice.

Deep change heavily impacted these goals, as we will see. It created new strains on the constitutional system. It produced new values and argued for their acceptance. It altered patterns of society and systems of thought. It transformed the problem of government, as the Founders saw it, to a broader and more diffuse problem, of which government was only one part. It enormously complicated American life.

Fear became an abiding element of the American response to change. Americans developed a fear of bigness, a fear of impersonality, a fear of new and disturbing ideas, a fear of lost autonomy, a fear of compromised innocence, a fear that enemies once held distant could now threaten their shores, a fear of strangers within.

Yet hope became an equally abiding element in the American response to change. The hopes of the Founders proved adaptable to the world of deep change. Americans continued to believe in Progress with a capital "P." They continued to believe in Justice with a capital "J" as well, even though it proved to be as elusive as progress. They became ever more convinced of their founding principles even as they grew wary of the Founding itself. And they felt good enough about the government they had created that they would turn to it over and over again, almost instinctively, as anxiety and uncertainty shadowed their path.

Chapter 11

Progressives and Private Power

Americans have typically mistrusted large organizations. After all, in colonial times their own organizations—families, businesses, town or colony governments—were small and easy to supervise, while the only large organization they knew, the British Empire, seemed out of control to them. The problem of large organizations was like the problem of government: they wielded a great deal of power over people's lives. After Americans had fought their Revolution, they wanted no further part of gigantic bureaucracies. Indeed, it was only with the greatest difficulty that they could be persuaded to adopt the federal Constitution.

But government exercised *public* power—what about *private* power? Americans had few worries on that score before the Civil War. After Appomattox, it was another matter. Among the deep changes they now had to contend with was the increasing reality of private power, which Americans encountered in all manner of organizations capable of shaping their lives. Private power would be exercised by labor unions and employer associations; by political parties; by federated interest groups; by railroads, steamship companies, and stage lines; by hospitals; by banks; by colleges and universities; by turnpike builders, power companies, and the owners of telephone exchanges; by ferryboats and trolley lines; and by a hundred other services in the increasingly complex and sophisticated urban environment. Americans would be bothered by all of these. Most of all, however, they would be bothered by two organizations: political machines and cartel monopolies—the so-called "trusts."

In this chapter we want to explore the sources of American discomfort with these institutions and come to understand how in their response to private power, Americans came to see themselves as "Progressives."

The Era of Big Business

Like Americans, Adam Smith mistrusted the power of large organizations. For him the ideal economic world was one of small producers, individual and autonomous, flexible in their response to market situations. Smallness and individuality were romanticized by American transcendentalists like Ralph Waldo Emerson and Henry David Thoreau. (One could hardly imagine retreating to Walden Pond to start a business corporation.) But the Civil War brought an end to such dreams. To oppose the "slave power"—which itself represented private power run amok—it was necessary to create an organization mightier still. In the course of the struggle the federal government tripled in size and came to exercise powers beyond the Founders' imagination. Both Emerson and Thoreau, ironically, ended the war as government employees.

Something similar began happening to American industry. Even before the war, Americans had discovered that certain kinds of industry were by nature not small. Take railroads, for example. A railroad from one town to another was of limited value. The whole point was to transport goods *anywhere* they might be desired. Thus, by definition, the larger the railroad, the better it worked. Large railroads could not be built by a few investors either, even very rich investors. It took a corporation able to sell stock and amass capital. Railroads gained from economies of scale. Once tracks were laid and bridges and trestles were built, the more trains that utilized them the better. Size and efficiency went together. The same general considerations held true for canals, steamship companies, and mining and timbering operations. Increasingly, size and efficiency held true for factories as well, such as the textile mills that began dotting New England. The first ones were very small, on the order of a few dozen employees. Soon the great mills at Lowell, Massachusetts, had payrolls running into the hundreds—then thousands.

The growth of corporations had a significant impact on employer-employee relations. In colonial America, as it had been in Europe for a thousand years, such relations were generally characterized by *paternalism*. That is, the factory owner was more than just a boss to his employees. He was something of a lord, something of a friend, and something of a father figure. Workers went to him with their personal problems, sought his advice on financial matters, made him godfather to their children. With the large corporation, none of this applied. On the contrary, the impersonal employer—whom employees may never meet—became something of an adversary. Workers began to form trade unions to protect themselves against his power.

Large corporations often competed differently in the marketplace. Most businesses compete in a market where they assume their individual actions do not determine or influence prices. That is, the wheat farmer or the shoemaker assumes that they have no influence over the price of wheat or shoes. They produce their products as efficiently as possible and sell at the prevailing price. But a large corporation or a group of corporations acting together may dominate the market and be able to set the price of a product by withholding production from the market. Market power was often the goal of large corporate interests. The path to market power could involve destroying competitors, buying them out, or in the case of trusts, making agreements to dominate a market. The size of corporations often caused people to assume they had more market power than they actually had. Just as businesses were growing in size, markets were also growing because of rapid population increase as well as economic expansion.

Large corporations, however, that faced few competitors used their monopoly power. They could set prices artificially high and maintain them by reducing supply. The artificial restriction of supply created distortions and inefficiencies in the economy. Other corporations formed cartels to behave like monopolies. They simply got together in the time-honored fashion and carved up the market like a Christmas turkey; or they developed legal subterfuges, such as the "trust agreement," whereby a parent company could hold all producers in a kind of feudal bondage and dictate terms among them.

A few industries were inherently monopolistic. If a railroad passed through a small town in Ohio on its route from Chicago to New York, chances were that it would be the only mode of transportation available, for the competing line would take a different route between the two large cities. Farmers and other shippers soon

The Central Pacific Railroad monopolized all railroad traffic crossing the Sierra Nevada Mountains into California.

noticed that rates from small towns to the cities were much higher than rates between the major hubs where railroads competed with one another. Or, even worse, there was no competition. When the builders of the Central Pacific Railroad succeeded in breaching the Sierra Nevada Mountains, they conveniently monopolized all rail traffic in California—and soon all other forms of transport as well.

Technology made its own contribution to monopoly. Frank Sprague's electric traction motor, which made the urban trolley possible, led to the creation of a giant corporation holding the Sprague patents. General Electric came about through Thomas Edison's patents, and the Westinghouse Corporation resulted from George Westinghouse's invention of the air brake.

How did Americans feel about monopoly? Certainly, there were feelings of ambivalence. The rags-to-riches stories of some of the leaders of corporations were inspiring. In the story of Andrew Carnegie, for instance, people saw real life reflections of the American Dream. Carnegie came to the United States as a poor immigrant boy from Scotland. He lived the life of a Horatio Alger hero, studying nights to learn accounting, honing skills on the job, winning the attention of powerful figures who could foster his career. He got into the steelmaking business at the right time and in the right place, and made the most of his opportunities. J. P. Morgan, the quintessential banker and a less sympathetic figure than Carnegie, eventually combined Carnegie Steel with other companies to create a corporate behemoth, United States Steel. Carnegie retired to spend his vast fortune on philanthropy and libraries. He returned to Dumferline, Scotland, whence his family had come to America, and bought a castle.

Library of Congress

Andrew Carnegie (1896) led a rags-to-riches life and monopolized the steel industry.

Journalists often portrayed the leaders of corporations in dark and sinister terms, labeling them "Robber Barons" to reflect their power and an unscrupulous nature. In turn journalists were called "muckrakers" and their stories characterized as "yellow journalism." John D. Rockefeller represented the kind of businessman who was the target of journalists. The Standard Oil Company, founded by Rockefeller, came to dominate the oil industry from drilling to refining to retail sales. Rockefeller bought out many of his competitors and ruthlessly competed with others. He amassed a fortune which was valued at about $1 billion in 1912, perhaps $20 billion in contemporary terms. To ordinary Americans, he looked much more powerful than even the president of the United States.

The game of monopoly acquired legal and political overtones. The well-paid lawyers of the "Robber Barons" found loopholes in the statutes that enabled their patrons to escape the constraints of the law. Indeed, corporate leaders often used local courts to issue rulings and injunctions to tilt the business field into their favor. Once in power, monopolists used their considerable political clout to push for high tariffs—which saved them from having to compete with foreign suppliers.

Some monopolies grew so powerful that they towered over state and local government. In California, for example, the transportation trust set up its own political bureau under a man named William F. Herrin and funneled huge resources into its operations. The bureau eventually controlled every aspect of state government, from the legislature, to the governor's office, to the courts. Agencies set up to regulate railroad traffic and ensure the fairness of freight rates fell under the bureau's domination as well. Californians began referring to it as "the octopus."

Beginning in the 1880s, Americans reacted against the presumption and power of such corporations. Many believed that railroads exercised unfettered power. America saw bloody strikes—Carnegie's Homestead Plant among them—dramatizing callous treatment of workers. And they had seen firsthand what happened to streetcar fare or heating oil prices the moment a trust tightened its grip. Best sellers of the day included Frank Norris's *The Octopus*, recounting the depredations of the California railroads, and Upton Sinclair's *The Jungle*, exposing sins of the Chicago meatpacking plants. Rough treatment of immigrant labors was one thing, but the meatpacking tycoons were also poisoning the American consumer with wormy beef, ground-up rats, even the carcasses of a worker or two who tumbled into the processing vats.

One proposed remedy to the situation was socialism, which began making inroads with the American voter. In 1912, socialist candidate Eugene V. Debs garnered more than a million votes for president—a

The Granger Collection, New York

A strike at the Carnegie Homestead Plant protested the treatment of workers.

breathtaking tally. Other voices were more strident still. Groups calling themselves Anarchists, Syndicalists, or the International Workers of the World prophesized an industrial Armageddon in the United States: workers would rise up and take charge of the factories once and for all, and all forms of government would melt away. Yet socialism or more radical variants were never as powerful in the United States as they were in Europe. America was still seen as a land of economic opportunity where you or your children could climb the ladder to economic success.

The problem of the trusts and corporate power did not go away. Corporations that weren't viewed as outlaws were often viewed as powers unto themselves. Individuals—workers, farmers, small shopkeepers—felt powerless in the face of corporate power. Correctly and incorrectly, they saw the corporations as all-powerful economically, setting wages, determining working conditions, setting prices, and manipulating the political process. In principle, competitive markets were supposed to eliminate economic power. Businesses competed to obtain workers. Prices were the result of impersonal forces of demand and supply rather than the personal prerogative of corporate leaders. In short, individuals felt powerless.

Yet, at the same time Americans feared a tyranny of private power, the economy had been delivering a higher and higher standard of living. Between 1870 and 1910, as the fear of corporate power grew, income per person doubled, forty million immigrants were absorbed into the economy, and new consumer products such as electric lights and automobiles were being provided to many American households. Moreover, the work week had decreased slightly, more young people were graduating from high school, infant mortality was decreasing, and life expectancy was increasing. While individuals distrusted and feared the economic power of corporations, they were living better.

Political Machines and Their Bosses

The corporation wasn't the only form of organization that Americans found threatening. The era of big business was also the era of the political machine. Politics by machine might be said to be inherent in the idea of democracy. Democracy supposes virtue on the part of citizens but it does not and cannot compel virtuous conduct. Once voters become detached from a sense of responsibility, their votes become a commodity like any other, available to the highest bidder.

After the Civil War, political machines became the order of the day in many American cities. New York, Chicago, Kansas City, San Francisco, and other urban centers found themselves under the thumb of the owners and operators of the machines, the *political bosses*. Some of these, to be sure, were only dignified saloon brawlers, at home in a smoke-filled room. Others were known as distinguished citizens. What all of them had in common was private power, the same kind of power wielded by the trusts, and during the Gilded Age that power became enormous.

New York's Tammany Hall was the grandfather of American political machines. It was started in 1789 and was soon controlled by the infamous Aaron Burr as a kind of fraternal lodge with a political agenda. Its primary purpose was to promote the election of its own candidates to state and local office, the assumption being that Tammany men were somehow more fit than other office seekers owing to their clubby interest. In a world without political parties or other concentrations of voting power, Tammany came to move like a tank among archers. Come election day, by fair means or foul, it could almost always deliver the vote.

Machines that were successful at the polls found themselves with more than just harmless prestige

POLITICAL MACHINE

Most big cities were characterized by huge blocks of immigrant voters. Politicians appealed to these groups in straightforward ethnic terms. Good things happened to the ethnic group responsible for electing the local politician (In this case the Irish). The politicians, as part of a political machine, maintained power by transforming public authority into private power—power for themselves and their limited constituency. It was a twisted perversion of self-government.

for a reward. Governments paid careful attention to the sources of electoral power and went out of their way to make sure that brokers of such power were kept happy. People who needed favors performed by the mayor's office learned that it was expedient to go through Tammany Hall. Such favors, of course, came at a price.

The nature of political machines was revolutionized by foreign immigration. Thousands of immigrants, lost and alone in the city, not only clustered together in ethnic neighborhoods, they were easily mobilized by political bosses of the same ethnicity, who pledged to take care of them, see to their special needs, and shield them from hostile forces. The immigrants voted unquestioningly for a certain slate of candidates because Big Jim Kelly or Giovanni Luciano told them to. And the bosses were usually as good as their word. They found jobs for their constituents, helped them out of scrapes, furnished occasional legal services, and saw to their happiness and welfare. At Christmastime there might be a turkey for the family dinner table, or new shoes for the kids.

Political machines became as well organized as corporations—and better organized than political parties. Following the city's plan of districting, they divided into wards or other units and appointed specific individuals as "heelers," to visit constituent families regularly and see to their needs, and, at election time, get out the vote. Machines had their strong-arm side as well. Squads of "bully boys" could be made available at a moment's notice to disrupt an opponent's activities or even to trash a

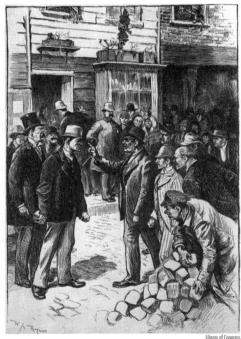

Library of Congress

Wood engraving by W. A. Rogers (*Harper's Weekly*, Nov. 16, 1889, p. 920). Tammany "workers" at a poll in 1889. Tammany workers could almost always "deliver the vote."

polling place. In the notorious Five Points district of New York, rival gangs were known to fight pitched battles at election time.

Graft and stealing were the political machines' bottom line, of course, for once in power the bosses were in a position to make the fullest use of their influence. Of the many and varied forms of corruption, these were most prominent:

- Gambling, prostitution, dope dealing, and other forms of vice were allowed in specific precincts as long as the machine was well paid.

- Contracts were awarded to chosen contractors, often at vastly inflated sums, in exchange for under-the-table kickbacks to the machine.

- Corporations paid bribes to the machine for special privileges, such as the right of trolley companies to run overhead wires or the right of restaurants to serve alcohol.

- Monopolies and franchises were simply sold to the highest bidder.

All told, political machines levied an astronomical toll on the American taxpayer. Under Boss William Marcy Tweed, for example, the Tammany Hall machine managed to steal as much as $2 *billion* (in current dollars) from the people of New York. While other cities did not run up tallies as high as this, neither did they have pockets as deep.

Venal bosses and venal corporations often went hand in hand. In California, for example, the railroad's political bureau worked closely with political machines to tighten its hold on state and local government. A famous graft investigation conducted in San Francisco in 1906 revealed that the city's major corporations worked hand in glove with the notorious Abe Ruef machine. The same was true of political machines elsewhere.

The Constitution and the American Founding were meant to be a long-term answer to the problem of unacceptable exercise of power. Markets were to disperse economic power to the point that no one controlled prices in the economy. Government was to be controlled by repeated exercise of consent through elections and by the structural devices in the Constitution. An ordinary free American in 1800 had very little contact with government and did not see businesses or other institutions as powerful or oppressive. But the change reviewed in the previous chapter changed the scale of America, and the change in scale created either private power in the hands of large corporations or the appearance of such power. Business was so much bigger and so impersonal that individuals felt small and threatened by this new power. Moreover, state and local government had also grown because of the growth of cities. Now a city government could become corrupt and tyrannical in ways not imagined earlier. Thus, Americans from 1880 to 1914 looked for ways to offset the new sources of power generated by the change in scale of America. Ultimately, they turned to the source of power that could always trump other sources—government.

The Progressive Response

Political responses to the problems of private power and government corruption took several forms. All of them had this much in common: they assumed that the problem could only be solved by the federal government. The answer to private power, so it seemed, was public power. But if the solution was public power, then reformers had to be sure that government at all levels stayed subservient to the people.

Populism

An early response was that of the Populists. Populism arose in the 1880s and 1890s. It was centered in the South and Midwest, and was essentially a rural phenomenon. Farmers in the Gilded Age were pressed by many problems, ranging from drought to overproduction to currency deflation. Farming was a hard life in the best of times, and these times were far from best.

As Populists analyzed their difficulties, they concluded that the blame essentially lay with two kinds of organizations they couldn't control: banks and railroads. Populists blamed the banks for currency deflation and falling prices—meaning that they had to pay back their loans with money that was harder and harder to come by. Populists blamed the railroads for monopolistic freight rates that drove the prices of farmers' produce downward. Eventually, the rural Populists were joined by disgruntled factory workers, whose difficulties with the conditions of industrial labor were becoming acute.

Influenced by the increasing popularity of socialism, Populists proposed that banks and railroads be nationalized and operated by the federal government. They also proposed that currency be inflated by means of the free coinage of silver to augment the supply of gold. Populists won many state and local elections in the South and Midwest. However, when they attempted to form a viable third party on the national scene, they were essentially co-opted and absorbed by the Democratic Party, which nominated the Populist candidate, William Jennings Bryan, for president in 1896. The election campaign was intensely emotional and accompanied by much demonizing of those who held private power—whom Bryan compared to the crucifiers of Jesus.

Bryan's loss of the election (to William McKinley) more or less spelled the end of Populism. But the difficulties that had spawned it were not soon to go away.

Progressivism

A second and rather different response to the problem of private power was mounted by the Progressive movement. Progressivism was an urban phenomenon and much different in character than Populism. Where the Populists had looked backward nostalgically, Progressives (as their name implied) looked hopefully to the future—to progress. There was much in Progressivism of science and technology, of the cult of the expert, of universities, of the emerging fields of sociology, psychology, political science, and social work. The movement was filled with cutting-edge intellectuals, crusading editors, and people with clipboards and stopwatches.

Progressivism was heavily influenced by the ideas of Charles Darwin, especially as these had been refined and applied to society by Herbert Spencer and others. Society, like everything else, said the Social Darwinists, was in a state of constant change and development, evolving into ever higher and more complex forms. What we perceived as social or political problems were simply the strains of evolutionary progress. The issue for the Progressives, then, was whether evolution would be random and haphazard or intelligently guided.

There were Progressives in every part of the country and in every level of government. There were Progressives in both national parties, too, Theodore Roosevelt being the great Republican Progressive and Woodrow Wilson the great Democratic. Progressives addressed themselves to all kinds of problems, from cleaning up city slums to increasing the efficiency of schools, from reducing hazards in the workplace to providing better care for expectant mothers, from conserving natural resources to designing an improved banking system. But their main struggle was with private power—

PROGRESSIVES REFORM OF CHARACTER

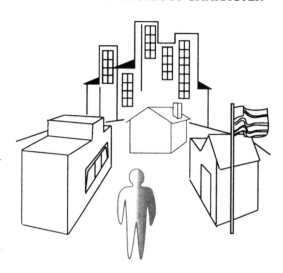

Progressives sought to reform character by reforming those institutions such as the home, school, workplaces and community which were assumed to affect character.

with the trusts on one hand and political machines on the other.

Progressives saw both evils essentially as wrong turns in the evolutionary process. They had evolved from something simpler and would in turn evolve into something more complex. The point was to see if the something more complex could also be made better.

Progressive reformers built their new construction of America on both economic and political reform.

Economic Reform

Economic reform started with the problem of monopoly or the trusts. There were two possible strategies and both were employed. The first strategy was to break up the monopolists or trusts, and thereby create economic competition. In 1890, Congress passed the Sherman Antitrust Act which made it illegal to conspire to restrain trade. The Sherman Act was the basis for government breakup of Rockefeller's Standard Oil into five separate companies, with the hope that these "baby Standard Oils" would compete with one another. Other laws fostering competition were also passed, most notably the Clayton

PROGRESSIVES AND THE TRUSTS

One approach to the trusts was to break them into smaller pieces, forcing them back into economic competition (above). The other approach was to regulate them with bigger and more powerful government (below).

Antitrust Act in 1914. These laws were aimed at fostering economic competition and breaking up monopolies.

The second strategy was to regulate business power rather than attempt to destroy it. Regulation of business started early in the Progressive Era when, in 1887, the Interstate Commerce Commission (ICC) was organized to regulate railroads and the rates they charged. States also initiated regulatory agencies to control public utilities such as power and subway systems. When Upton Sinclair wrote an exposé of the meatpacking industry, political pressure increased for regulation of the safety and cleanliness of foods, which led to creation of the Food and Drug Administration (FDA). The precedent of government regulation of business, whether to control monopoly or to regulate business for some proposed public interest, was well established by the end of the Progressive Era.

One of the major complaints of the late nineteenth and early twentieth centuries was directed toward banking. Ordinary Americans traced the problems of declining prices or farm foreclosures to banks. Moreover, in bad times when people needed the support of the banking system, banks sometimes closed their doors or simply refused to give customers back their deposits. A particularly bad banking panic in 1907 provided the push for creation of a central bank. In 1913, Congress and the President created the Federal Reserve System, a group of regional reserve banks headed by a Board of Governors in Washington, DC. Eventually the "Fed," as it is called by the financial community, would become a dominant government institution in the control of the economy. Creation of the Federal Reserve was one of the most important outcomes of the Progressive Era.

Much of the regulation during the Progressive Era of the economy was actually at the state level. States were especially active in passing labor laws. Workmen's compensation programs were initiated to insure workers against on-the-job injuries. Laws regulating the hours and conditions under which women could work were also passed in many states as well as laws requiring compulsory schooling of children under age fourteen or sixteen.

Governmental Reform

Reformers of the Progressive Era were also intent on making government more responsive to the people. States amended their constitutions to inject more democracy into government. The typical approaches usually included:

- *Initiative*. Citizens could put propositions directly on the ballot through petition. If the proposition received majority vote, it became law.
- *Referendum*. Laws passed by legislatures could be directly submitted to the people for a vote at an election. If a majority of the people voted against the law, it was taken off the books.
- *Recall*. By petition, citizens could call a special election to consider the recall of an elected official. If a majority voted for the recall, then the person was removed from office.

All these measures were designed to bypass a legislature or elected official who might have been corrupted by private power.

At the federal level, the most important change directed at increasing democracy was the Seventeenth Amendment, which shifted the selection of senators from the state legislature as provided in the Constitution to popular election of senators by the people. State legislators were perceived to be too close to large economic interests of that state. However, the most far-reaching change may have been the Sixteenth Amendment, which finally made a direct tax on the incomes of individuals and businesses constitutional. Though income taxes had been passed during the Civil War and the 1890s, the Supreme Court had held that an income tax was unconstitutional because the Constitution prevented direct taxation. The Sixteenth Amendment allowed direct taxation. Income tax would soon grow to be the favorite method of generating government revenue. To Progressives, the income tax held promise as a way of redistributing economic rewards within the economy. With an income tax, rates could be increased with income, shifting the burden of supporting the activities of government to upper-income groups. To politicians, the income tax proved to be a simple way to raise increasing revenues for government. Economic growth itself pushed more and more money into government coffers.

Growth of Government in the Progressive Era

In 1870 the federal government had one civilian employee for every eight hundred people in the country. By 1927, after World War I and the completion of the Progressive reforms, the federal government had one employee for every two hundred people. In 1902, when statistics combining all levels of government first became available, government accounted for 8 percent of the output of the economy. By 1927, government had grown to 12 percent. There is no question that the Progressive Era expanded the scope and size of government. Government had taken on the regulation of significant aspects of the economy. With a new important source of revenue, government had taken the first tentative steps toward social programs to help the poor.

During the 1920s, Progressivism visibly faltered, in part because the economy was booming in most sectors. However, the stock market collapse in 1929 and the New Deal response to the Great Depression pushed the United States back on the track of reform and government expansion. At one point or another, the Franklin Roosevelt administration embraced virtually every solution proposed by Populists and Progressives as well as many new proposals.

Progressivism and the Founding

Using the term *Progressivism* in a broad, generic sense, we can observe a number of ways the Progressive struggle against private power has impacted the Founding.

As the Founding developed, it assumed an essentially *laissez faire*, hands-off attitude toward the market place. By the end of Andrew Jackson's presidency, Americans had come to stand more or less against mercantilism and other forms of intervention. While there would be significant exceptions to this rule—the federal government, for instance, essentially financed the building of the first transcontinental railroad—the exceptions often proved the rule.

Certain clauses in the Constitution were interpreted by the Supreme Court to support *laissez faire*. The "due process clause" of the Fifth Amendment, for example, which was also included in the Fourteenth Amendment after the Civil War, had not been drafted with market economics in mind. But with a bit of semantic tweaking, it was possible for courts to interpret the wording that way—and to conclude that "due process" meant that government should keep its hands off economic matters entirely.

The same thing happened with the commerce clause. The wording of the clause appeared to give the federal government a broad grant of power in dealing with commercial matters, but in the era of big business the Supreme Court began to suppose otherwise. (This process will be treated more fully in chapter 15.) Because "commerce" was a vague term and subject to a variety of interpretations, Supreme Court Justices adopted a very narrow construction of it and applied it only to the physical transit of goods across state lines. Congress, in other words, was essentially barred from delving into the economy at all.

Progressives became incensed by what they viewed as malefactors hiding behind the Constitution. The government's hands were tied, as they saw it, because the Founding stood against—or could be made to stand against—Progress. State attempts to curb the trusts supposedly violated the due process clause of the Fourteenth Amendment. And when the federal government tried to step in, it was told that the commerce clause gave it no authority to do so. In one famous case, the Supreme Court held that the American Sugar Company, which sold its product in every state of the Union, did not engage in "commerce" insofar as the Constitution was concerned.

It is no mere happenstance that the first assault mounted against the Founding came at the hands of Progressive historians. In 1911, at the height of Progressivism, Charles A. Beard wrote his soon-to-be-famous book titled *An Economic Interpretation of the Constitution*, arguing that the Framers in Philadelphia had had personal motivations for writing the Constitution—mostly having to do with investments—or in other words, that the use of the Constitution to confer private advantage was nothing new. If the Founding was going to be used to block Progress, Beard and others seemed to conclude, then the Founding must be shown for what it was, an artifact of the eighteenth century, and a shabby one at that.

Woodrow Wilson adopted a similar stance. In a famous speech before the Commerce Club in Washington, Wilson, who had been a professor of political science early in his career, argued that the structure set up by the Constitution was mechanical in nature, a thing of springs and wires and balances, and that in practice it tended to create gridlock rather than meaningful action. A Darwinian world, Wilson asserted, called for a constitution of growth and development and change. How could Americans guide their own evolution if they were hampered by outdated rules?

Library of Congress

Woodrow Wilson (1916) argued that the Constitution created political gridlock and that modern America needed a constitution that would promote growth and development.

In this same spirit, Franklin D. Roosevelt, himself an old-line Progressive, argued that the Bill of Rights needed to be broadened and deepened to address difficulties during the Depression Era. Americans, he said, had a right to economic security along with the rights on Madison's list. He became so angry with the Supreme Court's interpretations of the Constitution that he proposed to redesign the Supreme Court! But as Peter Finley Dunne noted, "The Supreme Court reads the election returns." Supreme Court interpretations of the commerce clause and other important aspects of the Constitution changed to accommodate the Progressive reforms. Furthermore, the Progressive Era led to structural reforms—direct election of senators, the creation of the Federal Reserve, and income tax—leading to profound changes in government in successive decades.

Chapter 12

The Great Depression and the New Deal

The American Founders energetically debated contrasting visions of the republic they had in mind. We have seen, for example, how the Federalists and Anti-Federalists projected very different ideas of American nationhood to voters. And the ongoing dialogue between Thomas Jefferson and Alexander Hamilton was in large measure a debate about two dissimilar visions of American life. Even though a powerful sense of nostalgia for Jeffersonian America lingered into the twentieth century, it was clearly Hamilton who won the debate. The Constitution set up an "extended republic," one that would come to be known for its geographic size, its expanding population, its industrial development, its urban way of life, its influence in global affairs—and its commerce.

Commerce had not been a kindly term in ancient Greece. It denoted such things as moneygrubbing, price gouging, advantage taking—the narrowest and shabbiest kind of self-interest. True virtue could never flourish in a commercial society, it was assumed.

With similar thoughts in mind, critics of the Constitution argued that the Founders were turning their backs on the idea of virtue when they opted for the commercial republic. In reading *Federalist* 10, for example, these observers pointed out that Madison was no longer talking about moral behavior in explaining the Constitution's operation, but rather only about interest clashing with economic factions in a patchwork of constant conflict.

Adam Smith would have had a reply for these critics of the market economy. Those who seek their own self-interest in the marketplace are not necessarily bad neighbors, bad friends, or bad citizens, he would say. On the contrary, they tend to exhibit qualities that make for peace and social happiness.

Whichever side was right, the U.S. soon grew into the largest single free market in human history—a direct result of the Founding. For better or worse, this fact would shape the American experience in innumerable ways.

American Prosperity

During the course of the nineteenth century, American prosperity became something of a phenomenon, as we noted in chapter 10. What we think of as prosperity today has not been an abiding feature of the human experience. In most societies there were a few haves and many have-nots, with poverty the typical experience of most. One of the distinguishing features of the Good Society was a generalized prosperity, where all were well off—or at least better off than they would have been elsewhere.

This kind of prosperity was essentially mandated by democracy. For in a society with widespread political power, economic disparity must always lead to difficulty. The have-nots, if they feel victimized, will always be tempted to gang up on the haves in the political arena and seek to even up the score. In a democratic society, then, there needs to be:

- A comparatively narrow disparity between rich and poor.
- A sense that even the poor are adequately fed, housed, and cared for.
- A feeling that equality of opportunity exists across the board, that anyone, rich or poor, has a reasonable chance to succeed.

Such a situation can only be created by economic growth. Thus, when we speak of American prosperity, it is really the phenomenon of growth that we are talking about.

Growth is the steady increase in the per capita performance of an economy. It is measured by computing the GDP (gross domestic product, the sum total of all final goods and services produced) and dividing that number by population to get the GDP per person or per

MEASURING ECONOMIC PERFORMANCE

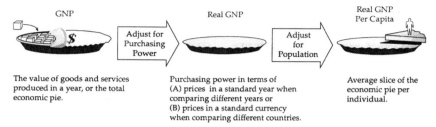

GNP must be adjusted for differences in purchasing power and population before comparisons can be made with previous years or other countries.

capita. When measured over time, GDP per capita must be adjusted for increases or decreases in the average level of prices to calculate what economists call *real GDP per capita*, the most accepted measure of the standard of living in an economy. If this real per capita income is rising from year to year, the economy is experiencing economic growth.

Beginning roughly at the time of the American Revolution and the ratification of the Constitution, the U.S. economy, like many of the European economies, embarked upon a long period of growth, which in more than 200 years has averaged close to 2 percent growth per year. While 2 percent may not seem breathtaking, it essentially means that real income per capita will double every thirty-five years. In the entire human experience, such a growth rate over an extended period of time is without precedent. Only in the past two centuries, both here and abroad, has a large part of the world's population experienced consistent increases in the standard of living.

Economic growth is an artifact of the modern world, unknown before the Industrial Revolution. Broadly speaking, it was made possible by the market system of production and the application of scientific technology through improved machines and improved processes. By creating an ever-greater division of labor and using ever better tools, we have learned to generate unheard-of abundance.

Until recently, only a handful of economies have been able to bring together the specific factors that promote economic growth. Great Britain was conspicuous among this group. And America, as England's child, was favorably poised from colonial beginnings to follow suit. Beyond this, Americans found themselves on the upside of most of those growth factors, of which there are basically five.

1. Resources

From the beginning, American resources were vast, consisting of timber, coal, metallic ores, petroleum, minerals, and extensive tracts of arable land.

2. Labor Quality

Labor itself does not bring economic growth since more labor typically means more mouths to feed. An important key to economic growth is more productive labor. American society also promoted good health, education, hard work, and personal achievement—qualities that steadily improved the quality of the labor force and accounted for a large part of economic growth.

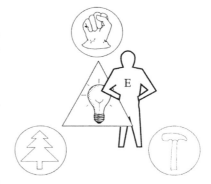

3. Capital Accumulation

To give workers ever better tools, Americans worked hard at capital accumulation, stressing saving and investment, and developing a banking system that answered the needs of an expanding economy. As U.S. industry burgeoned, foreign investment also became a significant factor, as did the laws of incorporation that facilitated capital development.

Economic growth formula.

4. Technology

Innovation became a significant factor in American industrial development. Americans proved to be extremely adept at machine technology, forging ahead of the British early in the nineteenth century. Americans would remain on the cutting edge from that point on.

5. Entrepreneurship

All the resources described above have to be put together to contribute to a productive economy. The person who organizes and innovates is called an entrepreneur. Americans excelled in imagination and chance taking, the two principal qualities of entrepreneurship.

American prosperity was driven by a variety of social and cultural factors as well. An ethic of personal success grew out of American individualism. Materialistic values stoked a demand for ever better housing, personal transportation, labor-saving appliances, newfangled gadgets, and symbols of higher status.

In the burgeoning, dynamic society that economic growth created, wealth tended to circulate rapidly. Where in the Old World wealth tended to remain in the same families from generation to generation, here there was a high degree of social mobility, both upward and downward. But social mobility was more than just economics. It tapped into an American founding myth and gave it fullest expression. We saw in chapter 2 that the Puritans created myths of the Lost Eden and the New Jerusalem. To these two founding myths Americans now added a third, which in some

Rough and Ready, a book in the Ragged Dick series by Horatio Alger Jr., explores the American Dream.

sense grew out of both of them—the American Dream. In America, this myth held, a poor boy could go from rags to riches.

The American Dream was explored in a series of fictional works written for youth by Horatio Alger Jr. In the saga of *Ragged Dick,* for example, readers learned that a poor bootblack in the streets of New York could battle his way to business success so long as he hewed to the traditional virtues of industry and frugality. As with the Puritans, wealth became a sign of God's pleasure.

In sum, Madison's commercial republic became the booming, buzzing, market-driven society favored by Alexander Hamilton, a society capable of turning poor bootblacks into flush capitalists—as witness Andrew Carnegie. Its phenomenal economic growth owed to many things, of course, but most of all it owed to the Founders' insistence that there be no trade barriers among the states. The greater the area of exchange, as Adam Smith had pointed out, the greater the total benefit—and America was a free-trade zone larger than any to be found in Europe. Combine free trade with a stable democracy, and America's prosperity seemed assured.

American Dream, American Nightmare

We have seen that the process of exchange is governed by the law of comparative advantage, which states that every individual, every group, every nation will tend to produce those goods and services for which they are the low-cost producer. As long as there are differences in opportunity cost, everyone will be the low-cost producer of *something*. The law of comparative advantage helps us to make sense of American prosperity. Owing to the nature of its resources, its transportation networks, and its diverse population, the U.S. was able to create a balanced economy, which is to say that Americans became low-cost producers of a wide array of goods and services, exchanging food stuffs, cotton, and wool for the manufactured goods of Europe. But most exchange in the U.S. was within or between regions of the country. Profitable exchange could take place between western farmers, eastern manufacturers, northern merchants, southern producers of staples, and so on.

One of the key implications of the law of comparative advantage is full employment of resources. Every resource should have a comparative advantage or a least comparative disadvantage that should direct the employment of that resource. No resource should remain unemployed. To be sure, there would be temporary unemployment while adjustments are made, but long-term unemployment of a resource would violate the law of comparative advantage.

While Americans were discovering the benefits of trade, they were also discovering vagaries of the business cycle. Market economies, it seemed, did not proceed in a steady upward course of economic growth, even under the most favorable of circumstances. They would surge ahead in periods of growth and expansion and then falter in periodic recessions. Economists were never completely certain what caused recessions to occur, though there was much theorizing on the subject. The general thinking now is that recessions are brought about by shocks to the economy. The economic shock could come from any number of directions—crop failure, a collapse of stock prices, outbreak of war, or dislocation in banking or some other key sector of the economy. By the laws of supply and demand, markets should quickly readjust themselves to the new realities created by a shock, even a bad one. Unfortunately, in the real world, prices prove to be "sticky" or inflexible and unable to change quickly enough to absorb all the necessary change in the economy. The result is a fall in output and unemployment, sometimes catastrophic in scale.

Major recessions have punctuated American history, and almost always with political fallout. In 1837, for example, a frenzy of wild-cat banking led to the collapse of many state banks and plunged the U.S. into a deep recession. Andrew Jackson's successor, Martin Van Buren, took a major hit at the polls and his party lost the election of 1840. Populism (mentioned in the preceding chapter) was largely the result of another recession, with mortgage foreclosures, bank and

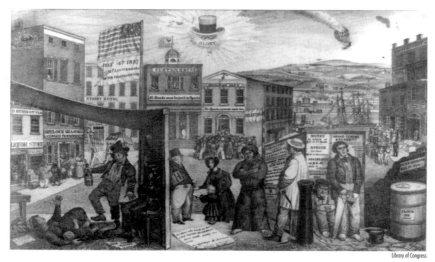

Library of Congress

"The Times" by Edward Williams Clay, 1837. A cartoon depicting the toll the recession of 1837 took on American workers.

investment house failures, and high unemployment in the 1890s. The election of 1896 was one of the most bitter and hard fought in U.S. history. William Jennings Bryan's famous "Cross of Gold" speech reflected a fear on the part of many Americans that capitalism entailed the "crucifixion" of ordinary laborers.

While markets did not involve crucifixion—despite socialist rhetoric—they did operate with blind impersonality. Market systems had no conscience, no sense of fair play, no idea of social justice, no regard for the environment, no highly refined taste. They simply delivered whatever consumers wanted, good or bad, and at the lowest opportunity cost. The upside was goods and services at costs so low that consumers could enjoy the fruits of prosperity. The downside might be long hours, low wages, harsh working conditions, and, most frightening to many workers, periodic bouts of unemployment.

Onset of the Great Depression

The prosperity of the 1920s created a widespread confidence that market maladies had been overcome. Agencies such as the Interstate Commerce Commission were supervising big business. Banking was now under the watchful eye of the Federal Reserve System. Real income marched steadily upward. And the stock market soared to dizzying new heights. The American Dream was becoming a reality for millions. But in 1929 there were signs that the rapid growth of the 1920s was coming to an end. Agriculture had not shared in the prosperity of the twenties. Many farmers were struggling and some were losing their farms. In summer 1929, industrial production began to decline. Then came the stock market crash in October 1929. The bubble in stock prices burst. General Motors stock, which had sold for $139 in 1928, was worth only $36 in November 1929.

In 1930, the bad economic news shifted to banks. Banks make money by loaning out deposits and collecting interest on the loans. Everything works well unless depositors all want their money at the same time. If depositors are fearful that the bank cannot make good on deposits, they immediately try to withdraw their money. Most depositors trying to withdraw their funds simultaneously is called a *bank run*. Faced with a run, a bank is likely to shut its doors or stop paying out funds to depositors. The decline in stock prices put pressures on banks and raised concerns about the stability of banks. In

1930, banks began to fail and shut their doors. As banks failed, the money supply of the economy fell and more economic disruption occurred. Inexplicably, the Federal Reserve, with both the responsibility and the capacity to stop the bank failures and control the money supply, failed to do so. The economy continued to spiral downward. Unemployment was 3.2 percent in 1929, 8.7 percent in 1930, 15.9 percent in 1931, 23.6 percent in 1932, and 24.9 percent in 1933 before beginning a slow improvement. A recession in 1929 combined with the bank failures of the 1930s and the total loss of consumer confidence created the Great Depression. The American dream changed abruptly to an American nightmare.

Hard Times

The Depression demonstrated how bad things could get in a market economy, though some economists laid the blame at the feet of the Federal Reserve. Layoffs and plant closures became daily events. By 1932 automobile production had slumped from its 1929 level of 4.5 million units to a scant 1.1 million. Ford Motor Company, once the bright star of U.S. industrial achievement, shut down completely for a time.

Nor was Ford alone. At the bottom of the Depression, one hundred eighty-five thousand businesses were bankrupt, 25 percent of the work force was idled, and per capita income had been wrenched back thirty years. Some four thousand banks closed their doors in 1933 alone, and with the collapse of each had vanished the personal savings of entire communities. In one case alone, more than four hundred thousand depositors were wiped out.

American farmers, victims of chronic overproduction, had not known real prosperity for two generations, and now their plight was truly pitiful. California growers left oranges to putrefy in the sun. Iowans burned their corn for fuel. And Minnesota dairymen emptied milk cans by the truckload onto the dusty road. "You don't pick three-cent cotton," explained a gaunt Mississippi sharecropper, "you just leave it sit."

Almost as hurtful as poverty and hunger was the damaged pride. Americans who had been climbing up the economic ladder for generations now began climbing down. Executives were demoted to shipping clerks, and shipping clerks to custodians. They stood on the

Library of Congress

New York City, 1933. Out-of-work business-men sold items on the street at junk markets during the Great Depression.

street corners and sold apples, still dressed in the suit and tie they had worn to the office.

Some strove to hide their pain, staying indoors so that neighbors wouldn't know the furniture had been repossessed. They told—and lived—complex lies. Finally, when the house went up for sale and dissembling became impossible, they did desperate things. Every so often someone put a gun to his head and pulled the trigger. Suicide rates increased.

More often, though, the down-and-outer simply took flight. He went off, supposedly to look for work, and never returned. Sometimes he wound up in a skid row hotel, paying a dollar a week and fending off the rats. Sometimes he took to riding the rails, sleeping in boxcars or haystacks. Sometimes he came to rest in one of the Depression's many shantytowns. And often he ended up on the pavement.

The woman he left behind was no more fortunate. Usually she was stranded with the children, often young, and thrown back upon the charity of neighbors. There are hundreds of surviving photographs of these truncated families. In almost all of them the faces reflect a hopelessness and despair beyond expression. An entire generation was stunted by the ordeal.

Herbert Hoover, who was president when the collapse occurred, did his best to combat the Depression by the means available. Although he used the power of government in unprecedented ways, he did so in the context of a belief that sooner or later the market system would right itself. Intervention, he believed, would come at a price, and the price might run pretty high.

Economic understanding was still rather limited at the time. Indeed, as the Depression's story unfolded, it became increasingly clear that many of the things government had done in response to the crisis only made a bad situation worse. The U.S. turned its back on tariff reduction talks and ran its own tariffs up even higher, inviting retaliation from trading partners and throttling foreign trade. Government at all levels slashed expenditures in an effort to balance the budget, dampening demand and throwing even more people out of work. And the Federal Reserve System, instead of inflating the money supply and stimulating demand, did precisely the opposite, stifling the economy all the more. Hoover's fear, in other words, proved to be all too well founded. Some government intervention in the economy was exacting a price. In the election of 1932, voters decided, justly or unjustly, that the Republican Party should also pay a price.

Election of 1932

The election of 1932 represented a dramatic change in American politics. The candidate of the Democratic Party, Franklin Delano Roosevelt, put together a coalition of Southerners, farmers, labor unions, and urban centers that would dominate American politics for fifty years. Voters in 1932 were ready to punish Republicans, the party that happened to be in power as the Depression began. After the 1928 election, Republicans held majorities in both the House (267 to 167) and in the Senate (56 to 39). After the 1932 election, there were only 117 Republicans in the House and 35 in the Senate. Democrats held larger majorities in both houses of congress and the presidency. The election of 1936 reduced Republicans to a shadow of their former power with only 89 house members and a measly 16 senators. Clearly, voters blamed the Republican Party and wanted a different approach.

The New Deal

Franklin Roosevelt pledged to offer the American people a "New Deal." The term had interesting connotations. If life was a poker game that had somehow become corrupt, then calling back the cards and dealing them over again amounted to a kind of refounding—something like Lincoln's "new birth of freedom." Roosevelt, who was committed to both capitalism and democracy, probably had nothing so revolutionary in mind. But owing to the desperation of the situation, he found himself driven forward by events. His New Deal would impact the Founding as heavily as the Civil War had done.

Experimentation

Roosevelt and his "Brain Trust"—which included advisors of considerable sophistication—concluded that the market system had broken down in some fundamental way and could not or would not repair itself. Therefore the system must be made to work differently. Instead of producers and consumers acting in their perceived self-interest and letting Smith's "invisible hand" guide the outcome, New Dealers decided to use cartel monopoly and its built-in negotiated agreements as their principal weapon against the Depression. All major industries would be allowed to collude together and set prices, wages, and conditions of labor, not in a spirit of self-interest but of public benefit. It was a bold experiment in pure virtue.

The National Recovery Administration (NRA) and its country cousin, the Agricultural Adjustment Administration (AAA), put the cartel monopoly theory into action. As with all cartel monopolies, they believed they could force up prices by artificially curtailing production, and that the higher prices, with accompanying higher wages, would then stimulate demand. However, with few exceptions, this approach to the Depression failed as completely as Hoover's efforts had. Like the market system itself, the New Deal was based on an understanding of human nature, and that understanding was simply not borne out. Given monopolistic power, big business used it to its own advantage, not the public good, shorting small producers and failing to benefit consumers. Fortunately, the Supreme Court declared the NRA unconstitutional. By 1935 the NRA was a dead letter.

The AAA had a more successful career, and vestiges of it still exist today in the form of price supports for certain agricultural commodities. It rescued the family farm for millions of Americans, where the market system might have simply cashed them in. But production quotas and price supports remained an artificial solution, imposed by the will of government, and artificiality would dog the heels of the American farmer forever after.

The early New Deal only proved Hoover's fundamental skepticism. Market failures are hard to fix.

Keynesian Economics

Roosevelt needed to find an intellectual foundation on which to base an economic policy. At the very time that the U.S. was struggling against depression, a brilliant British economist, John Maynard Keynes, was working out just such a foundation. Undoubtedly, it

THE RECESSION SPIRAL

If enough firms have pessimistic expectations of the economic future, business investment declines (A).

This causes a decline in aggregate employment and income and therefore a decline in consumer demand (B).

The lowered consumer demand leads to further decisions to reduce business investment (C).

This, again, causes employment and income to fall even further, reducing even more consumer demand (D).

was as much trial and error as any formal economic theory that convinced the New Dealers of the best strategy to follow. But Keynes's theory would prove to be influential with governments across the world over the next half century.

Most economists before Keynes believed that the economy would be self-regulating. They were guided by a maxim from a French economist, Jean Baptiste Say, that "supply creates its own demand." In other words, payments to those who produce goods and services would be sufficient to buy the goods produced. The prescription of most economists when confronted with recession was simply to wait—that in the long run, the economy would right itself. Keynes's retort was that "in the long run, we are all dead." In a technical treatise directed to economists, Keynes argued that the economy could fall into a trap that would not return the economy to full employment. Keynes argued that government had to be an activist in the face of recession. Keynes's main policy idea was fairly simple. Recession is characterized by a falloff in demand, and it is this falloff that causes the economy to spiral downward. Some businesses lay off workers. Laid-off workers spend less money. A small decrease in demand is multiplied many times as it works through the economy. Other businesses sell fewer goods and as a result lay off more workers. And so on. Keynes pointed out that it is within the power of government to turn this vicious cycle around through its powers of taxing and spending.

Since government, by its very size, is a key player in the economic game, it can artificially stimulate demand by increasing government spending or cutting taxes. Government spending can stimulate demand directly as the government builds roads and buildings, or embarks on a new program. Alternatively, the government can induce businesses or consumers to spend more by reducing taxes, leaving them with more of their income. Keynes's prescription to combat recession implied that government would run deficits in its budget during recession, adding to its national debt. But Keynes expected the government to run surpluses in its budget during periods of economic boom. As it turned out, politicians were much more attracted to budget deficits created by increasing government spending and cutting taxes than to budget surplus, which required spending

THE KEYNESIAN SOLUTION

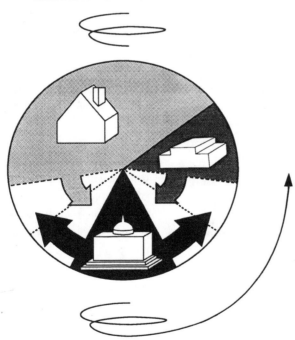

Keynes argued that through fiscal policy, government could reverse the recession spiral through
(A) increased government spending and/or
(B) lowered taxes which would increase household consumption and business investment.

restraint and tax increases. In practical terms, Keynes pushed public policy toward two tendencies—government assumption of responsibility to manage the economy to combat recession, and toward government deficits to "stimulate the economy" regardless of the state of the economy. Since 1936, when Keynes published his ideas in a book entitled *A General Theory of Employment, Interest and Money*, the U.S. government has run a deficit in its budget over 90 percent of the time—a tribute to human nature in politics and to the influence of Keynes's ideas.

New Deal Relief

After the initial confusion and experimentation with the NRA, the New Deal settled into a two-pronged effort—short-term relief and long-term economic regulation. First there were a series of short-term relief programs to soften the effects of the Depression. Unemployed young men were encouraged to join the Civilian Conservation Corp (CCC), organized to complete conservation projects on federal land and to build campgrounds in the national forests. To provide work for unemployed of all ages, a succession of work relief agencies were formed—Federal Emergency Relief Administration (FERA), Public Works Administration (PWA), and Works Progress Administration (WPA) for construction of public buildings and roads, sanitation projects, arts projects, writing projects, and so on.

Prior to the New Deal, relief of poverty or unemployment was considered a responsibility of local government. Roosevelt federalized relief, making poverty and unemployment primarily national responsibilities from then on.

New Deal Economic Regulation

Roosevelt and his "Brain Trust" were not satisfied to provide short-term relief from the effects of the Depression. They were convinced that a market system could not regulate itself. Yet they were, by no means, persuaded that socialism, complete government control of the economy, was better than capitalism. They simply wanted the government to exert guidance over a market economy. They wanted to replace Adam Smith's invisible hand with a visible hand operating with a light touch. With the support of an overwhelming Democratic majority in Congress, they rapidly passed law after law setting up regulation of the economy. Some of the more important regulatory changes included:

- Securities and Exchange Commission (SEC) to oversee the stock market.
- National Labor Relations Board (NLRB) to regulate negotiations between unions and corporations, giving unions better opportunities to unionize new industries.
- Federal Deposit Insurance Corporation (FDIC) to oversee bank safety and guarantee bank deposits.
- Fair Labor Standards Act to establish a federal minimum wage of $0.25 (about $3 in 2000 prices).
- Social Security Insurance to provide insurance against unemployment, disability, and most important in the long run, to provide retirement funds for most Americans.

The Granger Collection, New York

New Deal Cartoon, 1935. Roosevelt tried to heal the depression and supervise business through an "alphabet soup" of agencies and programs.

- Federal Communications Commission (FCC) to oversee radio, telephone, telegraph, and later electronic media.
- Civil Aeronautics Board (CAB) to regulate airfares. The CAB was dissolved in the 1980s.
- Tennessee Valley Authority (TVA) to provide power, flood control, and industrial development to the upper South. The TVA was meant to be a model for other massive reclamation projects.
- Rural Electrification Administration (REA) to subsidize bringing electrical power to rural areas.

The New Deal was followed by World War II, led by the same president and a Democratic congress. World War II required the full mobilization of the economy for the war effort. Government once again was substituted for markets in directing the economy. Government bureaucrats were essentially directing corporations in their efforts to produce ships, planes, tanks, and other armaments. Markets had to take a backseat to the planning of war production. The New Deal and, to some degree, World War II changed the relationship between the federal government and the economy in profound ways. Before the New Deal, government did not take responsibility for the functioning of the market economy. After the New Deal, almost any serious glitch in the economy was open to debate and possible action by the federal government. A serious increase in the price of a staple or necessity would elicit calls for government action. Sometimes the government responded; sometimes it did not. Every perceived problem within the economy was seen as a proper role for government. Politicians and policy makers could imagine an ideal course of action where government could eliminate or at least mitigate some economic weakness or problem. They didn't occupy themselves with much follow-up as to whether or not government actually made the situation better or worse.

The Constitution proved to be no serious impediment to expansion of government power over the economy. The commerce clause was interpreted broadly, providing plenty of stretch for government involvement to be declared constitutional. The "takings clause" in the Fifth Amendment of the Bill of Rights was interpreted narrowly, leaving private property subservient to government desires or intent. Rights considered economic were seen by the courts as less substantive than the rights of free speech, privacy, or exercise of religious expression. Criminal due process worried the courts much more than due process involving economic values.

As government grew after the Great Depression and World War II, Americans gradually became more cynical and questioning about government involvement in the economy. Leading intellectuals such as Milton Friedman argued that government intervention in the economy was nearly always a mistake, that the economic forces of the market were superior to mistake-prone government planners. In the late twentieth century, starting with Jimmy Carter's administration, but accelerating in Ronald Reagan's administration, deregulation was the watchword. Government pulled back in many areas such as airline pricing and regulation of the media. The Post Office, a government monopoly for two hundred years, faced heavy competition from FedEx and UPS. Some people even began to call for economic competition in education in place of public schools.

But neither side gained complete victory. Every economic issue provoked the old debate of markets versus planning. Many advocated government planning as a way to produce security and the right distribution of income or consumption. Others pointed to the efficiency of markets and the capacity of entrepreneurial energy to innovate and create new solutions. Health care and education were common battlegrounds, as was Social Security. No clear cut answer was in sight.

The promise of the market economy was closely akin to the promise of political democracy. Neither could guarantee the right answer in a given situation. The best either could provide was what the people themselves seemed to value. If there were faults in the public character—blind spots, distortions, moral lapses—they could not be papered over in the marketplace any more than in the voting booth. Both institutions revealed the human soul.

Chapter 13

America and the World

In chapter 11 we saw that rapid change brought Americans to confront private power. In chapter 12 that change brought them to confront the impersonal market. The anxieties arising from these two developments pale beside those arising from a third confrontation—one with the outside world.

Some find such a fear ironic. Since the end of World War II, they point out, the United States has had the capacity to destroy the entire planet several times over, making it the only true superpower. Its institutions have triumphed over those of determined adversaries. People all over the world look to it for guidance, inspiration, and security. What on earth is there to be afraid of?

The answer to this question is complicated, and once again it grows out of the Founding. By the very nature of that Founding, Americans came to embrace two contradictory beliefs:

- That they should withdraw from the world to whatever extent possible and chart their own course.
- That they should lead the world by example and become a beacon of virtuous conduct.

Reconciling these irreconcilable alternatives has provided a central tension in America's relationship with the rest of mankind.

Born in a Machiavellian World

The world of the ancient Greeks was torn with strife. Whatever may be said for the internal life of the Greek *poleis*, their external relations were tarnished by conflict, aggressiveness, underhanded diplomacy, and a constant urge toward imperialism. Virtue, it seemed, did not apply outside one's own borders.

Niccolò Machiavelli, the great Renaissance political thinker, helps us understand the reason for this paradox. In the human psyche, he noted, there is a disconnect between public and private morality. Those who might be scrupulously honest in their private lives often break all the rules in their public capacity. This is even more apparent for situations in which the self (myself, my family, my tribe, my country) is pitted in some way against the outsider—the Other.

Machiavelli's insight helps make sense of the world into which the American Republic was born, a world every bit as cynical as that of ancient Greece. In the 1600s and later, the various nation-states of Europe, well ordered internally, interacted without much compassion or common courtesy, following the rule of "every man for himself." When the American Revolution broke out, France and England had been at loggerheads for a century over the question of who was dominant in Europe. The contest was colored by alliances and counteralliances, by deal making and deal breaking, by sellouts, betrayals, landgrabs, power plays, and ultimately by war. Between 1702 and 1763, France and England had fought each other no fewer than four times.

Library of Congress

This complex game played directly into the hands of the American rebels and ultimately spelled their success. American diplomats, notably Benjamin Franklin, knew precisely how to play England against France and Spain and mobilize suspicions that each might have of the others. In the end, Franklin violated his agreement with the French and worked out a separate peace with the British, smoothly apologizing while hitting the French up for a loan.

Benjamin Franklin. "Poor Richard's" devious dealings with the French demonstrated a difference in private and public morality.

That "Poor Richard," as Franklin was known, might be capable of such cunning says much for Machiavelli's insight.

Most of the Founders realized that the enmity between France and England, however useful to their cause, might prove dangerous to the fledgling republic. To forge a permanent alliance with either of them would risk embroiling the United States in disastrous foreign wars. George Washington spelled out this danger clearly in his famous Farewell Address. But it was not a new idea.

In 1789 the French Revolution unleashed violence and bloodshed upon the whole of Europe. England forged an alliance against the revolutionary regime, and upon the execution of the French king in 1793, the two countries were at war once again. This war would continue in fits and starts for the next twenty years, sweeping from the English Channel to the gates of Moscow. Both sides fought desperately, the French for their Revolution, the British for monarchical order and stability. And the United States was caught directly in between.

We have already seen that Thomas Jefferson and the Anti-Federalists were sympathetic toward the French, accepting many of the goals of the Revolution, while Alexander Hamilton and the Federalists leaned toward the English. Still, most Americans preferred the neutrality that Washington had urged. There was nothing to gain and everything to lose by taking sides.

Yet as a commercial republic, the U.S. was vitally interested in foreign trade, and some Americans supposed that they could continue to trade with both the British *and* the French by proclaiming the rights of neutrals. But both belligerents pressed every advantage to the fullest—neutrals' rights be damned—and if the Americans got in the way, their ships were captured, their cargoes confiscated, their seamen hijacked, their neutrality trampled underfoot. In 1799 the U.S. fought an undeclared war with France, and in 1812 a declared war with Great Britain. The lesson? Involvement with the Old World could be risky.

Manifest Destiny

While Americans were learning about the harshness of the world, they were also learning to covet more of it for themselves. Actually they had done so from the very beginning. When it became clear to the colonists that American Indians were Others—that they were not eagerly awaiting conversion to Christian morals and European manners—hostility ensued. Colonial Indian wars were bloody, brutal, and horrifying, with abundant atrocities on both sides. And because the Indians occupied desirable lands, no matter how far west they were pushed, there was always a reason for further engagement. American dealing with these "foreign nations," as the Indian tribes were conceived, was no less cynical than European diplomacy.

The same attitude applied to other foreigners on the American continent. Americans resented the Spanish presence in Florida as well as the French presence on the Mississippi and conspired to undermine both. American leaders negotiated the purchase of Louisiana from Napoleon in 1803, and later the purchase of Florida. In the War of 1812 they made a determined effort to capture Canada, which they regarded as "the fourteenth colony," and abandoned that dream only with agonized reluctance.

American settlers moved into the rich lands bordering the Gulf of Mexico, and when the inevitable day of reckoning arrived, they staged a revolt against Mexican rule and broke away as the Republic of Texas. The welcoming of Texas into the Union in 1844 inflamed Mexican opinion to such an extent that war became unavoidable. In the ensuing conflict, American arms proved themselves on the battlefield in a dramatic way. The Americans, it seemed, were on the march.

The settlement of the Mexican War included the purchase of California, another outlying province of Old Mexico, together with all the territory separating it from Texas. At the same time, Americans voiced a willingness to take on the English yet again, this time over the Pacific Northwest. In American minds, the Oregon Territory included not only the present-day states of Washington and Oregon but also British Columbia. The warlike slogan "Fifty-four forty or fight!"—describing the longitude and latitude of the region—was meant to convince the English that Americans would settle for nothing less than the entire package, too, though they did finally agree to the present-day boundary.

Observers began to wonder how far Americans were willing to go in their headlong urge to expand. During the Mexican War, there was talk of taking the *whole* of Mexico, not just the northern half

Lithograph, 1848, by Nathaniel Currier. Some believed that America's expansionist tendencies, as depicted in this caricature of General Lewis Cass, would lead America into war.

of it, and later on of adding Central America and the Caribbean as well. The phrase Americans kept invoking was "Manifest Destiny"— meaning that they were fated to engulf the entire continent. It was the old dream of Columbus in a new guise.

One explanation of Manifest Destiny was that Americans were engaged in European-style empire building. After all, this was the time when Britain, France, Russia, Germany, Italy, and Belgium were pushing their way into the far corners of the earth, planting colonies, claiming possessions, and assuming various forms of political control. Yet American imperialism was fundamentally different. The Founders made an important decision with regard to the West. It would be organized not as an empire but as an extension of the republic, enjoying all the rights and privileges of the original states. In other words, the areas that Americans now sought to attach to the republic were not targeted for exploitation but rather enlisted for cooperative partnership—Jefferson's "empire of liberty."

Of course, this noble purpose did not soften the blow for those Others who stood in the American path. Many Mexican-Californians saw their lives destroyed by the American influx. It was far worse for the hapless Indians.

The Winning Cards

While Americans looked to the West, they also took a second look at Europe. So adamant were they that European powers should not intermeddle in the Western Hemisphere that in 1821 they enunciated the famous Monroe Doctrine. This manifesto declared that "recolonization" would not be tolerated by the United States. That is, if other colonies in the Americas successfully broke free from their European overlords, there must be no English-style wars of reconquest. The Monroe Doctrine stated, in effect, that Europeans ought to remain on their own side of the globe.

As time passed, Americans grew increasingly fond of this idea. They saw Washington's Farewell Address (no entangling alliances)

Library of Congress

"Keep off! The Monroe Doctrine must be respected" (*Judge*, Feb. 15, 1896, pp. 108–9). The Monroe Doctrine put the United States between Europe and the Western Hemisphere.

and the Monroe Doctrine (keep out of the Western Hemisphere) as twin pillars of America's foreign policy. Simply put, the policy was called *isolationism.*

Isolationism was never meant to curb *commercial* involvement, only *political* involvement. As a commercial republic, the United States continued to trade all over the world. And, true, commercial relations did tend to entail political relations, at least to some degree. The United States fostered friendly interaction with its chief trading partners in Europe, Latin America, and the Far East.

Toward the end of the nineteenth century, the United States also began to feel the tug of Euro-style imperialism. It purchased Alaska in 1867 and began to show an interest in certain Pacific islands, such as Hawaii and Samoa. This was not Manifest Destiny. Rather, it expressed the fear all industrialized nations felt that markets for their manufactured goods might be pirated away by imperial rivals. Americans counted on lucrative trade relations with China, for example, but China was being carved into "spheres of influence" by England, Germany, and Russia, not to mention a boldly aggressive Japan. It behooved the United States to stake out its own position in the western Pacific.

Such feelings were given shape and clarity by an influential professor of naval science at the U.S. Naval War College at Newport, Rhode Island, Captain Alfred Thayer Mahan. In his writings, Mahan argued that naval power was the decisive power in human history, and that economic and political power tended to follow on its heels. The United States, said Mahan, was ideally situated to take full advantage, for it fronted both the Atlantic *and* the Pacific, and thus could approach Asia directly. If only America had a powerful navy, Mahan lamented.

As a highly industrialized nation, the U.S. was fully capable of building such a navy. Moreover, technological innovations in naval armament had grown out of the American Civil War. (Remember that famous battle of the ironclads at Hampton Roads.) Americans were in the forefront of developing armor plating, heavy artillery, powerful explosives, rapid-fire gunnery, and submersible vessels.

Mahan had followers in high places, and some of them—Senator Albert Beveridge of Indiana, Senator Henry Cabot Lodge of Massachusetts—were responsible for building a sleek, modern navy in the

THE BIG STICK IN THE CARIBBEAN SEA

The Granger Collection, New York

Theodore Roosevelt and his "big stick."

late 1880s. Another Mahan devotee, Theodore Roosevelt, pushed forward the Panama Canal, which had significant naval value.

Industry, technology, and naval armament proved to be the winning cards in the game of empire. Even though the United States did not see itself as an imperial power, it held those cards by the turn of the century. And it began throwing its weight around accordingly, especially in the Western Hemisphere. When Colombia dragged its feet on the Panama Canal project, Theodore Roosevelt staged a revolution in Panama and struck a deal with the breakaway Panamanian government. "I took Panama," he boasted, "and let the Senate debate." And the U.S. dispatched gunboats to several Caribbean hot spots to protect American investments and make sure that the inhabitants played by the rules. "Speak softly," Roosevelt advised, "and carry a big stick."

Matters came to a head in summer 1898. An insurrection against Spanish rule had been sputtering in Cuba for almost a decade, with American opinion solidly behind the insurrectos. When the battleship *Maine* was blown up in Havana Harbor in February (probably the victim of a stray mine), the United States declared war on Spain and sent an expeditionary force to Cuba. Then, significantly, the U.S. dispatched a naval squadron to the Philippine Islands, a world away from Cuba, and thrashed the Spanish fleet stationed there. The United States had stepped onto the world stage at last.

Mission and Moral Leadership

The Spanish-American War sparked a great debate among Americans about fundamentals. That debate would continue in various guises throughout the twentieth century. In some ways it continues to this very day.

The problem, as many saw it, was that the United States had crossed the line into full-fledged imperialism, no different from that of Britain, France, or any of the world powers. To begin with, the United States more or less kept Cuba, despite a sort of sham independence, then it took charge of other Spanish possessions, such as Guam and Puerto Rico, as well as the Hawaiian Islands, where American missionaries had inspired a revolution against the native monarchy. Most controversially, the U.S. took over the Philippine Islands, then proceeded to construct a huge naval base at Subic Bay.

The presidential election of 1900 became a referendum on these actions, which were opposed by a powerful coalition of "anti-imperialists" led by William Jennings Bryan. We need to consider the arguments they marshaled against taking such a path:

- Manifest Destiny did not apply to the case at hand. There was no mandate for the U.S. to start taking over Caribbean islands or the assets of defunct empires.

- Danger lurked in all these commitments, for the U.S. would be drawn into ever dicier imperial rivalries. How, for example, could the U.S. possibly defend the Philippines, which was on the very doorstep of Japan?

The underlying question ran deeper still, and it grew out of the American Founding. Was it the proper business of a democratic republic to play the international power game? Did such conduct reflect virtue as Americans understood it, or only naked self-interest?

As a people, Americans have never been able to answer these questions conclusively. Self-interest, of course, was accepted as a legitimate basis of the Founding, and much of the American story could be told in no other terms. Equally plainly, self-interest was not all there was—not for Americans.

The anti-Imperialists came to employ another term in describing their conception of the American role. This was the word *Mission*. Like Manifest Destiny, there was something almost mystical about Mission. It held that Americans must be a beacon to the world, teaching by example how free peoples are to behave. Let Europe's benighted monarchies bicker and squabble about imperial possessions— America must be above all that. America must stand for peace, for human brotherhood, for international understanding, for democratic self-determination, for the dignity of man. Such was its appointed Mission.

AMERICAN MISSION: ISOLATIONISM

Isolationists believed that America could best serve as a beacon to the world by avoiding entangling alliances with other nations.

Mission lost out in the referendum of 1900, for the United States retained all its winnings in the Spanish-American War. But Mission by no means lost out in the long run, as we shall see. It is still alive and well in the twenty-first century.

The clearest example of Mission in U.S. foreign policy occurred at the end of World War I. When the war broke out in Europe, the United States attempted to stay clear, as it had during the Napoleonic Wars, asserting the right of neutrals to trade with both sides. Of course neither side allowed trade with the other under any circumstances. The situation was far too desperate for that. Inevitably the

U.S. was drawn into the conflict.

Woodrow Wilson, who was president at the time, vowed that this must be a war "to make the world safe for democracy"—disdaining the shabby war aims of his European allies. At the war's conclusion, victors and vanquished alike had battered one another almost beyond endurance, while the American president with his shining idealism had gained breathtaking prestige. Wilson proclaimed his famous Fourteen Points to guide the postwar settlement, the last of which was to organize a League of Nations. So horrific a conflict, he vowed, must never happen again.

If Wilson had pointed the way for American Mission, he also pointed out its limitations. The opinion of the citizens was sharply divided over the issues of the war, over the harsh settlement that was embodied in the

AMERICAN MISSION: INTERNATIONAL INVOLVEMENT

The moralistic detachment of America's isolationism gave way to moralistic involvement in international affairs *(above)*. The ultimate justification was to establish a League of Nations with characteristics of American structure *(below)*.

Peace of Versailles, and most of all, over the League of Nations. Many Americans feared that any League of Nations would call for active, day-to-day participation on the part of the U.S.—the very antithesis of isolationism. The U.S. would not only be involved with Europe, it would be involved up to its eyebrows, with no chance of withdrawal.

And so, gradually, Mission became watered down into something else, something we might call *moral leadership*. Where Mission presupposed active, dynamic, and ongoing engagement, moral leadership presupposed only the power of a good example. The U.S. would retreat back into isolationism, but it would be an isolationism aimed at lighting the way for mankind.

Accordingly, during the 1920s and 1930s, while the Peace of Versailles frayed apart and Europe saw the rise of Hitler, Stalin, Franco, and Mussolini, the U.S. tried to behave in exemplary ways. It

AMERICAN MISSION: MORAL LEADERSHIP

Moralistic leadership involved less direct moralistic involvement in world affairs. America would be part of the world its influence would be in purely moralistic terms.

made clear its own intention to back away from imperialism, setting a date for Philippine independence and putting Alaska and Hawaii on the road to statehood. The U.S. negotiated arms-reduction agreements with other naval powers, notably Japan, and spoke earnestly against military buildup. The U.S. scolded Hitler and Mussolini for aggressive moves in Europe, and refused to recognize Japan's 1931 annexation of Manchuria. The U.S. pleaded with all powers to refrain from aggression, to let others live in peace, to keep open the doors of world trade. The one thing Americans did not do was cooperate with European democracies to stem the tide of totalitarianism. That, alas, would have spelled involvement.

How futile moral leadership was became dramatically clear on December 7, 1941, when the Japanese attacked the U.S. fleet at Pearl Harbor, bombing it into oblivion.

The Good War

At the time of this writing, the generation of Americans who fought World War II is elderly and disappearing at a rate of more than one thousand veterans a day. While little has been done to honor them formally—the World War II Memorial in Washington, DC, for example, was constructed in 2004—they have been celebrated in any number of popular histories, novels, and movies, of which *Saving Private Ryan* is perhaps the most memorable. Such artifacts powerfully remind us of the Good War.

What made World War II the "good war" furnishes an important key to understanding America's relationship to the world. For it was not until the experience of that war that Americans achieved a satisfying sense of their role on the world stage. World War II reprised many of the themes we have touched upon in this chapter: isolationism, Mission, even a dash of imperialism. We can identify plenty of self-interest in the American desire to secure a world that was sane, orderly, law-abiding, and, most importantly, open to American trade. But we can also identify works of exalted virtue, especially on the part of American men and women at arms.

Despite the rise of the dictators and all their works of evil, American isolationism survived right up to the eve of Pearl Harbor. A bill for military conscription passed by a single vote in 1940—*after* the war in Europe had broken out. Even so, Americans were coming to realize that the world would not work properly without their active involvement. Such measures as Lend-Lease—where the U.S. supplied massive quantities of military hardware to a beleaguered England—indicated that the light was beginning to dawn at last.

In a left-handed way, Japan performed a valuable service in surprising the Pacific Fleet, for in one stroke all doubt and uncertainty disappeared. Americans were in the war at last and consciously in a

A small craft rescues a seaman from ships under attack in Pearl Harbor on December 7, 1941. America's moral leadership proved insufficient to keep it free from international entanglements after Japan bombed Pearl Harbor.

leadership role. Even though the price they would pay on the battlefield in terms of human life was dwarfed by that of the British (to say nothing of the Russians), it seemed clear in all minds that U.S. participation would prove decisive. When he heard of Pearl Harbor, Winston Churchill joyfully threw his hat in the air, knowing the U.S. would enter the conflict.

In the "total war" of which this would be the world's harshest example, America once again held the winning cards. Only incidentally did these consist of skillful generals and admirals. Much more important were:

- A colossal industrial establishment (beyond the reach of enemy bombs) and the capacity to put it to use. The war would be won, in large measure, by sheer output.

- Technological sophistication and the ability to mobilize it. The war would be ended, dramatically, by a "secret weapon" almost beyond human imagination.

- Quiet resolve on the part of millions, both military and civilian, who would fight not for conquest, not for glory, not for imperial hegemony, not even for hatred of the enemy, but for the supremely democratic motive that it was a job that had to be done.

While there were no battles in which U.S. forces covered themselves in glory, there were many battles in which casualties ran very high. At Monte Casino in Italy; at Guadalcanal in the Solomon Islands; at Tarawa, Iwo Jima, and Okinawa along the approaches to Japan; and in the Belgian woods where the Battle of the Bulge was fought, Americans proved they could be tough and tenacious in engagements that seesawed back and forth for months. And in the D-day landings at Normandy, they proved their valor beyond question.

In some ways, however, the real war was the one described by Bill Mauldin's cartoon characters, Willie and Joe, who had no taste for glory and few illusions about life. Willie and Joe spent their days slogging through the mud, sleeping in the rain, trying to find comfort in a foxhole. When in one cartoon a medic offers Joe a medal, he replies: "Just gimme a couple o' aspirin. I already got a purple heart."

Equally important to the war's outcome were developments on the home front. Since industrial production became the war's crucial factor, victory was to become a matter of mobilizing the country's vast manufacturing establishment. Henry Ford converted his automobile plant at Willow Run, Michigan, to the production of B-24 Liberators, proving that heavy bombers could be turned out on an assembly line much like Model Ts. In Richmond, California, Henry J. Kaiser, an engineer-turned-shipbuilder, put together a monstrous operation for the rapid construction

The Granger Collection, New York

Technological developments, such as the rapid construction of liberty ships, helped win the war on the home front.

of armed freighters called "liberty ships." The first of these vessels required 196 days to build. The last took 4 days, 9 hours, 36 minutes.

The production miracles were made possible by high wages, grueling hours, and a labor force augmented by blacks, Hispanics, Filipinos, and Rosie the Riveters. They were also made possible by steely determination. Home-front heroism, less conspicuous than the battlefield variety, was no less relevant to the war's outcome.

As with production, so too with technology. Americans began the war with weapons from the turn of the century; they ended it with jet aircraft, radar-sighted gunnery, and an atomic bomb. The building of the bomb was a story unto itself. To make uranium fissionable, it was necessary to separate U-235, which was radioactive, from U-238, which was not. Since the two isotopes were chemically indistinguishable, the job required the combined efforts of a thousand scientists, engineers, and production specialists—all working in utmost secrecy.

At war's end, the Axis powers were simply overwhelmed. Hitler supposed that his "Fortress Europe," manned by abundant slave labor, could outsupply the Allied forces. He had no conception of the skies over Berlin, black with U.S. bombers that advanced in endless waves. His U-boats were sinking 600,000 tons of Allied ships a month in the Battle of the Atlantic, and yet American production made good the losses and *still* kept the British and Russians well supplied.

For these and other reasons, World War II became "the good war" in American memory. Its character tended to resolve many of the dilemmas Americans had faced in the past:

- With enemies as dastardly as these, Americans had no qualms about "entangling alliances" or engagement in European turmoil.

- By assuming a leadership role, Americans no longer had to worry about a cynical peace settlement. President Roosevelt specified early on that there would be no peace short of total surrender, together with a complete reconstruction of defeated enemies.

- Not only did Americans renounce their own flight into imperialism—the Philippines would be set free at the war's end—they could require similar renunciations from their allies. Franklin Roosevelt made Winston Churchill promise to pull out of India in the aftermath.

In sum, there was little or no disconnect between virtue and interest in World War II. Americans could fight for a better world for themselves while at the same time seeking a better world for everyone. The U.S. immeasurably strengthened its own defenses while simultaneously freeing captive peoples, destroying oppression, and empowering democratic principles. Americans helped defeated enemies back onto their feet and rebuilt their political and economic systems from scratch—and in the process acquired three valuable trading partners (Japan, Germany, and Russia) in the postwar world.

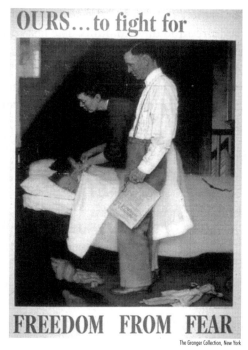

OURS... to fight for

FREEDOM FROM FEAR

The Granger Collection, New York

Freedom from Fear. One of President Roosevelt's Four Freedoms, illustrated by Norman Rockwell.

Just as Woodrow Wilson had spelled out his Fourteen Points at the end of World War I, Franklin Roosevelt enunciated his Four Freedoms in a speech that imparted a higher meaning to the latter conflict. All of mankind, he said, ought to be free to speak out, free to worship as they choose, free from want, and free from fear. As a crusade to secure such freedoms, World War II made sense.

The Bad War

What came to be called the Cold War began virtually the moment the Axis surrendered, and it stretched through the latter half of the century. In essence, it took the form of an armed stalemate between the United States and the Soviet Union, with all others impelled to take one side or the other. It was portrayed as a war of freedom versus tyranny, of democracy versus totalitarianism, of capitalism versus communism. It was complex and many-sided, and it kept changing like a chameleon as power relations shifted, or as one side or the other developed some new weapon, or as chance events favored the East or the West. This type of dynamic created a bad war in the minds of many Americans.

Where World War II had brought things together for Americans, the Cold War seemed to pull them apart:

- Now there were "entangling alliances" all over the place, and the dullest American could see that they truly *were* entangling. The smallest spark in some remote corner of the earth might set off a general conflagration.

- American leadership of the free world was no longer in question—instead it was leadership, but at what cost! Some so-called allies were actually dictatorships themselves, angling for their own advantage. Others were simply playing one side against the other. And still others (France, for instance) made no bones about despising the American role.

- Technological advantage became ephemeral, then meaningless, for in a world of nuclear warheads and global-range missiles, who cared whether one side could destroy the other a greater number of times.

- America's professed ideals came to seem shabby in the Cold War environment, with sit-ins, boycotts, and violent protests. Placards screamed that "Amerika" (as Hitler would have spelled it) wasn't worth dying for.

- Imperialism reared its head once again, this time as "*Yanqui Imperialismo.*" The Americans, it was charged, had figured out how to gain all the benefits of imperialism without incurring any costs, simply by cowing others into trading on lopsided terms.

The Cold War provided a setting for several hot wars, and the U.S. was in the thick of every one. The first was Korea, a long, debilitating conflict that achieved little beyond a grudging stalemate. The second was Vietnam, much longer and even more debilitating, ending in abject defeat. Beyond these clashes there were air strikes, punitive actions, and brushfire miniwars from Africa to the Philippines. There were revolts to suppress, regimes to prop up, bullies to thwart, and flames to quench all over the world. There was the danger of

China invading Taiwan—and of Taiwan provoking China. There was the Berlin quagmire, a constant worry, one episode of which required a seven-month airlift to supply the beleaguered city. There was Cuba and its self-styled red caudillo, inciting a showdown that verged upon nuclear war. There was a revolution in Chile, a palace coup in Brazil, a Maoist uprising in Peru, a ghastly "secret war" in Argentina, and insurgencies throughout the length and breadth of Central America. And in the midst of everything, there arose in Cambodia a tyranny that was, if possible, more horrifying than Hitler's.

But for most Americans the Cold War came to center upon Vietnam. It would have been a hard war to win in the best of circumstances, but in the context of an East-West standoff it was impossible. The United States, battling a communist insurgency, fired more bullets and dropped more bombs than in all of World War II, and in the end had to pack up and leave. For in a world where one false move might have triggered a nuclear holocaust, the best the U.S. could hope for was a Korea-style agreement to stop fighting. And such an agreement didn't materialize.

The Granger Collection, New York

The Vietnam War caused Americans to take a closer look at their motives and position as a world leader.

In the soul-searching that followed Vietnam, Americans reopened all the old questions. Were their own motives truly pure? Was leadership of the free world desirable, or even possible? Did the U.S. really have an obligation to police the planet? Didn't a sort of neo-isolationism make better sense? Americans had entered Vietnam in that spirit of hopefulness which had seen them through World War II—and they retreated from it in futility and cynicism. From that moment on, they lived in a world beyond their control.

The Troubled Peace

The Cold War was followed by a hot peace. True, the Soviet Union quietly bowed off the world stage and the West was proclaimed the winner. Yet the same sort of chaos remained. Where once the threat had been international communism, now it was Islamic fundamentalism. Or it was ethnicity on the rampage. Or it was the Arab-Israeli conflict, with unfathomable beginnings and scant hope of an end. Or, worst of all, it was simple rule by terror—the notion that any group, *every* group, had means at hand to get whatever it wanted merely by blowing up something.

War clouds gathered in the Middle East. The trouble was Lebanon. Then it was Syria. Then it was Libya. Then Syria again. Then Iran, where a revolution toppled the Shah and installed a fundamentalist regime. And finally it was Iraq. Each installment was linked in some way to Israel, which the United States had pledged to support at all costs, and which Muslims had pledged to oppose. It flared into one conflict after another—1948, 1967, 1973—and then into a guerrilla war that sputtered and popped like a burning fuse. There were any number of peace talks, overtures, and tentative settlements—punctuated by raids, atrocities, car bombs, hijackings, and the murder of eleven Israeli athletes at the 1972 Olympics. There was evidently no solution.

To make a bad situation worse, it was in the Middle East that much of the world's oil supply was located. So whatever course the U.S. pursued, it was accused of acting in its own greedy interests.

In 1990, Iraqi President Saddam Hussein calculated that the Middle East situation might favor a bold move on his part, so he decided to invade neighboring Kuwait. Iraq's presence in the oil-rich area, together with the threat it posed to Saudi Arabia, prompted the U.S. to take drastic action. The Gulf War was the result.

The war was unpopular with many other countries, especially those in the Arab world, where it could not be divorced from U.S. support of Israel. Islamic fundamentalists had no difficulty portraying America as "the Great Satan," and they had more in mind than foreign policy. The Great Satan was seen to be a force for modernization, for liberal democracy, for scientific and technological progress, for the equality of races and genders—for a view of the world that was incompatible with Islam.

The stage was now set for a different sort of war carried out in a different sort of way. It burst forth on September 11, 2001, when Islamic terrorists, organized, trained, and financed by a renegade Saudi oil sheik, hijacked four American airliners and used them as ballistic missiles. Two of the aircraft demolished the World Trade Center in Manhattan, with catastrophic loss of life, while a third slammed into the Pentagon in Washington, DC. It was every bit as infamous as Pearl Harbor.

But for many it was far less easy to sort out. Like all else in the Troubled Peace, the meaning of the assault was unclear, and Americans divided over an appropriate response. Some supported all-out war against "bandit nations," whether or not they had been involved in the 9/11 attacks. Others favored a go-slow approach, aimed at specific terrorists. And in some other countries, U.S. actions were seen as another bout of imperialism—or another Vietnam.

At the dawn of the twenty-first century, then, Americans had good reason to be wary of the world in which they lived. It was a world of terrifying vulnerabilities—unarmed aircraft, unguarded football stadiums, unprotected food and water supplies. Few of the U.S.'s historic allies supported them in their wars of preemption, though forty-eight countries stood with them. There was no doctrine, no idea, no catchphrase on which the U.S. could fall back on. Isolationism wouldn't work. Mission and Manifest Destiny seemed irrelevant. And moral leadership—indeed, any kind of leadership—appeared to be stuck in a political quagmire. All that was left was national self-interest—a very cold comfort.

Troubled peace indeed.

The America Question

All of this travail notwithstanding, Americans had earned the right to take some bows on the world stage. After all, whenever they had committed their lives and treasure on the battlefield, it had almost always been in the name of some higher good, call it justice, democracy, or human rights. And Americans had been uniformly magnanimous to defeated foes, helping them to build thriving economies and responsible democratic governments. The U.S. had not ignored national self-interest, to be sure, but it had not allowed it to be its only guide. Few other nation-states could make such a claim.

During the era of its spread-eagle foreign policy, the U.S. conquered the world in a different way as well, one that an observer termed "Coca-Colanization." American music, American movies, along with American products and values and lifestyles became all the rage in many parts of the globe, even among those who remained politically hostile. The fact that immigrants continued to pour in from everywhere remained a powerful commentary.

The deeper question was whether Americans had anything to say to the rest of mankind. By the terms of their Founding,

AMERICAN MISSION:
LEADER OF THE FREE WORLD

The leader of the free world role embodied both America's sense of mission and national self-interest. The productivity of the market system helped establish and maintain this leadership role.

they clearly did have a message for the world, an announcement of republicanism, democracy, constitutional government, human rights, self-determination, individual opportunity, and free-market economics. But was anyone really listening? For all that American *power* counted in global calculations, how about the American *example*? Was the world any different, fundamentally, from what it might otherwise be without the U.S.? There can be no final answer to this question—the America Question. Yet it provides a handy way of thinking about the ultimate meaning of the American experiment. If mankind really did turn a corner with the advent of America, perhaps the ambiguity and uncertainty of the twentieth century will not have been in vain.

Chapter 14

Confronting the Postmodern World

We have seen that the American Founding was rooted in concepts and values that had a long ancestry. Some went back to the classical world. Some were drawn from Christianity. Some had arisen in the European Enlightenment, which was much more recent but still over a century old. And some were distilled from the wisdom of the ages.

In the surge of rapid change that followed the American Civil War, many new ideas and values appeared in the Western World. Americans encountered these in books and newspapers; or they discovered them in college classrooms; or they found them in stage plays, vaudeville productions, radio programs, magazine stories, movies, television, videos; or they met them in their world travels.

Because Americans valued Progress, they generally received new ways of thinking the way they received new gadgets—as a blessing. There was much in the popular idiom about keeping up with the times, being in style, knowing the score. No one wished to be out of date or out of step. In his study of American culture, Alexis de Tocqueville noted a preoccupation with the opinions of others. Democratic Americans, he concluded, had only one another to look to for opinions—not those aristocrats who dominated opinion in Europe—and so they carefully observed what today we would call the polls.

Something else was happening too. As American society gradually became more consumption-minded in the twentieth century, there was a shift in emphasis from adulthood to youth in determining what was socially desirable. Where eighteen-year-olds once sought to pass for thirty, now thirty-year-olds (and forty- and fifty-year-olds) affected the manner of teenagers. It was yet another way of breaking from traditions.

Small wonder that the world of the American Founding began to seem quaint. Look at its clothing styles. Look at its stilted manners and formal speech. Look at Peale's portrait of George Washington on the face of the dollar bill—nothing hip there—or curl up with *The Federalist Papers* and try to keep awake. It was an out-of-date world indeed.

The Granger Collection, New York

George Washington by Rembrandt Peale, 1795.

So it was that Americans began to encounter modernity, and its more extreme form, "postmodernity." It came to Americans as a perception that the past was dead and gone, and therefore unimportant. So, why cling to it? Why not change with the times, and look to the new, the latest, the smartest, the coolest?

It was not a universal sentiment and not all Americans felt it. Yet enough of them did, in one way or another, to make it an important factor in American life. There was a marked tendency in the United States to loosen the ties of the past and seek guidance elsewhere. As Founding aged into Heritage, there was always the possibility that the Founding would become irrelevant and its Heritage as fleeting as the wind.

The Troubled Career of Virtue

We have come to appreciate how much the American Founding rested on what the ancient Greeks called virtue. Virtue was a troublesome concept, as we have seen, and some of the Founders mistrusted it themselves. Would people truly do the right thing simply out of a sense of honor, a respect for justice, or a belief in God? Yet the obverse was equally troubling. Would people do the right thing in a world devoid of honor, justice, or a belief in God? Could human selfishness and egoism be kept in bounds *solely* by the cop on the corner?

Civic virtue came to perform prodigious works in the course of American history. To consider only a couple of these, we might begin with the American Civil War. That conflict, as we have seen, was not simply the result of misunderstandings between North and South—it was caused by differences of opinion over human slavery and by the gathering perception that slavery was not just wrong but evil. Granted, most Northerners were not committed abolitionists. The fact remains that virtually all those who died—wearing gray as well as blue—died in the name of virtue, be it defense of the Constitution, the furtherance of republican values, or the safeguarding of one's own community. And many truly did die to end slavery. The war mushroomed into Armageddon precisely because Americans prized moral conduct.

Library of Congress

Adolf Hitler. In World War II, Americans fought for justice for Europeans tyrannized by Hitler.

The same can be said for U.S. participation in foreign wars. In a few of these, perhaps the Mexican War or the Indian wars, it is true that Americans fought to gain territory or some other booty, but in the conflicts of the twentieth and twenty-first centuries, right down to the war in Iraq, American servicemen and women have essentially fought for justice. In World War I it was the rights of neutrals and the pledges of treaties—the German Kaiser ignored both—that touched off U.S. outrage. In World War II the problem was Hitler, of whom no more need be said, and Japanese rulers for whom the attack on Pearl Harbor was only business as usual. In Korea and Vietnam, Americans fought to stem the tide of communism, which had shown itself to be pitiless with human rights. And in Afghanistan and the Gulf Wars, Americans fought, in large measure, to succor those who suffered under bloodthirsty dictators.

Civic virtue manifested itself in less dramatic ways as well. Honesty and probity characterized most areas of American life, including politics, even though corruptionists and boodlers continually made headlines. The overwhelming majority of Americans observed the law, respected authority, and led decent, constructive lives.

Participation in the political process remained high throughout most of U.S. history. Many Americans contributed time and energy to the party of their choice and usually for the right reasons. They abided the will of the majority, even in the most controversial of elections, such as the presidential balloting of 2000, which was decided by a statistically even vote in a single state.

America was swept from time to time by waves of reform, which also reflected the impulse of virtue. In Andrew Jackson's day, reformers sought to democratize the political process, as we have seen. They also sought to build better schools, humanize the penal system, take better care of the sick and the elderly, and eradicate the scourge of slavery. Progressive reformers had their own agenda of improvements: cleaner cities, sturdier families, a more honest and responsive political system, and much else. Their war against private power, as discussed in chapter 11, was itself a product of civic virtue.

Virtue was idealized in American books and movies. Many of these were tales of military heroism, but there were stories too of the forthright young sheriff of a western town who, upon learning of the cowardice of the townspeople, faces the bad guys all alone (*High Noon*), of the businessman who agrees to pose as a traitor to spy on Nazi Germany (*The Counterfeit Traitor*), of the young housewife who opts out of her suburban world to support civil rights in the South (*The Long Walk Home*). The films of Frank Capra—*Mr. Smith Goes to Washington, Mr. Deeds Goes to Town, It's a Wonderful Life*—were all parables of American virtue.

All of this said, virtue appeared to weaken substantially as an American ideal in the twentieth century. Audiences grew tired of all that

A policeman standing beside cases of moonshine, 1922. Millions of Americans "winked" at the Constitution as they violated the Eighteenth Amendment.

righteousness and soon branded virtuous ingénues like Lillian Gish "Little Goody Two-Shoes." Give them a Theda Bara or a Mae West, they said—someone they could relate to. After all, the 1920s had introduced Prohibition (the attempt to ban the sale of alcoholic liquors via the Eighteenth Amendment), and Prohibition had introduced the hip flask, bathtub gin, and "speakeasies"—bars that could be entered only by password.

This experience harmed the rule of law in the U.S. For when millions of Americans simply winked at the Eighteenth Amendment, they were winking at the entire Constitution. It was no accident that gangsters like Al Capone built empires from bootlegging and that eventually they took to battling one another in the streets. Americans had forfeited their right to public order.

In the 1960s there was a repeat performance involving the drug laws. Marijuana, hashish, peyote, and a growing list of uppers and downers supplemented the use of LSD, which in that decade became pandemic among the young. Those who violated the drug laws often felt compelled to stand against the rest of society and to dignify their lawlessness with terms such as "hip" and "cool." Once that line was crossed, they found it easier to evade draft laws, traffic laws, tax laws, and a host of other ordinances. What they learned, first and foremost, was contempt for "the system" and all its rules.

Crime became an American scourge in the 1920s and 1930s—and the gangster a sort of dark hero. Later on, in the 1960s, crime rates recommenced a jagged rise that would continue through the century. So-called white-collar crime made a hefty contribution to the statistics, and crimes of violence became absolutely appalling. Homicide rates in American cities rose from double digits at the beginning of the century to *quadruple* digits by its end. Americans learned to double-lock their doors, install burglar alarms, and withdraw into gated communities. Ever greater numbers of them purchased firearms.

While it was impossible to assign simple cause and effect to these alarming trends, observers noted the decline of virtuous paradigms in the media and the rise of their opposites. Crime was often glorified in movies, for example, after the Production Code worked out by Hollywood in the 1930s to keep film content morally elevated fell by the wayside in 1968. Violence followed a similar path.

The taste for mayhem in American culture goes back as far as old-time melodrama. Traditionally, as Richard Slotkin has noted, Americans found a kind of purification in stories of good guys blowing away bad guys and heroes avenging mortal wrongs. Beginning in the 1960s, however, violence in the media began to cast off its moralizing and shaded into violence for its own sake. In a film titled *Natural Born Killers*, for example, the serial carnage grew mindless and numbing, utterly devoid of moral content, while in dark comedies like *Pulp Fiction* and *Get Shorty* it seemed to have no meaning at all.

Contempt for the law came to pervade the lyrics of rap music— along with a broader contempt for civilized values. Songs of love degenerated into songs of lust, and these into songs of rape, torture, and murder. The point seemed to be assaulting standards of any kind—simply because they existed.

For the ancient Greeks, virtue was the path leading mankind out of barbarism. For some postmodern Americans, there was an apparent wish to turn around and go back.

Radicalizing the Founding

Americans of Jefferson's time often missed the radical implications of the Founding. This is because the Founders themselves honored the ancient virtues of wisdom and moderation. A Washington, an Adams, even a Jefferson himself (who was often accused of radicalism) would never read the words "all men are created equal" to argue for a compulsory equality of condition, or the words "life, liberty, and the pursuit of happiness" to mean that Americans could do as they pleased.

Once these words were canonized, however, there was a tendency to give them an ever wider scope of meaning, as is often the case with "scripture." Radical egalitarianism and radical individualism have haunted the American experience ever since.

Radical Egalitarianism

The Founders' understanding of equality may be summarized as equality of opportunity, the notion that persons of whatever birth or background deserve a roughly equal chance in the world. In a free society, equality of opportunity does not and cannot lead to equality of result, for the God-given talents and capacities of individuals vary enormously, as do the circumstances that life affords.

When we radicalize egalitarianism, however, we come up with entirely different notions. There is a tendency to limit freedom to achieve—and enforce—equality of result. In the race of life, as it were, we seek not only to insure that all runners get off to a fair start but that fast runners must be slowed down somehow, while slow runners must be artificially speeded up.

In the twentieth century, the quest for both kinds of equality would result in massive market intervention. To begin with, such things as free public education, antidiscrimination laws, and welfare programs like Head Start or school lunch would be aimed at securing equality of opportunity, that fair start off the blocks. The idea was to make everyone—black or white, rich or poor—as competitive as possible.

Yet the result of these traditional methods has often been disappointing. Public education, for example, could never break free from the handicap of the impoverished neighborhood, where the children

EQUALITY OF OPPORTUNITY

Each participant in the economy should have an equal chance of economic success or failure. All should start the race at the same place and run under the same conditions with outcomes depending on individual performance.

EQUALITY OF RESULTS

Each participant in the economy should receive the same economic rewards regardless of performance.

of hopelessness assure one another that school is unimportant. A similar fate befell antidiscrimination laws. It did no good to prohibit discrimination in hiring if there were no qualified minority applicants.

Increasingly, the inability of such measures to make a difference would lead to frustration, and this in turn would lead to more and more aggressive approaches. If equality of opportunity did not solve the problem, reasoned some Americans, then we should turn instead to equality of result. Public housing, public transportation, public health care, Social Security benefits, food stamps, and most forms of direct welfare assistance were thus aimed at redistributing income—making the poor a little richer and the rich a little poorer.

Accompanying social and economic egalitarianism, Americans developed a sense of what might be called intellectual egalitarianism. In a land encompassing a great diversity of cultures, lifestyles, religious beliefs, and value systems, intellectual egalitarians imparted a rough-and-ready equality to all of them—refusing to state preferences. The only value to be imposed in such a world was that of "openness," meaning that one must be open to new ideas, new lifestyles, new definitions of good and evil. To make choices was to "discriminate."

Where the Founders had embraced a strong belief in universal moral truth, the new egalitarians preferred moral relativism. Things were not absolutely good or bad in a relativistic world; they were good for one group or bad for another, depending on time, place, and circumstances. (Abortion, one argued, wasn't bad for the unwilling mother, only for the hapless fetus.) This, of course, made it easier to accommodate changes in American life that might otherwise be upsetting. Rappers who sang of killing cops or raping baby-sitters were, after all, merely expressing their own set of values.

Radical Individualism

As with radical egalitarianism, radical individualism was rooted in founding texts. That all people had a right to life, liberty, and the pursuit of happiness suggested that individuals ought to be free to live their lives as each saw fit. In the Founders' world, it was assumed that everyone would aspire to live more or less as everyone else did, the life of the yeoman farmer or the middle-class townsperson. A century of immigration and cultural ferment altered such expectations. The rise of cities and city ways gave Americans far more choices of lifestyle, and these continued to multiply. Immigrant groups had brought cultural baggage from the old country, and their concentrations were so great in some places that subcultures began to sprout like mushrooms.

Some ethnic groups had a rough time of it and were subjected to discrimination. Yet the logic of the situation eventually prevailed. In a land of so many groups, it made no sense for any single one of them to determine the norms. The result was a general, if sometimes grudging, acceptance of cultural differences. This lack of a single normative culture is called *pluralism*.

Pluralism celebrated self-expression. The Irish were invited to express their Irishness, the Italians their Italianness, and so on. Americans soon learned to make the most of ethnicity, expanding their tastes to include French wines, German beer, Italian pizza, Mexican burritos, Japanese sushi, and Chinese Moo Goo Gai Pan. They celebrated St. Paddy's, Columbus Day, Cinco de Mayo, Martin Luther King Day, Hanukkah, even the Chinese New Year, as though each holiday were their very own.

In time, ethnic groups were supplemented by other kinds of variety. On city streets thronged bankers in pin-striped suits, sailors on shore leave, farmers from the countryside, tradesmen with their lunch pails, shopkeepers, streetwalkers, hustlers, Jehovah's Witnesses, Hari Krishnas, bikers, skaters, Goths, pimps, drug dealers, panhandlers, cardsharps, Sikh Dharmas in their white turbans, and black-habited Sisters of Mercy—a kaleidoscope of color and diversity. The troubling question for some Americans was whether, and to what extent, this expanding array of self-expression was good. For some of it decidedly cut against American norms, however broadly conceived.

PLURALISM

MELTING POT

American Pluralism manifested itself in two ways. Originally, America was viewed as a Melting Pot of immigrants of various nationalities and races, melted down into a generic essence of American individuals (*above*).

Gradually, America became more like a Salad Bowl. Various group gained increasing pride in their original ethnic distinctions and attempted to keep these alive. The only thing that unified the American "salad" was an acceptance of the American Creed (*below*).

SALAD BOWL

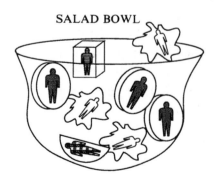

Counterculture

With its openness and toleration, America proved hospitable to a style of self-expression that in the 1960s would be called the *counterculture*. As its name implied, the counterculture ran counter to the manners and mores of the mainstream.

The first installment of the counterculture was imported from Paris in the mid-nineteenth century, calling itself "bohemianism." Bohemians consciously modeled their style as an antithesis of the middle class. Where the middle classes embraced materialistic values, financial success, genteel art, prudish manners, and moral respectability, bohemians celebrated poverty, failure, *avant garde* art, indecent manners, and moral licentiousness.

Bohemians succeeded in convincing some Americans, mostly the young, that running against the grain was a worthy pursuit. At Pfaff's Tavern in New York or Sanguinetti's Restaurant in San Francisco, bourgeois diners crowded in to watch the antics of the bohemians, which included loud recitations of poetry and graffiti-style drawings on the walls. Oddly enough, an exclusive organization of West Coast socialites dubbed itself the Bohemian Club. Going bohemian was becoming hip.

The question is why? The German philosopher Georg Wilheim Friedrich Hegel believed that any dominant system of ideas or values would tend to create its own opposite as a matter of course. Perhaps that explains it. Whatever the cause, American civilization was generating its own kind of discontentment, and nothing illustrated it better than the emerging counterculture.

After World War II, bohemianism broke out anew and continued in waves through the end of the twentieth century. The place of George Sterling and the old Sanguinetti's crowd was taken by Allen Ginsberg and Jack Kerouac in the 1950s, calling themselves the Beat Generation. And then by Timothy Leary and Ken Kesey in the 1960s, calling themselves hippies. And so on. Each new wave created a surge of enthusiasm among the young, who dressed outrageously, groomed experimentally, and adopted manners that were calculated to offend. They hung around the streets, threw frisbees in the park, took drugs, were promiscuous, attended rock concerts. Some groups affected tattoos, others body piercing, still others the shaved head or spiked hair or death-mask makeup. A growing number opted for homosexuality. The message was the same over and over: down with bourgeois normalcy.

Hollywood joined the crusade. Beginning in the 1950s, the movie industry created one tormented, angst-filled hero after another—Marlon Brando, James Dean, Dustin Hoffman—fighting lonely battles

The Granger Collection, New York

James Dean in *Rebel Without a Cause* epitomized a generation's rebellion against middle-class normalcy.

against a cold and uncaring establishment. Dean's role in *Rebel Without a Cause* was typical. The slouching, scowling young protagonist had had it with his shrewish mother, his feckless father and their whole empty, sterile, phony way of life. He just wanted to be "real."

With openers such as these, detractors went on to "deconstruct" the establishment in every way possible—chiefly in college classrooms. American life was shown to be shallow, shabby, hypocritical, and pretentious. It was blasted for false values, hollow sentiment, showy behavior, and drooling avarice. In one memorable example, a movie titled *The Graduate* (which won the Academy Award in 1967 for best picture), the establishment was personified in the character of Mrs. Robinson, a monster who would stop at nothing to indulge her corrupt pleasures.

The lesson was clear. Among a swelling chorus of critics, America had catastrophically failed.

The Power to Persuade

The Founders might wonder why anyone would pay attention to such critics in the face of America's remarkable achievements—of which the critics themselves were an evidence. We should understand the Founders' thinking on this point.

In the election campaign of 1800, Federalists and Democratic-Republicans alike had resorted to every means available to blacken their opponents. Thomas Jefferson's victory in the face of the Federalists' propaganda blitz convinced him of a proposition that would become one of the cornerstones of the Founding. In the free-for-all of political debate, Jefferson submitted, the truth would eventually win out. The people themselves would sort through all the lies and distortions and half-truths, and would sooner or later figure out what was what.

Armed with this belief, Americans became stonily serious about the conduct of political discussion. In the days of Andrew Jackson, for example, newspapers were filled with long and turgid essays on political topics that would put most of today's readers to sleep. In a similar vein, the famous Lincoln-Douglas debates stretched on for as long as *eight hours* at a time, with a lunch break in the middle. It was the duty of the people, Americans believed, to study the issues carefully and know them inside out.

Technological change altered this situation dramatically. As newspaper presses became able to print photographs, the character of many papers transformed. No more turgid political essays, vowed *New York World* publisher Joseph Pulitzer. His paper would ply the reader with bold headlines, shocking stories, lurid details, and above all, pictures. The style would soon be called "yellow journalism."

Pulitzer's competitor, William Randolph Hearst, demonstrated the power of yellow journalism 1898. There was a revolution in Cuba at the time, roiling along against the island's colonial government, and Hearst's *New York Journal* became so engrossed in its atrocities that a kind of hysteria began to grip the country. *Journal* readers eagerly awaited the next installment of Spanish brutality, Spanish ruthlessness, Spanish horror. When the U.S. battleship *Maine* was mysteriously blown up in Havana Harbor in February, readers knew immediately who

THE HIGH PRIESTS OF THE SACRED FLAME.

The Granger Collection, New York

A 1909 cartoon depicting the high priests of yellow journalism, William Randolph Hearst and Joseph Pulitzer.

had to be responsible. Hearst had painted the Spanish in such garish colors that few could doubt their culpability—no matter how little sense it made. The result, alas, was war.

Radio came into use during the 1920s, and public communication turned yet another corner. Franklin Roosevelt employed broadcasting for his famous "fireside chats," reassuring fellow Americans that the Great Depression could be beaten. But radio proved ideal for demagoguery too. Father Charles E. Coughlin, who came to be known as "the radio priest," proved he could stir up hatred and bigotry on the airwaves as effectively as Adolf Hitler. Within a few short months, he had built a following of alarming size.

Films were good vehicles of persuasion too. Audiences did not recognize them as such—which made them even better. Messages embedded in the background and characters of a movie slipped under the radar of most Americans and were received uncritically. Who would dream that John Ford's *Grapes of Wrath* was casting ballots for Roosevelt's New Deal, or that the famous western *High Noon* was a parable about the Hollywood blacklist.

That a blacklist even existed in Hollywood pointed up the problem. In the early 1950s, many Americans grew anxious about the alleged fact that Hollywood was "full of communists." The investigation that followed was not a pleasant one, nor did it honor American traditions of free speech and due process. In response to enormous pressure, film studios blacklisted—which is to say fired without recourse—scores of real and imaginary members of the Communist Party, believing that their role as producers, directors, and especially screenwriters gave them a dangerous political influence. Movies were under the radar no longer.

Movies were eventually supplemented by television, which was soon piped into every American home. In the new medium's infancy, producers were concerned about the accessibility of TV programs to viewers of all ages, and for that reason the industry adopted a voluntary code of production "don'ts" (for example, don't show blood and gore, don't show nudity). But Americans were tiring of don'ts, as we have seen, and public opinion began undermining the production code. Family shows—*Ozzie and Harriet, Leave It to Beaver*—slowly gave way to sex and violence.

And to various political agendas. During the Civil Rights Revolution, it was noted that unfavorable stereotypes of Hispanics or

African Americans were measurably affecting public prejudice. If the U.S. was going to make racial progress, such stereotypes would have to go. Images of servile blacks, for example, must be replaced with images of two-fisted, charismatic blacks, as in the films of Sidney Poitier. Soon every group, not just African Americans, was clamoring for a spruced up media image.

Images were largely created with smoke and mirrors. Where the American Founders had been concerned with the substance of things, image-engineering took appearance to be everything. Makeup, lighting, camera angles, press releases, and media gossip became the stuff of "reality" for many Americans, and public relations became a growth industry. An actor could become a star overnight if he or she were fitted with the right image.

It worked the same way for politicians. When Senator John F. Kennedy debated Vice President Richard Nixon on television in the 1960 election campaign, image became the decisive factor. Americans who listened to the debates on radio generally declared Nixon the winner, for the logic of his arguments seemed stronger. Those who saw the debates on television, however, came away with a different view. As one respondent put it, "Senator Kennedy reminded me of that handsome young sheriff on *Gunsmoke*."

What followed was image-engineering elevated to high art. Election campaigns were taken over by consultants trained in public relations, coaching the candidates in how to stand, how to speak, how to address the camera, how to affect the right gestures. Political arguments were reduced to "sound bites," positions to catchy slogans, values to whimsical one-liners. It was no accident that film star Ronald Reagan swept Jimmy Carter aside in the 1980 election, that Bill Clinton's

Film star Ronald Reagan (1981) beat Jimmy Carter in 1980 due, in part, to his media image.

performance in the 1992 primaries inspired a hit movie, or that he-man Arnold Schwarzenegger overwhelmed the lackluster Gray Davis for governor of California. Nor was it any accident that *West Wing* turned into a fabulously successful television series.

The mass media became a battleground of the "culture wars" that broke out at the end of the twentieth century. On one side of the conflict were those in favor of escalating freedom of expression, and on the other side were those who preferred traditional standards of restraint. Less obvious but equally important was the use of the media to glamorize indecency, obscenity, homosexuality, and the loosening of marital ties. Lifestyles of the stars became as important to the media audience as plot or characters. When the stars adopted body piercing or tattoos, millions of fans followed suit.

By the end of the millennium, it was doubtful that Jefferson had been right about truth always winning out. The very concept of truth was losing ground in political debate, and its place was being taken by "glittering things." The indulgences and excesses of democracy that had spelled the downfall of ancient Athens seemed all too plainly in evidence, their effects magnified many fold by the mass media.

Founding Heritage

The American Founding had begun as a more or less conscious project of modernization, for the Founders were convinced that what they struggled against were shackles from the dead past. Get rid of kings and aristocracies and state churches, they believed, and mankind would finally come into its own.

But modernization has no recognizable end point, so how do we know when the job is finally done? For the American Founders, this question would probably be answered by referring to the ancient idea of the Good. That is, a modern republic discards the baggage of the past up to a certain point only when injustice is replaced by real justice, or when prejudice becomes human understanding. The heritage of the American Founding was thus, by implication, a search for the "right" way to live, not simply a search for some newer and different way to live.

Beyond the name-calling of the culture wars, there were signs at the end of the twentieth century that civilization itself was becoming threatened in the West—and that did not exclude America. The endangering of the traditional family, the weakening of community, the alarming increase in crimes of mindlessness—such as the massacre at Columbine High School in Littleton, Colorado—the demonizing of those with whom one disagreed, the resurgence of gangs, the ethos of violence, the waning of compassion, the degradation of values were all straws in a wind turning ominous.

As individuals, Americans could find solace where they may. Specifically as Americans, however, they were prompted to search for it in their own national identity. What were their professed ideals, they asked themselves once again, and how did these apply? Or, put another way, what *was* their founding heritage?

Alas, there were no easy answers.

Chapter 15

The Search for Justice

We have seen that change brought many sources of anxiety and uncertainty to Americans. Their response to such fears was rarely passive. An important outgrowth of the Founding was the assumption that Americans were in charge of their own lives. (How else could the Founding itself be explained?) In politics, this assumption translated into surges of activism, often in state or local venues, sometimes in the national.

And so it was that Americans became committed to reform. In previous chapters we have touched on the work of Jacksonian reformers, Populist reformers, Progressive reformers, and New Deal reformers. Broadly speaking, all of these were in search of justice—meaning that they were measuring the realities of American life against the ideals of the Founding, and the realities were coming up short. The Just Society, like its first cousin the Good Society, seems to have sprouted among other founding principles.

Glancing briefly at a couple of these reform movements, we can gain some idea of the American sense of justice. Jacksonian reformers sought to broaden democracy, to remove bastions of special privilege such as the Bank of the United States, to increase opportunity for the common man. They began agitating for women to have a voice in the conduct of their lives—and for slaves to be set free. If the Athenian sense of justice was to play the game by the rules, the American sense of justice was to open the game to all players.

Justice, so described, was to become an American passion.

Economic Justice

Aristocratic societies, as Alexis de Tocqueville pointed out, are typically unconcerned with economic justice. If there are a few very wealthy families in the world and a host of miserably poor ones, well, that's life. But the American Founders did not agree. They knew many of the factional struggles that had destabilized ancient Greece had been between the haves and the have-nots, and that popular government could never work under such a handicap. People with nothing to lose did not make good citizens.

In America, where land ownership was common, there was a rough-and-ready equality of condition that served democracy well. Even those who did not own property knew that with hard work and careful scrimping one could always buy a farm in due time. Large landowners were vastly wealthier than small ones, of course, but with no artificial barriers to opportunity, one's own success or failure was held to be a matter of individual push.

The catch came with those artificial barriers. Jacksonian America was still a command economy in many ways, especially on the local level, and it bristled with franchises and monopolies. The idea of a truly free market made its way slowly and against dogged resistance.

The Granger Collection, New York

President Andrew Jackson toppled the Bank of the United States—the greatest franchise of them all.

But it gained encouragement from the political war that Jackson fought against the Bank of the United States—the greatest franchise of them all—which assumed a huge symbolic importance. Jacksonians understood themselves to be not just political democrats but openers of the doors of opportunity.

Later on, industrial America endangered economic justice in yet a different way. Where factories back in Jackson's day had employed highly trained artisans, able to command the respect of their bosses, the Carnegies and Rockefellers of a later era hired increasing numbers of low-skilled or unskilled workers, and the bosses no longer respected them—or even knew their names. To keep wages high and working conditions acceptable, laborers forged themselves into unions and took up "collective bargaining." Their only weapon in this new marketplace was to strike against employers or boycott their goods. Such tactics, alas, were not calculated to insure the peace.

Other Americans complained of economic injustice as well. We saw in chapter 11 how farmers in the South and Midwest, facing overproduction and falling prices (along with drought, pestilence, monetary deflation, and a host of other difficulties) became so stressed during the 1880s and 1890s that they formed their own political party and began winning victories at the ballot box. By the 1896 presidential election, these Populists, as they called themselves, were demanding serious and substantial changes in the U.S. economic system.

So went the quest for economic justice. In a complex and dynamic society, some group always seemed to be getting the short end of the stick. Now it was the miners, now the farmers, now the factory workers. Each group mustered as much political clout as it could in the American democracy and used it to best advantage. Each also flirted with forms of direct action, such as strikes (on the part of workers) or confrontations (on the part of farmers). In May 1880, in the San Joaquin Valley of California, settlers and railroad men staged a bloody shootout.

One aim of Progressivism was to develop a system for adjusting these stresses and strains. Progressives such as Theodore Roosevelt and Woodrow Wilson called upon government to intervene in economic affairs in such a way as to moderate the winning and losing. Their assumption was that a market economy could never deliver justice on its own. Only government, armed with science and technology, could determine fairness up and down the line, and then act in ways to insure that all Americans received it.

This theory was put to the test in the Great Depression. For complex reasons, the economic meltdown of the 1930s spared practically no one, as we have seen. Farmers could not sell their produce and left it rotting in the fields. Workers lost their jobs and ended up standing in bread lines. Factory owners closed their gates. Suburbanites lost their homes. Corporate executives wound up selling apples on street corners. The near universality of suffering helps us understand why Franklin D. Roosevelt's New Deal became the most striking political phenomenon of the twentieth century.

The New Deal attempted to solve the riddle of economic justice once and for all. With a host of new federal programs and agencies, New Dealers believed they could not only fix what had gone wrong with the market economy, they could at the same time rebalance the mechanisms of fairness in American life:

- Farmers would have their chronic overproduction curbed at last. Acreage would be taken out of cultivation and crops actually destroyed, if necessary, to force prices up in the marketplace.

- Industries would be permitted to form cartel monopolies, gaining the power to limit production and set prices at profitable levels.

- Workers would be paid a decent wage, adequate for home ownership and the raising of a family. Otherwise they could go on strike, with the government's blessing.

- The unemployed would be given jobs—make-work if necessary. The impoverished would be provided welfare. Those on the verge of losing homes, farms, or businesses would be floated emergency loans. The aged and infirm would be able to collect pensions.

- The government would see to it that companies played by the rules, that advertisers told the truth, that public utilities charged reasonable rates, that Wall Street behaved itself.

- And where pockets of desperation still remained—such as the impoverished Tennessee Valley—the government would promote regional development.

It was, in sum, America's only truly serious effort to secure economic justice for everyone.

Fort Loudon Dam, Tennessee, June 1942. After the Great Depression, government works projects, such as the Tennessee Valley Authority, tried to promote regional development.

The New Deal echoed far into the future. Harry Truman's "Fair Deal," John F. Kennedy's "New Frontier," and Lyndon Johnson's "Great Society" all pursued notions of economic justice. And even in the presidential election of 2004, candidate John Kerry invoked New Deal themes. "I seek a better America for *all* Americans," he said, "not just for the wealthy few."

Yet the more Americans struggled to secure economic justice, the more it seemed to elude them. There were several reasons for this. To begin with, it turned out that interventions into the market economy always bore hidden costs. Take minimum wage laws, for example. These were intended to provide higher wages for entry-level employment, and by and large they actually did so. By the laws of supply and demand, however, minimum wage laws made labor more expensive and thus reduced the number of jobs that employers could offer. Some workers earned more—but others stood idle. There was no way to win.

There was an even deeper difficulty. In many cases, Americans simply couldn't agree what justice was. If, say, manufacturing jobs migrated to third-world countries with resulting American layoffs, was that just or unjust? It seemed unjust to the workers whose jobs were lost but not to the consumers who could now afford cheap automobiles, stereos, and digital cameras. Point of view meant everything.

While it is difficult to generalize, Americans seem to have backed away from economic justice as something attainable by deliberation. It is not the fault of the ideal. It is simply that we don't know how to make the ideal a reality. So we fall back on the sort of justice that markets *can* deliver, flawed as that may be. Markets reward hard work, ingenuity, risk-taking, education, inheritance, and happy accidents. Above all, they reward productivity. They do not reward the aged, the infirm, the young and dependent, the membership of unpopular or suspect minorities, the hidebound, the rut-bound, and those who are unwilling to work.

While this may be justice up to a point, it seems to fall short of the truly just society.

Social and Political Justice

The American Founding was grounded in assumptions about political justice. "Is it just," cried Thomas Paine, "for an island to rule a continent?" The same question was stated more philosophically in the Declaration of Independence. If all men are created equal, is it just for *any* of them to rule others?

We have seen that the Declaration was not written as a philosophical treatise, however, but as a manifesto. Neither Thomas Jefferson nor most of his contemporaries were about to free their slaves, enfranchise their wives, or welcome Native Americans into political society. For this exclusiveness there was plenty of precedent. In ancient Athens—that beacon of republican idealism—justice was thought to be obtainable only among citizens. Since slaves were not citizens, it seemed perfectly congruous to hold them in bondage. Since women were not citizens, why worry about other rights for them? As for foreigners, even long-time resident foreigners, well, they belonged to some other polity.

Of course, precisely such parsing could be (and was) done by the British as well. Why treat colonials as full-fledged Britons when they were obviously something else? Why extend legal protections, such as jury trial, to cases where juries were sure to be lenient? And so on. Anyone could be just to friends, as Socrates pointed out—it was being just to *others* that posed the problem. Political justice, in sum, is hard to define, hard to pin down, hard to apply, and extremely hard to separate from one's own selfish interests.

In time, Americans developed their own notion of justice, which went something like this. Human beings, *as* human beings, are indeed more or less created equal. True, they have different talents and capacities, but the differences among them don't begin to compare with, say, the differences between a man and a horse. So, while Aristotle might argue that men were fitted by nature to rule over horses, you couldn't really say that they were fitted by nature to rule over one another. There was no strain of mankind so clearly superior as to be designated "natural rulers." Thus, according to justice, the people must rule themselves.

The trouble with this theory is that it contradicted so much that was long and clearly established. The world simply didn't work the way Jefferson thought it should. In his world, women *were* regarded as inferiors; chattel slavery was deeply entrenched; and Native Americans *were* viewed as outsiders, even if they were here first. The discrepancy between theory and practice has remained a challenge for Americans from the Founders' time to our own.

Much of the difficulty lay in ideas about nature. It was believed at one time or another than nature fitted Native Americans to be wild and unruly, women to be wives and mothers, Africans to be servile, and various immigrant groups to be hot-tempered, slow-witted, dishonest, slacking, or slovenly. How could self-rule be imagined, much less achieved, among so motley a throng?

Equality of Opportunity

The American answer to this question grew out of experience, much of it painful. In essence, it was that prejudice ought to step aside for opportunity. That is, in the name of justice, Americans should open the doors of opportunity and see whether or not any given prejudice is justified. Here are three examples.

1. New Kinds of Immigrants. In the 1830s and 1840s, when thousands of dispossessed Irish and Germans began pouring into the United States, so-called "nativists" loudly objected, claiming that "America is for Americans." The Irish especially, many of whom were poor and uneducated and almost all of whom were Catholic, faced massive discrimination. They were consigned to festering slums in a few large cities and forced to accept whatever jobs went begging. Signs saying "No Dogs or Irishmen Allowed" became commonplace.

Nativists would have permanently disfranchised such groups and found plenty of reason for doing so. They did *not* believe that prejudice should step aside for opportunity. But, with the Founding in mind, most Americans reasoned that immigrants, however humble, should not be condemned to everlasting and irredeemable inferiority—*not if all men were created equal.*

The Granger Collection, New York

In a cartoon by Thomas Nast, 1871, Columbia protects a Chinaman, warning an Irish mob that "America means fair play for all men."

Once armed with the ballot, the Irish and Germans made their way handily in America. Indeed, they forged voting blocs to be reckoned with and thus opened doors of opportunity for themselves. It was no accident, for example, that so many New York policemen came to speak with an Irish brogue.

This story was told over and over in the American experience. Immigrants from Southern and Eastern Europe who poured into the United States after the Civil War encountered much of the same hostility as the Irish and Germans had a generation earlier. But the same logic applied. Let prejudice step aside for opportunity and allow the newcomers a chance to prove themselves.

2. Women. Women posed another problem for equality of opportunity. Many Americans believed that nature had fitted women for roles of subordination. Even here, however, there were seeds of doubt, running back to the Revolution. If women were so dependent, it was asked, why were so many of them able to run the family farm while husbands and fathers went off to fight the British? And if they were incapable of high thinking, why did so many of them support the Revolution and advance its ideals? Did nature really create women *that* different from men?

There commenced one of the longest and most important dialogues in American history, a dialogue between—and about—men and women. While its details are beyond our scope, we can guess at their general character. Men reasoned that as dependent beings, women must be shielded and protected, kept unsullied by the political arena, and focused on domestic life. Women counter-reasoned that all this shielding and protecting masked a patronizing air, gross exploitation, and often outright abuse.

There was merit on both sides of the argument. Radicalized notions of women's liberation raised questions about the future of the family, the health of the community, even the survival of the political state—just as radicalized notions of women's subordination raised questions about personhood. How could one argue that

ARE NOT THE WOMEN HALF THE NATION?

The Granger Collection, New York

Justice looks on as a woman begs Uncle Sam for her rights in a pro-suffrage cartoon, 1919.

women were fit *only* to be wives and mothers without arguing that personhood was unimportant—and thus that human equality was a pipe dream?

Americans have never resolved these issues. After all, gender discrimination still exists. But Americans have grappled with the issues and have grudgingly come to accept that whatever else we think about the battle of the sexes, prejudice should not stand in the way of opportunity. Allow women to vote. Allow their full participation in politics and society. Allow them to compete with men in every vocation—from brain surgery to military combat. And try to be as open-minded as possible in assessing the results.

Where this leaves the family, the raising of children, the teaching of values, the health of the community, and the practice of what might be called the gentle arts we have more or less agreed to leave up in the air. In this instance, equality of opportunity may have come at a high price.

3. Race and Ethnicity. Race and ethnicity posed still another challenge to justice. In the case of most immigrants, the doors of opportunity could be opened with a tacit proviso in mind: the "melting pot" would eventually do its work. Irish, Germans, Scandinavians, Italians, Hungarians, Serbs, Latvians, and Poles could be counted on to look like and behave like the descendants of Paul Revere within a generation or two of their arrival. Their uniqueness would literally melt away. But some groups were unmeltable, either because they possessed distinctive racial characteristics or because they represented cultures that were essentially melt-proof. What of these?

Much of the sad story of American racism could be told here. It is an epic tragedy, as most Americans know. However they were able to extend the logic of equal opportunity to the mainstream cases, many simply balked at extending it to the unmeltables. To welcome the full participation of Asians, Africans, Hispanics, Polynesians, Indians, Jews, and others was in the eyes of the doubters to pollute racial purity and mongrelize American society. If every sort of difference was to be recognized and accepted, they asked, what did being "American" even mean?

The situation of the unmeltables was essentially the same in every case, though with varying degrees of intensity. They were subject to assorted forms of discrimination, public and private. They

An African American uses the "colored entrance" of a theater in Belzoni, Mississippi, 1939.

were often denied political rights and thus also denied any means of redress. They were forced to live in "ghettoized" neighborhoods, were barred from attending desirable schools, and were generally segregated in public transportation, in theaters and restaurants, in hotels and motels, in churches, on public beaches, and so on. Many areas of mainstream life were simply off limits to them. And when push came to shove, they were consigned to a criminal justice system in which they had no voice whatever.

The precise manner in which discrimination impacted the lives of individuals ranged all the way from exclusion at the local country club to death by lynching. Lynch law prevailed in the South from the end of the Civil War until well beyond World War II. Literally thousands of African Americans were beaten, branded, dragged to death behind automobiles, or strung up on a handy lamp-pole—simply to insure the intimidation of others. Police commonly looked the other way.

What such practices said about American justice may go without comment. However they were rationalized as "keeping the races separate" or "maintaining public order," no one ever bothered to call them just. And injustice troubled the American soul.

Accordingly, efforts at reform go back a long way, even to the Founding itself. And always the arguments have been the same: How could people be singled out solely because of the color of their skin or the God to whom they prayed? How could the freedom of some be abridged without abridging the freedom of all? How could America claim to be a Good Society while preserving such relics of barbarism?

Equality of Result

There were two kinds of equality, as we saw in chapter 14. The struggle for social and political justice initially focused on equality of opportunity. Reformers took aim at segregated schools, discriminatory laws, and other barriers to a fair and equal chance. As these barriers began coming down in the 1950s and 1960s, another dark truth soon emerged. Equality of opportunity may or may not make much difference. In some cases, of course, it made an enormous difference. Some groups made great strides forward as soon as the obstacles were removed from their path. They enrolled in the best schools and proved themselves to be worthy competitors. They bought property, started businesses, entered the professions, joined clubs, and moved into upscale neighborhoods. They took part in the political process and found their voice in the national forum.

Other groups continued to lag behind, however, some of them far behind. Hispanics, on the whole, have not done as well as Asians in the post–Civil Rights era, but both have done better than blacks. African Americans and Native Americans have had a hard go of it. Reasons for this have been linked to culture, to values and traditions, to the experience of slavery in the one case, or to the experience of genocidal war in the other. While impressive numbers of both groups have made the most of their opportunities, still the incidence of poverty, alcoholism, drug abuse, broken marriages, teen pregnancy, and other symptoms of dysfunction remain high.

The issue that now came to trouble American reformers was the old question of justice in a new guise. Perhaps American life had been so unfair to certain groups that no amount of equal opportunity could atone. Some Americans, as the argument went, simply had no chance.

And so, by degrees, equality of opportunity came to be superceded by equality of result—a new and entirely different pathway

The Granger Collection, New York

A poor black sharecropper in Georgia, 1938. Despite government intervention, many African Americans remained in poverty.

to the Good Society. With equality of opportunity, the focus is on
freedom, allowing each individual an unfettered chance to compete.
With equality of result, the focus is on replacing freedom with something else. Americans have developed three possible alternatives.

1. Redistribution. We have seen that market economies penalize the
victims of discrimination. Thus, if a black brain surgeon is less productive than her white counterpart solely because of patients' prejudice, markets ignore the injustice of the case and reward the white
surgeon's higher productivity. One approach to this problem is to tax
the white brain surgeon and subsidize the black one. This is called
income redistribution.

Redistribution has been a theme in American politics ever since
the New Deal. Welfare programs redistribute income, taxing from
the haves for the benefit of the have-nots. So do public housing, public transportation, and public health programs such as Medicare and

Medicaid. Even public education is a kind of redistribution, since it is funded by those of means rather than those with children.

Not all redistribution programs specifically benefit the poor. Agricultural price supports, for example, may redistribute on behalf of the rich, since the producers of some commodities are not struggling family farmers at all but well-heeled agribusinesses. Such examples illustrate one of the difficulties of redistribution as a means of securing justice. What is and isn't "just" in a given situation? There are as many answers to this question as there are perspectives in viewing it.

2. Affirmative Action. Affirmative action has been called "reverse discrimination," for it singles out disadvantaged minorities for preferential treatment. Thus, in typical cases, black or Hispanic law school applicants have been chosen ahead of Caucasians with higher LSAT scores, or women have been admitted to medical school in preference to men. The theory of affirmative action is to right past wrongs by giving a leg up.

Once again, however, we seem to beg the question of justice. While most Americans concede the injustice of past discrimination, they divide vociferously about privileging certain groups in the present. What does one say to the white male student who cannot be admitted to a graduate program even though his qualifications are higher—that he has been singled out as a scapegoat? Many Americans have backed away from affirmative action for just such reasons.

3. Political Correctness. Even though political correctness has more to do with semantics than substance, it too represents an attempt to secure justice. Referring to a black person as an African American rather than, say, a "darky" affords a measure of human dignity that was sadly lacking before World War II. The same holds true for so-called sexist language. Many Americans are willing to accept awkward and prolix modes of expression—chairperson, mail carrier, server—to avoid giving offense.

Precisely because political correctness *is* semantic, however, it becomes arbitrary by nature. While it would never do to call an African American a "colored person," yet "person of color" is now the term of choice. "Negro" was pronounced unfit by the political-correctness authorities back in the 1960s, to be replaced by the word "black," whose meaning is identical. "Black" was then edged out by "Afro-American," which was in turn eclipsed by "African American," and so on. That the terms are never quite satisfactory may suggest, symbolically, that we will never completely redeem ourselves from the injustice of the past.

Even supposing that the correct terms could be agreed upon, would the speech of justice amount to justice itself? Possibly so. Yet for many, it remains a pale sort of justice that employs dignified terms of address while turning a blind eye to so much else.

Equality of result has been a little more successful than equality of opportunity at redressing the wrongs of the past. Statistics indicate that the poorest fifth of Americans receive essentially the same slice of the economic pie as they did a century ago, that women in the workplace still lag behind men in compensation, and that most minority groups remain significantly handicapped.

Social justice remains an American ideal—it is not yet an American reality.

Criminal Justice

The Founders believed that the Good Society must also be just to those who violate its laws—another concern borrowed from the ancient world. When Socrates discoursed on justice, this was the kind of justice he usually had in mind.

The Founders realized that standards of justice had changed radically over the centuries. It was common in their own time for thieves to be sent to the gallows and those who went bankrupt to be thrown into prison. The Founders hoped that in their own society, punishments would be reasonable, proportionate, and suited to the crime for which they were given. The Founders wanted no part of the "cruel and unusual" punishments that were common in Great Britain. At the same time, the Founders sought to retain the procedural guarantees that had become a part of English law. In the Fifth to Eighth Amendments, the Framers spelled out some of the more important of those guarantees, such as *habeas corpus*, right to counsel, and trial by jury.

Since the time of the Founding, standards of justice have continued to change. We no longer lock up those who go bankrupt or hang children for stealing bread. In part, such changes have come about as the result of democratic empowerment. That is, as the common people have assumed more and more political power, they have insisted that criminal justice be brought into line with social and political justice. After all, what we commonly call crime is strongly tainted with a class bias. The laws, say the reformers, should not punish what the lower classes may do—such as robbery or burglary—while ignoring what the upper classes may do—such as embezzlement or fraud.

The search for criminal justice has also been complicated by racial and ethnic minorities. One test for the rule of law, as we have seen, is that the laws be general, applying to all persons regardless of race, gender, or religious affiliation—an ideal we sometimes call "equal protection of the laws." Equal protection was not the rule in Thomas Jefferson's America—or even in Teddy Roosevelt's. After the Civil War had supposedly freed the slaves, African Americans found themselves burdened with "Jim Crow laws," some as harsh as the old slave regulations. Blacks were restricted in buying and selling property, in contracting for a job, in residing where they might wish to, even in traveling where they might wish to, and they faced a world of discrimination in public amenities.

While other groups bore less stigma, the stigma was still there. Chinese and Japanese in most places could not vote, hold property, or sit on juries. Hispanics in the borderlands found they had few rights enjoyed by other immigrants, while Native Americans were treated like enemy aliens. In most states, women were subjected to a range of discriminatory laws, everything from control of their own property to custody of their own children.

Equal protection of the laws was denied to others besides minorities. Union organizers and strike leaders, for example, found that the cards were usually stacked against them as well. Courts commonly looked after the property rights of factory owners while ignoring hazards faced by the strikers. Other legally disadvantaged groups included seamen, dockworkers, coal miners, tenant farmers, working women, and those who labored in the country's ten thousand sweatshops.

It was little wonder that ethnic minorities and the poor accounted for a sizable chunk of the U.S. prison population. By the

Library of Congress

Two African American prisoners work on a road in Georgia, 1900. Almost two-thirds of prisoners in 1900 were minorities.

early twentieth century, those two groups accounted for almost two-thirds of all convicts serving time—partly because of the conditions they lived under and partly because of the way they were singled out. Comparisons of the sentences handed out to different groups for similar crimes left no doubt about the dire condition of criminal justice.

It was with such distortions in mind that Congress passed the Fourteenth Amendment in 1868. The purpose of the amendment was to forbid discrimination as a matter of constitutional law. No state could deny to any of its citizens the "privileges and immunities," "equal protection of the laws," or "due process of law" available to all others. It represented a bold attempt to secure justice once and for all.

To succeed, however, the Fourteenth Amendment, like all other constitutional provisions, must first be "interpreted" by the Supreme Court—and there lay a considerable rub.

Justice and the Judiciary

In chapter 7, we saw how the practice of judicial review came into being with *Marbury v. Madison*. In that monumental Supreme Court decision, Chief Justice John Marshall argued that the judiciary in general and the Supreme Court in particular had the power to expound the Constitution and determine what its language actually meant.

In his long tenure as Chief Justice, Marshall invoked judicial review very sparingly. If the law were to remain predictable, he believed, its meaning must be stable. Besides, the rules of jurisprudence held that once a particular word or phrase was officially interpreted, all courts (including the Supreme Court itself) were bound by that precedent. Successive Chief Justices, in other words, couldn't go back and rework Marshall's interpretations to suit themselves. Or *could* they? It turned out that there was nothing to stop them from doing just that. After all, who was going to overrule the Supreme Court?

By turns, then, the process of constitutional interpretation gradually led to constitutional *re*interpretation. That is, a group of justices debating the meaning of a certain constitutional phrase may or may not chose to follow the thinking of their predecessors. Take the commerce clause (Article I, section 8), for example. Depending on one's understanding of such vague terms as "commerce" and "regulate," it was possible to come down many different ways on commerce-clause issues, and over the years the Court changed its mind repeatedly. Some quick examples:

- In an early decision (*Gibbons v. Ogden*, 1824), John Marshall, who was a strong nationalist, gave the commerce clause a very broad interpretation, stretching federal regulatory power to the max.
- A later Court, that of Chief Justice Roger B. Taney, distrusted federal power and sought to trim it back. In a series of cases decided in 1847 (the License Cases), Taney and his colleagues reinterpreted the meaning of the commerce clause to allow for concurrent *state* power in commercial regulation.
- A later Court still, that of Chief Justice Melville Fuller, took issue with both precedents and advanced a libertarian view of the commerce clause. In *U.S. v. E. C. Knight* (1895), Fuller interpreted the meaning of the word "commerce" so narrowly that neither

U. S. SUPREME COURT

The Granger Collection, New York

The Supreme Court is the ultimate authority on constitutional language.

federal nor state governments were left with much authority to regulate it.

- Finally, in the 1960s, Chief Justice Earl Warren and his colleagues used the commerce clause to advance the cause of civil rights. The power to "regulate commerce," they argued in *Katzenbach v. McClung* (1964), included the power to enact antidiscrimination laws—so long as discrimination had some conceivable commercial impact. Of course, anything under the sun had *some* conceivable commercial impact.

With decisions such as these, the Supreme Court was doing more than simply expounding the Constitution. It was using constitutional language as a springboard for innovation. The Constitution was being warped and stretched this way and that to accommodate political agendas, intellectual fashions, and felt needs of the time.

Prominent among those felt needs was that of justice. Many of the perceived wrongs discussed earlier in this chapter had come to weigh heavily on the consciences of Supreme Court Justices like Earl Warren. Going back to the idea of natural law, Warren supposed that there was a kind of moral constitution—a constitution of right and wrong—embedded within the document written in Philadelphia. Supreme Court Justices, as Warren saw it, were in a position to invoke that shadowy instrument every now and then when the interests of justice required it.

For instance, when Warren became Chief Justice in 1953, school segregation was still alive and well in the United States. "Separate but equal" educational facilities for black and white children had been pronounced constitutional by the Supreme Court back in the case of *Plessy v. Ferguson* (1896). In theory, as we have seen, Warren's Court was honorbound to reaffirm the doctrine of *Plessy*. But Warren persuaded his eight fellow justices—some of whom needed little prodding—to appeal to that higher law, the

Library of Congress

Chief Justice Earl Warren made several rulings based on a belief in a "moral constitution."

one holding that school segregation was inherently wrong. In the now famous case of *Brown v. Board of Education* (1954), the Warren Court struck down segregation as unconstitutional. To find authority for this bombshell, they turned to one of those vague clauses in the Fourteenth Amendment, affirming that no state shall deny the "equal protection of the laws" to its citizens.

Conservatives gasped in dismay. They pointed out that Warren and his colleagues had taken it upon themselves to overturn a well-established social practice, and in so doing invoked a power that was never mentioned in the Constitution. If the Supreme Court could abolish segregation, they reasoned, it could do virtually anything.

Subsequently, the Warren Court confirmed some of these fears. In the even more controversial case of *Roe v. Wade* (1973), Warren and his fellow Justices upheld the practice of abortion as a matter of constitutional law. Abortion was (and still is) intensely controversial. Instead of letting Americans resolve that controversy via the political process—as the Founders undoubtedly intended—the Supreme Court took it upon itself to make the decision for them. And once again, it was made in the name of justice.

The Civil Rights Revolution

Justice and the issues surrounding it came to center stage with the *Brown* decision and have been there ever since. We have learned anew that there are no easy answers. But in the half century since *Brown*, we have at least sharpened the questions.

Earl Warren appears to have been right that notions of justice are tied to the Founding. We can't sort out the right and wrong of discrimination, segregation, affirmative action, public assistance, "freedom of choice," and the like without asking who we are as a people, what we stand for, and on what terms we have come together as a nation-state.

Most Americans have at least a shadowy idea how events unfolded from the *Brown* decision. Desegregation provoked clashes and confrontations between the federal government and the states, many (but not all) of them Southern. In at least one of these face-offs, at Little Rock, Arkansas, in 1958, it was necessary to call out the U.S. Army in full battle array.

Heartened by a sense that the federal government was now on their side, African Americans took up other matters of segregation. They sat in at off-limits lunch counters and suffered themselves to be beaten and arrested. They boycotted the transit system in Montgomery, Alabama, and walked five to ten miles a day for the right to sit in the front of the bus. They marched in protest in one American city after another, until hotels and restaurants and theaters grudgingly removed the "whites only" designations. They faced police clubs, attack dogs, fire hoses, and dank jail cells to win for themselves the freedoms that others took for granted. Once in a while they were bushwhacked in the streets or dumped into shallow graves in a mangrove swamp.

They understood that political justice was a necessary precondition for social and economic justice, and they began agitating for the right to vote, which in many states had been denied them by means of legal subterfuge. After a massive march on Washington in 1963—culminating in Martin Luther King Jr.'s "I Have a Dream" speech—Congress passed a tough new Civil Rights Act, followed by an equally tough Voting Rights Act. In the following months, literally millions of black Americans registered to vote for the first time.

Political power made a monumental difference. Shouting at black activists was one thing—facing their wrath at the ballot box was quite another. Almost overnight, some of the nation's leading white supremacists dramatically changed their tune and began seeking racial harmony.

It was clear by now that the genie was out of its bottle once and for all. Other minorities—Asians, Hispanics, Native Americans—took up the cry for equal rights. Techniques that had been honed to perfection by the National Association for the Advancement of Colored People (NAACP) worked just as well for the other groups. And for women. While women were neither ethnic nor a minority, and while they had enjoyed full political rights since the passage of the Nineteenth Amendment in 1920, they clearly faced similar discrimination, as we have seen. Modern-day feminism caught fire in the general conflagration. Soon it was obvious that America was witnessing not just a series of parallel protests but a full-scale movement.

The road ahead for civil rights was to be long and arduous, strewn with every sort of pitfall. The assassination of Martin Luther King Jr.

Library of Congress

Participants, some carrying American flags, marched for civil rights from Selma to Montgomery, Alabama, in 1965.

in 1968—to name just one of these setbacks—resulted in widespread urban rioting. The phrase "Burn, baby, burn!" made its way into the American lexicon.

Since the 1960s, we have paused from time to time and looked back for a course correction. Clearly there has been a sea change of attitudes regarding justice. We would not dream today of using "the N word" in polite conversation, of refusing to hire qualified Hispanics, of doubling the rent for a Native American family, of arresting felons without reading the "Miranda rights," of calling women colleagues "the girls." Our movies and TV shows are filled with attractive ethnic faces, conspicuous role models. In many areas of American life we give a tacit leg up wherever we can to the female or minority applicant.

But does all this add up to justice? For some it does and for others it doesn't. Whatever else justice may do, it eludes consensus. Moreover, if we have made substantial progress since the Civil Rights Revolution, we have also chalked up substantial costs. We have often replaced overt discrimination with one or more of its covert cousins—mistrust, hostility, fear. We have exchanged our patronizing air toward disadvantaged groups for a punctilious correctness, to be sure, but one devoid of warmth and humanity. We have often leaned so far in the direction of criminal rights that we have forgotten the rights of victims. We have come to accept justice-by-lawsuit as a way of life.

Once again, the viewpoint of the Founders may be relevant here. While prizing justice, the Founders also prized liberty, and they often linked the two together, as in that famous closing line: *with liberty and justice for all*. For a John Adams or a Thomas Jefferson, the highroad to the just society was the free society. Make people truly free, as Abraham Lincoln observed, and justice tends to take care of itself. With that in mind, we may note that many of the barriers to justice in America have been barriers to freedom as well: schools that were closed to *some* children, businesses that refused *some* customers, agencies that red-lined *some* neighborhoods.

Freedom as a heritage of the American Founding may provide another clue to the justice puzzle. At the beginning of the twenty-first century, Americans may recall that true freedom, and the responsibility that accompanies it, can be an antidote to suspicion, mistrust, pettiness, and much else that divides us in the "culture wars." By and large it is the unfree who sooner or later become the unjust.

Chapter 16

The Philosophy of the Founding

The American Founders were not philosophers. They worked from no carefully formulated set of premises, embraced no overarching design. On the contrary, much of what they did was simply respond to situations as these arose, muddling through in the best English fashion. Still, they embraced a common background and worldview, and despite their many quarrels and reluctant compromises, they fundamentally agreed on many things. Had they not done so, no Founding would have been possible.

Later on, when Americans looked back, they sought to impose some sort of order on the Founders' work. How, they asked, did the various elements of the Founding fit together? What general ideas and concepts gave it coherence? What was there for future generations to remember and cherish? What Heritage would the Founding give rise to?

What we want to do in this chapter is think about such questions in the way the Founders themselves might have thought about them, based on what we know of them and their world.

American Exceptionalism

The Founders regarded themselves as transplanted Englishmen. Like colonials everywhere, they were eager to conserve the traditions of their homeland, and they were more than a little fearful of losing these in the American wilderness. Consequently, they often wore their Englishness on their sleeves, so to speak, and were angry and insulted when they thought they were being patronized.

Yet the Founders also recognized the American experience as unique. There was something innocent and purifying about it, something that Columbus had glimpsed long before, an escape of some kind from human corruptions and follies. Viewed from America, Europe looked different. Those corruptions and follies seemed a lot clearer. To a John Adams or a Thomas Jefferson, Americans were not destined simply to replicate the Old World.

During the great turmoil that swelled into the American Revolution, Americans became convinced that British tyranny had specifically set about to corrupt *them*. Some of this paranoia undoubtedly was a reflection of their Puritan heritage. But some of it may have sprung from the very rocks and trees, as it were, for something about the terrain of America, the soil of America, had become sacred to

Kindred Spirits by Asher B. Durand, 1849. The land of America became sacred to Americans and represented their innocence and freedom.

them. We can still hear echoes of that sacredness in such hymns as "America the Beautiful." It helps us understand why Americans had such a strong affinity for the commonwealth ideology, with its emphasis on the country party. If those "purple mountain majesties" and "fruited plains" were not yet a country in the sense of *patria,* they were surely a country in the sense of a life close to the land.

The land in America was beautiful and bountiful. More important, the colonists believed it was unbounded. Land available to ordinary people had special meaning for colonial Americans. They had not only come from cramped and crowded Europe, they had come from a place so destitute that homelessness and joblessness were accepted conditions of life. In America colonists were able to acquire the thing that for thousands of years had given substance and dignity to human existence. Land accorded them space, livelihood, opportunity, self-mastery, and the command of their own destiny. Small wonder that Americans saw the Old World's corruptions and follies so clearly.

As with the land, so, too, with the institutions; freedom of the one implied freedom of the other. Thomas Jefferson was one American who thought he knew the reason why, for he subscribed to the myth of an ancient Saxon democracy. In the lost world before recorded history, Jefferson believed, men tilled their own land, managed their own lives, and *elected their own kings.* Things could never be that way again, not in Europe. Kings had become tyrants, lords had become oligarchs, and freedom had simply perished, basically because there wasn't enough land to go around. In America, though, free land stretched clear to the Pacific, and with it the promise of liberty.

As the Founding began taking shape, Jefferson and Madison pondered such matters. How, they asked, could they preserve the best in their English heritage and rid themselves of the worst? How could they create a modern society, not by starting from scratch (as the French would attempt to do) but by selectively pruning away those Old World corruptions and follies? Get rid of kings. Get rid of lords. Sever the tie between church and state. Lift the bans on speech and opinion, and throw open the windows of the soul. In America all this seemed possible.

Such was the meaning of *American exceptionalism.* The United States would become that city upon a hill dreamed of by John Winthrop. It would not have to follow the dreary road that so much of humankind had trod. It could break the mold—break the rules. Someday, perhaps, the country could even *make* the rules, as John Adams dared to suppose. The United States had slipped beyond the confines of history.

The Social Compact

As Locke and others imagined the social compact, there was more to it than a hypothetical agreement to form government. Equally important was the idea of an active and ongoing agreement among the living, to accept the terms and conditions of their society.

Accordingly, in places where the social compact was alive and well, people abided by the laws and supported the governing system—both signs of social health. In places where the social compact had become derelict, less fortunate circumstances prevailed. There was lawlessness, dissention, and political turbulence. People rejected the system in ways large and small, and in the end they often rose up against it. A broken social compact led to a broken society.

Whatever else they faced, the American Founders saw their social compact as flourishing. Perhaps this was due to the essentially middle-class nature of American society. After all, there were no radical extremes on this side of the Atlantic, no lords peering down from shining palaces, no ghettos full of homeless beggars. Or perhaps it was due to the relative homogeneity of colonial culture, marked by agricultural pursuits, a simple lifestyle, and a straight-laced Protestantism. But something else was at work as well.

A prominent feature of American exceptionalism had to do with the way the social compact operated. Because Americans had more or less fashioned their own institutions, they were basically happy with them. Some of the colonies had essentially governed themselves from the outset—Connecticut, for example—while others were privately owned, which had amounted to the same kind of self-governing. Some of the colonies had literally drafted their own charters, too, and submitted them for the king's signature. Out on the frontier there were many communities that had sat down and worked out their own government. In the United States, in other words, the social compact wasn't theoretical or implicit—it was an everyday reality.

Americans created their laws and expressed confidence in the Constitution in this late eighteenth-century printer's cut.

While the colonies weren't democratic by modern standards, political participation was high in most of them—and that was much higher than it had been in Great Britain. Most adult males could meet the property requirements for voting. Many of them also held local office, such as town selectman, and as a result were treated with a certain dignity. The benign neglect the colonies received from the mother country strengthened their sense of autonomy and gave them a comfortable feeling of self-mastery. People migrated *to* them, not *from* them.

Classical political theory had often stressed a connection between the city and the soul. Autocratic *poleis* made for autocratic person-alities among their citizenry (and vice versa), while the same held true for democratic or aristocratic *poleis*. The de facto freedom of the colonies in America made for the personal freedom of their inhabit-ants, and personal freedom made for a social compact that worked. The American "city" tended to produce an American "soul."

This background proved to be crucial to the American Founding. The important fact about that Founding was that the people literally created it themselves. They decided, citizen by citizen, whether or not to support the patriot cause, whether or not to join the militia, whether or not to acknowledge the authority of Congress. They sent their own delegates to the state constitutional conventions, and when the proposal for a federal government emerged, they sent delegates to accept or reject it. There was nothing here about government com-ing down from on high. It was something the people themselves had worked up, tinkered with, overhauled on the work bench when it failed to perform properly, and then put back into operation. Never had the social compact operated in quite so literal a way.

Republic of Virtue

Like the English Whigs before them, the American Founders paid close attention to the ancient world, for its lessons seemed to speak to them directly. They were not classical scholars by any means, but part of being a gentleman was to have the essentials of a classical edu-cation, which basically consisted of memorizing passages of ancient learning in the original Greek or Latin.

Thus equipped, the Founders couldn't fail to be impressed by the significance of virtue as the lifeblood of republics. It was everywhere they looked. Nor could they fail to see the relevance of virtue to their own situation. Republics were hardly the order of the day in 1776. No one knew exactly how they worked. If Plato, Aristotle, and Cicero all affirmed that republics operated by dint of public virtue, that was good enough.

There was an important shift, however, in precisely what Ameri-cans took virtue to be. For the ancients, virtue had been *aretē*—excel-lence—and its whole point had been to fortify the *polis* with the wisdom, courage, temperance, and justice of its citizens. Examined closely, these virtues tended to be competitive in nature, reflecting the Greco-Roman passion for contest. There were winners and losers in the virtuous society, as each tried to outdo all others in civic zeal. Christian virtues, on the other hand, tended to be less about winners and losers but more about social accommodation. Love your neighbor, go the extra mile, turn the other cheek, forgive seventy times seven—there was nothing here about outshining someone else, only about making your community a good place to live. Societies that practiced ordinary kindness, however imperfectly, turned out to be more durable than those that strove only for excellence. For all its achievements, Greek values tended to self-destruct, whereas Christian values survived the centuries.

When the American Founders spoke of virtue, they may have used Greek terms, but the substance they alluded to was mainly Christian. The religious background of the colonies had amplified Christian values generally, and the Great Awakening of the 1740s had ignited an ardent Christian evangelism. Gone forever was the old Calvinist despair. Americans now believed in the freedom of the individual to choose salvation, and they worked hard to bring it to pass. There were incentives to practice virtue as never before.

The awareness of this spiritual infrastructure became a great source of confidence for the Founders. Interlocking with American exceptionalism, it created a world in which republicanism could thrive, not because Americans could emulate a George Washington in the exercise of excellence, but because they could care for

AMERICAN VIRTUE

A compound of Classical virtue and Christian value.

their families, attend church, look to the health of their communities, and live lives of common decency. Virtue such as this truly could be made to work, the Founders told themselves, unlike the *aretē* of ancient Greece—which had burned out.

The Revolution had the effect of proving American virtue, at least to some of the Founders. Take, for example, the sacrifices Americans had been willing to make—everything from backing the boycotts to facing enemy guns. Or the Joseph Warrens and Nathan Hales—patriots who had serenely faced death. Or the young men who suffered privation at Valley Forge, or worse, in British prison camps, where they died of illness and starvation and were left lying in their own filth.

Other Founders weren't so sure, however. Some aspects of the war had not cast American virtue (Greek *or* Christian) in a favorable

The Granger Collection, New York

Nathan Hale was hung by the British on September 22, 1776, for being an American spy.

Arnold and Andre, by C. F. Blauvelt. Benedict Arnold attempts to persuade Major John Andre to conceal the plans of West Point in his boot at their meeting on September 21, 1780.

light. What about all the spies and turncoats? What about traitors such as Benedict Arnold? What about the self-important generals who botched battle after battle; the militiamen who fired once and took to the woods; the merchants who sold to the highest bidder? What about all the greedy, grasping politicians who swarmed like ants in the state governments and cared not a whit for the public good? Could this be called virtue?

After reflecting on such developments, some of the Founders scrapped the idea of virtue altogether. People, they said, were too narrow and selfish to care about public values, much less to love their enemies. These Founders placed their faith in a structural solution to the Republican Problem, seeking out ways to set interest against interest, ambition against ambition, all through a constitutional government. If the structure could be made good enough, they thought, human nature could be made to control *itself*.

Most of the Founders, however, didn't abandon virtue completely, though they did become more sophisticated about it. They came to see virtue as being largely situational. In other words, the human capacity for noble conduct tended to emerge better in some situations than others, as, say, with the politician who fearlessly does the right thing but only in the glow of the limelight. This understanding of virtue provided a new approach to the use of structure. Rather than simply playing off interest against interest, structure could be used to create circumstances in which virtuous behavior becomes more likely. Here is an example:

Owing to alleged misdeeds, there is a popular outcry against a religious group known as the Druids. Rather than simply prosecuting individual offenders, Congress passes a bill banning *all* Druids from public life. (Assume for the moment that there is no Bill of Rights.) The president abhors this bill for both political and moral reasons. Politically, he was elected by all the people, including Druids, in a very tight race. Morally, he views the world from a higher perspective than most congressmen do, and thus he sees greater value in tolerance. Upon reflection, the president decides to veto the bill in question. In his veto message, he pointedly appeals to the virtue of the lawmakers, urging them to do justice. Note he doesn't have to convince all of them, only a small fraction. In fact, think how small it is. In democratic politics, a substantial number will side with the president anyway, regardless of his position, so all he has to do is add enough to that number to total one-third of the whole, enough to block an override. Chances are good that his appeals will win out. If they do so, we have the structure to thank (along with the president's own virtue of course), for it has enabled the president to mobilize latent virtue.

With such scenarios in mind, most of the Founders continued to believe in the importance, even the necessity, of republican virtue to sustain and fortify the American nation.

Rule of Law

In the ancient world, political societies were commonly run by tyrants or oligarchs. In either case, will ruled. The rule of will was not necessarily bad, and in a few cases it turned out to be rather fortunate, but it was generally bad enough, especially for anyone who ran afoul of the ruler. Will, so it seemed, was often capricious, nasty, and malevolent.

Among their contributions to political thought, the classical Greeks developed the idea of the rule of law. They discovered that when a society is given general, prospective laws that everyone recognizes and understands, the rule of will simply doesn't work any longer—the laws themselves take its place.

For the ancients, the rule of law encouraged peace and prosperity. It didn't necessarily encourage personal freedom, for that was not a value they often prized. In the modern world, however, we have seen that the rule of law also creates a private world in which the individual is free of state interference. Once the laws become stable and predictable, like the laws of nature, individuals become agents of their own destiny.

Founders such as John Adams placed great faith in the rule of law, which he took to be the very heart of the Founding. Since Adams's time, we have gradually come to realize that maintaining the rule of law can be a tricky business. While the principles of generality, prospectivity, publicity, and the like seem simple enough, they are often scarce in the world of politics. Take generality, for instance.

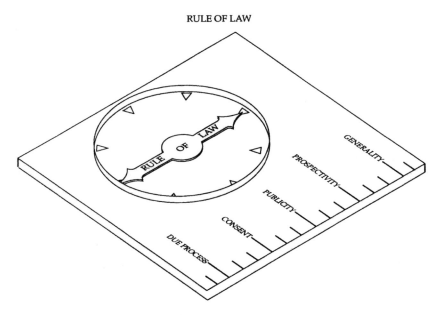

The concept of the "rule of law" represents the philosophical ideal that government may not act except in the impartial enforcement of a known general rule. The actions of such a government are predictable, much like the laws of nature. Those living under the rule of law can chart the course of their destiny in predictable self-determination.

The concept is clear and compelling: the laws must apply to everyone. In practice, however, we come up with all sorts of reasons why "everyone" shouldn't really include *everyone*. We believe some groups deserve special protections. We believe other groups pose special risks. We feel sorry for those who have faced, say, a natural disaster and need help getting back on their feet. We want the rich to pay more than their share of the taxes, and the poor to receive more than their share of the benefits. Generality becomes very dicey.

We have devised clever ways of getting around generality. If we vote an aid package for all cities whose elevation exceeds 5,000 feet and whose population exceeds two million, we don't have to mention Denver by name. With such cleverness in mind, the British government often violated the rule of law, in what was taken to be the best interests of the empire. The result, for Americans, was the rule of will, or tyranny. Many political societies have painted themselves into precisely such a corner.

The principles of the rule of law are philosophical ideals, not laws in themselves that could be adopted by a legislature. Their only real existence is in the human heart. This explains why some societies have little awareness of the rule of law. They are so used to being pushed around by government that they barely realize it is happening. Other societies, though perhaps unable to explain why, sense immediately when the rule of law is violated, for they perceive a glaring injustice. This describes the American colonies when Parliament passed the Stamp Act or revoked jury trial for accused smugglers.

The Founders were concerned about the rule of law and recognized its peculiar fragility. They insured that provisions in the Constitution specifically prohibited bills of attainder (violating generality) and *ex post facto* legislation (violating prospectivity). In the interest of publicity, the Founders required that Congress publish its own proceedings, and that the president give an annual accounting of the Union. In the Bill of Rights they spelled out precisely what they meant by due process of law.

Structure may also be understood in terms of the rule of law. With faulty government structures, both the states and the Confederation had failed to establish the rule of law convincingly, violating one after another of its principles. The federal government, the Founders believed, would do much better. With all of its mechanisms, the government still might err, but it would be unlikely to rule by simple will. For instance, in the example given above, the bill passed against the Druids violates the principles of generality and prospectivity by singling out a specific group and punishing it for past actions. Simple structures consisting of a unicameral legislature often did precisely the same thing. By adding a bicameral legislature and an executive with a mind of his own, the Constitution made it less likely that these principles would be ignored. Structure served the cause of freedom.

Empire of Liberty

As Britain's various colonies grew and prospered, the constitutional monarchy of 1688 was transformed into an empire, the richest and most extensive since imperial Rome. The key issue of empire, as the British came to understand it, lay in establishing a proper relationship of the parts to the whole. It was well, perhaps, for the colonies to see advantage in their imperial membership—that kept them happier—but the crucial advantage must be that of the imperial center. London must benefit, whether or not Boston or Halifax or Calcutta did. And to maintain such advantage, the British came to realize that they must enforce the subordination of their colonies by whatever means necessary.

As a federal republic, the United States found itself in a roughly similar situation. The thirteen original colonies occupied less than one-third of the land mass recognized by the peace treaty with Great Britain, and with the later addition of Louisiana and the Mexican Cession, that fraction would be much smaller still. What would be the proper relationship between the original polity and this continental sprawl?

Many of the Founders assumed that the relationship would have to be imperial in some way, assuming that the West must necessarily be subordinated to the East. Otherwise power would drain toward the Pacific, and America might lapse into barbarism. The wildness of the frontier seemed threatening.

Thomas Jefferson saw the case much differently. He had great faith in the "common man," especially once he was liberated from European artificiality. What he saw happening in the West was not the loss of civilized values, but the restoration of that ancient Saxon democracy, with all its dignity and justice. The West, for Jefferson, was the American future.

A map showing U.S. territorial expansion between 1776 and 1884. Thomas Jefferson proposed that new territories become states rather than have a conquered "empire" status.

When the question of organizing western territories arose under the Confederation, Jefferson was called upon to formulate a specific set of principles. Thinking carefully about what was at stake, the Virginian reasoned that if the West were to become America's empire, it would bring the same sort of calamities experienced by the British. The subordinate areas would assume various political shapes: territories, possessions, colonies, protectorates. Issues of equality and justice would arise between one of them and another, and among all of them and the East. In the end they would grow restive and scheme to break away.

Jefferson opted for a radically different model. Let the West be organized into full-fledged states, he said, of roughly the same size and population as the original thirteen. Congress would administer each territory and supervise its incubation into statehood. And as each achieved a threshold of political maturity, it would take its place among the others, on a wholly equal footing. Let the American empire be, in Jefferson's words, an "empire of liberty."

The United States as we know it today grew from this profound insight.

National Character

In 1831 a young Frenchmen named Alexis de Tocqueville toured the United States and took careful notes. Among the things that caught his eye was the character of Americans; for Tocqueville, like the ancient Greeks, assumed a connection between city and soul. To the extent that a founding establishes a people, not just a government, what *would* the character of Americans be, he wondered. In his two-volume report, titled *Democracy in America* (1835), Tocqueville pointed to Americans' ingrained optimism, to their restlessness, to their sense of equality and community, to their ready display of mechanical ingenuity, and to their distrust of Old World learning.

Tocqueville's book marked the beginning of an abiding interest in the character of the United States. Later, a historian named Frederick Jackson Turner famously explained the American character in terms of the frontier, pointing out that self-reliance, an ambitious spirit, and an egalitarian turn of mind would naturally develop among those who cleared forest and plowed land. Other historians argued that it was mobility that explained the American character, still others that it was material abundance, and yet others that it was immigration and the melting pot.

There is a concept that encompasses all of the foregoing perspectives—*self-invention*. The self-invented *patria* naturally gave rise to the self-invented citizen. After all, at the heart of the Founding lay the liberty of individuals to work out their own destinies. So if United States citizens began inventing themselves—if they studied nights to learn accounting, or went to Hollywood for a screen test, or sold the farm and moved to the city, or took up the practice of yoga—it might simply have reflected that pursuit of happiness the Founders regarded so highly.

The pursuit of happiness made it difficult for Americans to think with a single mind or speak with a common voice. By definition, individuals see the world in their own separate ways. From colonial days, Americans have questioned and disputed every aspect of their beliefs, their values, their politics, their morals, their very identity, never settling anything to the satisfaction of all. Never was there a body politic open to such ongoing self-scrutiny.

By creating a world of rocklike stability—together with agreement on fundamentals—the Founding made it possible for U.S. citizens to divide over everything else, and for each to pursue his or her own sense of meaning. The American character will probably remain elusive because the questioning and disputing will go on and on. Americans will continue to invent themselves because their Founding frankly bids them to do so.

The Founding as a Moral Enterprise

The three founding documents of the United States laid down a set of moral propositions. Those of the Declaration of Independence and the Bill or Rights are more or less obvious, as we have seen. The Declaration affirmed that all men were created equal and endowed with basic rights, that they were free to create any government they saw fit, and that they could expect any government they created to honor and protect the rights in question. The Bill of Rights listed some specifics, and further underscored their inviolability, so that citizens could repair to the courts if the government let them down. Both documents became banners of freedom.

But what of the Constitution? Is it not a moral document as well? Some have noted that, unlike the other founding texts, the Constitution appears only to lay out a structure of government, proposing no ethical principles. Readers of *The Federalist* came to know better. The Constitution's moral dimension was there, even if subtle. The framers had never proposed to lay out just *any* government, not even any republican government, but a government that somehow embodied Truth—with a capital "T."

To grasp the ethics of the Constitution, we need to note something else of importance about freedom. Americans, having actually experienced personal liberty, understood that there was much about it that couldn't be explained philosophically, having to do with such mundane things as buying a farm, starting a business, inventing a new contraption—*feeling* that one was free.

Americans had also come to appreciate the fragility of free institutions. Both in the experience of state governments and that of the Confederation, they had seen such institutions fail, and history demonstrated that the failures were only too common. Thus, for Americans, the Republican Problem wasn't just an exercise in logic; it was a pressing and daunting difficulty, and their very lives depended on finding a solution. How could they gain the benefits of republican life without incurring its dreadful costs?

Madison's insight about the extended republic comes into play here. The picture he painted in *Federalist* 10 of faction contending against faction was specifically the picture of a *free* society. Similarly, when Adam Smith described the bustle of producers and consumers in the marketplace, he too was depicting freedom. For both Smith and Madison, liberty was robust and dynamic. It was not about mystics in a state of bliss, but ordinary people in the scramble of life.

For Madison, as for Smith, the pursuit of happiness could, and sometimes did, lead to conflict. That was precisely the problem. Much of the tyranny and anarchy in the world derived from the clash of self-interest. But both Madison and Smith believed that cooperation among human beings was more likely than conflict *if* the conditions were right. Everything depended on the conditions. The point of Madison's extended republic, like the point of Smith's free market, was to achieve those conditions—to create an empire of liberty.

Smith noted that market behavior tended to harmonize individual interests so that competition did not lead to conflict. Madison might have said the same of his extended republic. Yes, there would be factions, hundreds of them, but in the end their pulling and hauling against one another would render them strangely harmonious, like producers and consumers in the marketplace. There was another point, too. People accumulating wealth and goods in the marketplace had their minds on something else besides politics. It was not that way in ancient Greece. The Greeks had frowned on materialism, and as a result *their* factions were composed of true-believing fanatics.

The large, extended, commercial republic, then, was a crucial element of that regime of liberty. Both as marketplace and political arena, the commercial republic tended to neutralize self-interest. That left less self-interest for government to deal with, and less government became possible. Yet government must still exist, if only to deal with the hard cases—one couldn't simply proclaim human rights and hope for the best. The question was, How to insure that government refrains from compromising the very freedom it was supposed to protect, as it had done so often in the past?

Here we glimpse the moral text of the Constitution. By creating a government that was powerful, well disposed, and securely under

A photograph of the South Market Street market, Chicago, 1919. Strong economic development created a "commercial republic."

popular control, the Constitution made real freedom possible. The federal government was made powerful by design. The government was made well disposed by its ability to mobilize virtue. Through structural counterpoise, the government was kept under the control of the people. Rights now meant something, for there was an agency capable of defending them.

We see, accordingly, that our triad of founding documents fits together. With all three of them working in concert, Americans came to enjoy the dignity and self-mastery that freedom alone could bring. It was in this sense that the authors of *The Federalist*—and the Founders themselves—could regard the American Republic as "True."

The Inspired Founding

Several of the Founders also believed that the American Republic needed to be inspired by God. After all, divine authority was the ultimate authority, as King James understood so well. Government might be a human invention, as the social compact affirmed, but without some higher sanction it forfeited the sense of mystery which set it above mortal institutions.

The specific problem here was the Constitution's amendability. Unlike the Articles of Confederation, the Constitution was designed to be altered. This fact emphasized the social compact within. The people themselves had written and approved it; in time they could amend it as they saw fit. But if they did so too often or too casually, the mystery would be gone. That's why the framers made the amending process just cumbersome enough to discourage habitual use.

There is a deeper question, however. Was the American Founding *really* inspired? In the early years of the republic, it was common for Americans to assert that it was inspired, and there was more to the claim than empty chauvinism. The idea was that God had inspired the American Founding not solely for the benefit of Americans but for the benefit of all mankind—that it marked a turning point in human history.

Several of the Founders appeared to accept this themselves, and these men had no illusions about the bare-knuckle politics, the serial compromises, the appeals to power and interest that ran through their labors from beginning to end. Here, for consideration, is a short list of supporting evidence for that belief of divine inspiration.

First, by any measure, the founding generation was a remarkable one. It would have been remarkable in Enlightenment Europe—and how much more so out on the Atlantic frontier. Take, for example, a roster of those who served in the Continental Congress, of those who guided the first state governments, of those who met in Philadelphia to forge the Constitution. Think of a George Washington, an Alexander Hamilton, a Thomas Jefferson, a James Madison, a John Adams, a Benjamin Franklin, not as marble statues but as men who knew one another, liked one another (for the most part), kicked around ideas, and hammered out difficult agreements. There has never been such a generation in U.S. history, before or since.

Second, the peculiar mix of personalities in the Founding is remarkable in another way. At every crucial point in the story, forceful characters played off against receptive characters, idealists against pragmatists, visionaries and innovators against compromisers and facilitators. At the Grand Convention, to name a single instance, there were energetic, take-charge individuals and there were subtle, manipulative individuals. Fifty-five of either variety would have spelled disaster. As it was, the personal chemistry was nearly perfect.

Third, there were several junctures in the Founding where the turn of a single card might have altered the entire outcome. What if the attack at Princeton had failed—as it very nearly did? What if Admiral Francois de Grasse had been delayed a few hours in arriving at Yorktown? What if Daniel Jenifer hadn't missed that particular roll call in Philadelphia, or Abraham Baldwin hadn't abruptly changed his vote? What if Edmund Randolph hadn't supported the document in Williamsburg that he had refused to sign previously in Philadelphia? What if George Washington had been killed by any of those six bullets in the battle of the Wilderness?

Fourth, there was a curious serendipity attending the American Founding. One saw it clearly at the Philadelphia Convention. Compromises that seemed ill-starred not only turned out for the best, they turned out as if touched by genius. Federalism wasn't brilliant political theory—it was a bizarre accommodation. Separation of powers didn't fall out of the pages of Montesquieu—it emerged from a weary committee. We look back on the Constitution as an achievement of western civilization, but the men who wrote it saw it as a mishmash of concessions.

Finally, when we consider how surprisingly (and often disappointingly) structural models often work in practice, it is little short of amazing that the Constitution worked at all—much less worked as it did. Several of the document's carefully contrived mechanisms utterly failed and had to be scrapped. (For example, the method of counting votes in the Electoral College, for example, produced deadlock ties and soon led to a constitutional crisis.) What if in practice the Constitution simply hadn't functioned, or, more probably, had functioned in a limp-along fashion like the Articles of Confederation? Would forces ever have mustered for another try? Unlikely.

None of these points absolutely proves the work of the Founders to have been divinely inspired. All the same, it creates just enough mystery to bathe the Founding in an aura it has never lost. Americans came to believe that their republic was more than just a sum of its parts, more than any of the Founders could have created by himself, more than all of them could have created together. And there was more to its Founding than simple serendipity.

The Declaration of Independence

Action of Second Continental Congress, July 4, 1776

The unanimous Declaration of the thirteen united States of America

WHEN in the Course of human Events,
it becomes necessary for one People to dissolve the Political Bands which have connected them with another, and to assume among the Powers of the Earth, the separate and equal Station to which the Laws of Nature and of Nature's God entitle them, a decent Respect to the Opinions of Mankind requires that they should declare the causes which impel them to the Separation.

WE hold these Truths to be self-evident, that all Men are created equal, that they are endowed by their Creator with certain unalienable Rights, that among these are Life, Liberty and the Pursuit of Happiness—That to secure these Rights, Governments are instituted among Men, deriving their just Powers from the Consent of the Governed, that whenever any Form of Government becomes destructive of these Ends, it is the Right of the People to alter or to abolish it, and to institute new Government, laying its Foundation on such Principles, and organizing its Powers in such Form, as to them shall seem most likely to effect their Safety and Happiness. Prudence, indeed, will dictate that Governments long established should not be changed for light and transient Causes; and accordingly all Experience hath shewn, that Mankind are more disposed to suffer, while

Evils are sufferable, than to right themselves by abolishing the Forms to which they are accustomed. But when a long Train of Abuses and Usurpations, pursuing invariably the same Object, evinces a Design to reduce them under absolute Despotism, it is their Right, it is their Duty, to throw off such Government, and to provide new Guards for their future Security. Such has been the patient Sufferance of these Colonies; and such is now the Necessity which constrains them to alter their former Systems of Government. The History of the present King of Great- Britain [King George III] is a History of repeated Injuries and Usurpations, all having in direct Object the Establishment of an absolute Tyranny over these States. To prove this, let Facts be submitted to a candid World.

HE has refused his Assent to Laws, the most wholesome and necessary for the public Good.

HE has forbidden his Governors to pass Laws of immediate and pressing Importance, unless suspended in their Operation till his Assent should be obtained; and when so suspended, he has utterly neglected to attend to them.

HE has refused to pass other Laws for the Accommodation of large Districts of People, unless those People would relinquish the Right of Representation in the Legislature, a Right inestimable to them, and formidable to Tyrants only.

HE has called together Legislative Bodies at Places unusual, uncomfortable, and distant from the Depository of their public Records, for the sole Purpose of fatiguing them into Compliance with his Measures.

HE has dissolved Representative Houses repeatedly, for opposing with manly Firmness his Invasions on the Rights of the People.

HE has refused for a long Time, after such Dissolutions, to cause others to be elected; whereby the Legislative Powers, incapable of the Annihilation, have returned to the People at large for their exercise; the State remaining in the mean time exposed to all the Dangers of Invasion from without, and the Convulsions within.

HE has endeavoured to prevent the Population of these States; for that Purpose obstructing the Laws for Naturalization of Foreigners; refusing to pass others to encourage their Migrations hither, and raising the Conditions of new Appropriations of Lands.

HE has obstructed the Administration of Justice, by refusing his Assent to Laws for establishing Judiciary Powers.

HE has made Judges dependent on his Will alone, for the Tenure of their Offices, and the Amount and Payment of their Salaries.

HE has erected a Multitude of new Offices, and sent hither Swarms of Officers to harrass our People, and eat out their Substance.

HE has kept among us, in Times of Peace, Standing Armies, without the consent of our Legislatures.

HE has affected to render the Military independent of and superior to the Civil Power.

HE has combined with others to subject us to a Jurisdiction foreign to our Constitution, and unacknowledged by our Laws; giving his Assent to their Acts of pretended Legislation:

FOR quartering large Bodies of Armed Troops among us;

FOR protecting them, by a mock Trial, from Punishment for any Murders which they should commit on the Inhabitants of these States:

FOR cutting off our Trade with all Parts of the World:

FOR imposing Taxes on us without our Consent:

FOR depriving us, in many Cases, of the Benefits of Trial by Jury:

FOR transporting us beyond Seas to be tried for pretended Offenses:

FOR abolishing the free System of English Laws in a neighbouring Province, establishing therein an arbitrary Government, and enlarging its Boundaries, so as to render it at once an Example and fit Instrument for introducing the same absolute Rules into these Colonies:

FOR taking away our Charters, abolishing our most valuable Laws, and altering fundamentally the Forms of our Governments:

FOR suspending our own Legislatures, and declaring themselves invested with Power to legislate for us in all Cases whatsoever.

HE has abdicated Government here, by declaring us out of his Protection and waging War against us.

HE has plundered our Seas, ravaged our Coasts, burnt our Towns, and destroyed the Lives of our People.

HE is, at this Time, transporting large Armies of foreign Mercenaries to compleat the Works of Death, Desolation, and Tyranny, already begun with circumstances of Cruelty and Perfidy, scarcely paralleled in the most barbarous Ages, and totally unworthy the Head of a civilized Nation.

HE has constrained our fellow Citizens taken Captive on the high Seas to bear Arms against their Country, to become the Executioners of their Friends and Brethren, or to fall themselves by their Hands.

HE has excited domestic Insurrections amongst us, and has endeavoured to bring on the Inhabitants of our Frontiers, the merciless Indian Savages, whose known Rule of Warfare, is an undistinguished Destruction, of all Ages, Sexes and Conditions.

IN every stage of these Oppressions we have Petitioned for Redress in the most humble Terms: Our repeated Petitions have been answered only by repeated Injury. A Prince, whose Character is thus marked by every act which may define a Tyrant, is unfit to be the Ruler of a free People.

NOR have we been wanting in Attentions to our British Brethren. We have warned them from Time to Time of Attempts by their Legislature to extend an unwarrantable Jurisdiction over us. We have reminded them of the Circumstances of our Emigration and Settlement here. We have appealed to their native Justice and Magnanimity, and we have conjured them by the Ties of our common Kindred to disavow these Usurpations, which, would inevitably interrupt our Connections and Correspondence. They too have been deaf to the Voice of Justice and of Consanguinity. We must, therefore, acquiesce in the Necessity, which denounces our Separation, and hold them, as we hold the rest of Mankind, Enemies in War, in Peace, Friends.

WE, therefore, the Representatives of the united States of America, in General Congress, Assembled, appealing to the Supreme Judge of the World for the Rectitude of our Intentions, do, in the Name, and by Authority of the good People of these Colonies, solemnly Publish and Declare, That these United Colonies are, and of Right ought to be, FREE AND INDEPENDENT STATES; that they are absolved from all Allegiance to the British Crown, and that all political Connection between them and the State of Great-Britain, is and ought to be totally dissolved; and that as FREE AND INDEPENDENT STATES, they have full Power to levy War, conclude Peace, contract Alliances, establish Commerce, and to do all other Acts and Things which INDEPENDENT STATES may of right do. And for the support of this Declaration, with a firm Reliance on the Protection of divine Providence, we mutually pledge to each other our Lives, our Fortunes, and our sacred Honor.

John Hancock

Josiah Bartlett
Wm Whipple
Saml Adams
John Adams
Robt Treat Paine
Elbridge Gerry
Steph. Hopkins
William Ellery
Roger Sherman
Saml Huntington
Wm Williams
Oliver Wolcott
Matthew Thornton
Wm Floyd
Phil Livingston
Fran^s Lewis
Lewis Morris
Richd Stockton
Jno Witherspoon
Fra^s Hopkinson
John Hart
Abra Clark
Robt Morris
Benjamin Rush
Benj^a Franklin
John Morton
Geo Clymer
Ja^s Smith

Geo. Taylor
James Wilson
Geo. Ross
Cæsar Rodney
Geo Read
Thos M:Kean
Samuel Chase
Wm Paca
Thos Stone
Charles Carroll of Carrollton
George Wythe
Richard Henry Lee
Th. Jefferson
Benj^a Harrison
Thos Nelson, Jr
Francis Lightfoot Lee
Carter Braxton
Wm Hooper
Joseph Hewes
John Penn
Edward Rutledge
Thos Heyward, Junr
Thomas Lynch, Junr
Arthur Middleton
Button Gwinnett
Lyman Hall
Geo Walton

The United States Constitution

We the People of the United States, in Order to form a more perfect Union, establish Justice, insure domestic Tranquility, provide for the common defence, promote the general Welfare, and secure the Blessings of Liberty to ourselves and our Posterity, do ordain and establish this Constitution for the United States of America.

Article I.

Section 1.

All legislative Powers herein granted shall be vested in a Congress of the United States, which shall consist of a Senate and House of Representatives.

Section 2.

Clause 1: The House of Representatives shall be composed of Members chosen every second Year by the People of the several States, and the Electors in each State shall have the Qualifications requisite for Electors of the most numerous Branch of the State Legislature.

Clause 2: No Person shall be a Representative who shall not have attained to the Age of twenty five Years, and been seven Years a Citizen of the United States, and who shall not, when elected, be an Inhabitant of that State in which he shall be chosen.

Clause 3: Representatives and direct Taxes shall be apportioned among the several States which may be included within this Union, according to their respective Numbers, which shall be determined by adding to the whole Number of free Persons, including those bound to Service for a Term of Years, and excluding Indians not taxed, three fifths of all other Persons. The actual Enumeration shall be made within three Years after the first Meeting of the Congress of the United States, and within every subsequent Term of ten Years, in such Manner as they shall by Law direct. The Number of Representatives shall not exceed one for every thirty Thousand, but each State shall have at Least one Representative; and until such enumeration shall be made, the State of New Hampshire shall be entitled to chuse three, Massachusetts eight, Rhode-Island and Providence Plantations one, Connecticut five, New-York six, New Jersey four, Pennsylvania eight, Delaware one, Maryland six, Virginia ten, North Carolina five, South Carolina five, and Georgia three.

Clause 4: When vacancies happen in the Representation from any State, the Executive Authority thereof shall issue Writs of Election to fill such Vacancies.

Clause 5: The House of Representatives shall chuse their Speaker and other Officers; and shall have the sole Power of Impeachment.

Section 3.

Clause 1: The Senate of the United States shall be composed of two Senators from each State, chosen by the Legislature thereof, for six Years; and each Senator shall have one Vote.

Clause 2: Immediately after they shall be assembled in Consequence of the first Election, they shall be divided as equally as may be into three Classes. The Seats of the Senators of the first Class shall be vacated at the Expiration of the second Year, of the second Class at the Expiration of the fourth Year, and of the third Class at the Expiration of the sixth Year, so that one third may be chosen every second Year; and if Vacancies happen by Resignation, or otherwise, during the Recess of the Legislature of any State, the Executive thereof may make temporary Appointments until the next Meeting of the Legislature, which shall then fill such Vacancies.

Clause 3: No Person shall be a Senator who shall not have attained to the Age of thirty Years, and been nine Years a Citizen of the United States, and who shall not, when elected, be an Inhabitant of that State for which he shall be chosen.

Clause 4: The Vice President of the United States shall be President of the Senate, but shall have no Vote, unless they be equally divided.

Clause 5: The Senate shall chuse their other Officers, and also a President pro tempore, in the Absence of the Vice President, or when he shall exercise the Office of President of the United States.

Clause 6: The Senate shall have the sole Power to try all Impeachments. When sitting for that Purpose, they shall be on Oath or Affirmation. When the President of the United States is tried, the Chief Justice shall preside: And no Person shall be convicted without the Concurrence of two thirds of the Members present.

Clause 7: Judgment in Cases of Impeachment shall not extend further than to removal from Office, and disqualification to hold and enjoy any Office of honor, Trust or Profit under the United States: but the Party convicted shall nevertheless be liable and subject to Indictment, Trial, Judgment and Punishment, according to Law.

Section 4.

Clause 1: The Times, Places and Manner of holding Elections for Senators and Representatives, shall be prescribed in each State by the Legislature thereof; but the Congress may at any time by Law make or alter such Regulations, except as to the Places of chusing Senators.

Clause 2: The Congress shall assemble at least once in every Year, and such Meeting shall be on the first Monday in December, unless they shall by Law appoint a different Day.

Section 5.

Clause 1: Each House shall be the Judge of the Elections, Returns and Qualifications of its own Members, and a Majority of each shall constitute a Quorum to do Business; but a smaller Number may adjourn from day to day, and may be authorized to compel the Attendance of absent Members, in such Manner, and under such Penalties as each House may provide.

Clause 2: Each House may determine the Rules of its Proceedings, punish its Members for disorderly Behaviour, and, with the Concurrence of two thirds, expel a Member.

Clause 3: Each House shall keep a Journal of its Proceedings, and from time to time publish the same, excepting such Parts as may in their Judgment require Secrecy; and the Yeas and Nays of the Members of either House on any question shall, at the Desire of one fifth of those Present, be entered on the Journal.

Clause 4: Neither House, during the Session of Congress, shall, without the Consent of the other, adjourn for more than three days, nor to any other Place than that in which the two Houses shall be sitting.

Section 6.

Clause 1: The Senators and Representatives shall receive a Compensation for their Services, to be ascertained by Law, and paid out of the Treasury of the United States. They shall in all Cases, except Treason, Felony and Breach of the Peace, be privileged from Arrest during their Attendance at the Session of their respective Houses, and in going to and returning from the same; and for any Speech or Debate in either House, they shall not be questioned in any other Place.

Clause 2: No Senator or Representative shall, during the Time for which he was elected, be appointed to any civil Office under the Authority of the United States, which shall have been created, or the Emoluments whereof shall have been encreased during such time; and no Person holding any Office under the United States, shall be a Member of either House during his Continuance in Office.

Section 7.

Clause 1: All Bills for raising Revenue shall originate in the House of Representatives; but the Senate may propose or concur with Amendments as on other Bills.

Clause 2: Every Bill which shall have passed the House of Representatives and the Senate, shall, before it become a Law, be presented to the President of the United States; If he approves he shall sign it, but if not he shall return it, with his Objections to that House in which it shall have originated, who shall enter the Objections at large on their Journal, and proceed to reconsider it. If after such Reconsideration two thirds of that House shall agree to pass the Bill, it shall be sent, together with the Objections, to the other House, by which it shall likewise be reconsidered, and if approved by two thirds of that House, it shall become a Law. But in all such Cases the Votes of both Houses shall be determined by yeas and Nays, and the Names of the Persons voting for and against the Bill shall be entered on the Journal of each House respectively. If any Bill shall not be returned by the President within ten Days (Sundays excepted) after it shall have been presented to him, the Same shall be a Law, in like Manner as if he had signed it, unless the Congress by their Adjournment prevent its Return, in which Case it shall not be a Law.

Clause 3: Every Order, Resolution, or Vote to which the Concurrence of the Senate and House of Representatives may be necessary (except on a question of Adjournment) shall be presented to the President of the United States; and before the Same shall take Effect, shall be approved by him, or being disapproved by him, shall be repassed by two thirds of the Senate and House of Representatives, according to the Rules and Limitations prescribed in the Case of a Bill.

Section 8.

Clause 1: The Congress shall have Power To lay and collect Taxes, Duties, Imposts and Excises, to pay the Debts and provide for the common Defence and general Welfare of the United States; but all Duties, Imposts and Excises shall be uniform throughout the United States;

Clause 2: To borrow Money on the credit of the United States;

Clause 3: To regulate Commerce with foreign Nations, and among the several States, and with the Indian Tribes;

Clause 4: To establish an uniform Rule of Naturalization, and uniform Laws on the subject of Bankruptcies throughout the United States;

Clause 5: To coin Money, regulate the Value thereof, and of foreign Coin, and fix the Standard of Weights and Measures;

Clause 6: To provide for the Punishment of counterfeiting the Securities and current Coin of the United States;

Clause 7: To establish Post Offices and post Roads;

Clause 8: To promote the Progress of Science and useful Arts, by securing for limited Times to Authors and Inventors the exclusive Right to their respective Writings and Discoveries;

Clause 9: To constitute Tribunals inferior to the supreme Court;

Clause 10: To define and punish Piracies and Felonies committed on the high Seas, and Offenses against the Law of Nations;

Clause 11: To declare War, grant Letters of Marque and Reprisal, and make Rules concerning Captures on Land and Water;

Clause 12: To raise and support Armies, but no Appropriation of Money to that Use shall be for a longer Term than two Years;

Clause 13: To provide and maintain a Navy;

Clause 14: To make Rules for the Government and Regulation of the land and naval Forces;

Clause 15: To provide for calling forth the Militia to execute the Laws of the Union, suppress Insurrections and repel Invasions;

Clause 16: To provide for organizing, arming, and disciplining, the Militia, and for governing such Part of them as may be employed in the Service of the United States, reserving to the States respectively, the Appointment of the Officers, and the Authority of training the Militia according to the discipline prescribed by Congress;

Clause 17: To exercise exclusive Legislation in all Cases whatsoever, over such District (not exceeding ten Miles square) as may, by Cession of particular States, and the Acceptance of Congress, become the Seat of the Government of the United States, and to exercise like Authority over all Places purchased by the Consent of the Legislature of the State in which the Same shall be, for the Erection of Forts, Magazines, Arsenals, dock-Yards, and other needful Buildings;—And

Clause 18: To make all Laws which shall be necessary and proper for carrying into Execution the foregoing Powers, and all other Powers vested by this Constitution in the Government of the United States, or in any Department or Officer thereof.

Section 9.

Clause 1: The Migration or Importation of such Persons as any of the States now existing shall think proper to admit, shall not be prohibited by the Congress prior to the Year one thousand eight hundred and eight, but a Tax or duty may be imposed on such Importation, not exceeding ten dollars for each Person.

Clause 2: The Privilege of the Writ of Habeas Corpus shall not be suspended, unless when in Cases of Rebellion or Invasion the public Safety may require it.

Clause 3: No Bill of Attainder or ex post facto Law shall be passed.

Clause 4: No Capitation, or other direct, Tax shall be laid, unless in Proportion to the Census or Enumeration herein before directed to be taken.

Clause 5: No Tax or Duty shall be laid on Articles exported from any State.

Clause 6: No Preference shall be given by any Regulation of Commerce or Revenue to the Ports of one State over those of another: nor shall Vessels bound to, or from, one State, be obliged to enter, clear, or pay Duties in another.

Clause 7: No Money shall be drawn from the Treasury, but in Consequence of Appropriations made by Law; and a regular Statement and Account of the Receipts and Expenditures of all public Money shall be published from time to time.

Clause 8: No Title of Nobility shall be granted by the United States: And no Person holding any Office of Profit or Trust under them, shall, without the Consent of the Congress, accept of any present, Emolument, Office, or Title, of any kind whatever, from any King, Prince, or foreign State.

Section 10.

Clause 1: No State shall enter into any Treaty, Alliance, or Confederation; grant Letters of Marque and Reprisal; coin Money; emit Bills of Credit; make any Thing but gold and silver Coin a Tender in Payment of Debts; pass any Bill of Attainder, ex post facto Law, or Law impairing the Obligation of Contracts, or grant any Title of Nobility.

Clause 2: No State shall, without the Consent of the Congress, lay any Imposts or Duties on Imports or Exports, except what may be absolutely necessary for executing it's inspection Laws: and the net Produce of all Duties and Imposts, laid by any State on Imports or Exports, shall be for the Use of the Treasury of the United States; and all such Laws shall be subject to the Revision and Controul of the Congress.

Clause 3: No State shall, without the Consent of Congress, lay any Duty of Tonnage, keep Troops, or Ships of War in time of Peace, enter into any Agreement or Compact with another State, or with a foreign Power, or engage in War, unless actually invaded, or in such imminent Danger as will not admit of delay.

Article II.

Section 1.

Clause 1: The executive Power shall be vested in a President of the United States of America. He shall hold his Office during the Term of four Years, and, together with the Vice President, chosen for the same Term, be elected, as follows:

Clause 2: Each State shall appoint, in such Manner as the Legislature thereof may direct, a Number of Electors, equal to the whole Number of Senators and Representatives to which the State may be entitled in the Congress: but no Senator or Representative, or Person holding an Office of Trust or Profit under the United States, shall be appointed an Elector.

The Electors shall meet in their respective States, and vote by Ballot for two Persons, of whom one at least shall not be an Inhabitant of the same State with themselves. And they shall make a List of all the Persons voted for, and of the Number of Votes for each; which List they shall sign and certify, and transmit sealed to the Seat of the Government of the United States, directed to the President of the Senate. The President of the Senate shall, in the Presence of the Senate and House of Representatives, open all the Certificates, and the Votes shall then be counted. The Person having the greatest Number of Votes shall be the President, if such Number be a Majority of the whole Number of Electors appointed; and if there be more than one who have such Majority, and have an equal Number of Votes, then the House of Representatives shall immediately chuse by Ballot one of them for President; and if no Person have a Majority, then from the five highest on the List the said House shall in like Manner chuse the President. But in chusing the President, the Votes shall be taken by States, the Representation from each State having one Vote; A quorum for this Purpose shall consist of a Member or Members from two thirds of the States, and a Majority of all the States shall be necessary to a Choice. In every Case, after the Choice of the President, the Person having the greatest Number of Votes of the Electors shall be the Vice President. But if there should remain two or more who have equal Votes, the Senate shall chuse from them by Ballot the Vice President.

Clause 3: The Congress may determine the Time of chusing the Electors, and the Day on which they shall give their Votes; which Day shall be the same throughout the United States.

Clause 4: No Person except a natural born Citizen, or a Citizen of the United States, at the time of the Adoption of this Constitution, shall be eligible to the Office of President; neither shall any Person be eligible to that Office who shall not have attained to the Age of thirty five Years, and been fourteen Years a Resident within the United States.

Clause 5: In Case of the Removal of the President from Office, or of his Death, Resignation, or Inability to discharge the Powers and Duties of the said Office, the Same shall devolve on the Vice President, and the Congress may by Law provide for the Case of Removal,

Death, Resignation or Inability, both of the President and Vice President, declaring what Officer shall then act as President, and such Officer shall act accordingly, until the Disability be removed, or a President shall be elected.

Clause 6: The President shall, at stated Times, receive for his Services, a Compensation, which shall neither be encreased nor diminished during the Period for which he shall have been elected, and he shall not receive within that Period any other Emolument from the United States, or any of them.

Clause 7: Before he enter on the Execution of his Office, he shall take the following Oath or Affirmation:—"I do solemnly swear (or affirm) that I will faithfully execute the Office of President of the United States, and will to the best of my Ability, preserve, protect and defend the Constitution of the United States."

Section 2.

Clause 1: The President shall be Commander in Chief of the Army and Navy of the United States, and of the Militia of the several States, when called into the actual Service of the United States; he may require the Opinion, in writing, of the principal Officer in each of the executive Departments, upon any Subject relating to the Duties of their respective Offices, and he shall have Power to grant Reprieves and Pardons for Offenses against the United States, except in Cases of Impeachment.

Clause 2: He shall have Power, by and with the Advice and Consent of the Senate, to make Treaties, provided two thirds of the Senators present concur; and he shall nominate, and by and with the Advice and Consent of the Senate, shall appoint Ambassadors, other public Ministers and Consuls, Judges of the supreme Court, and all other Officers of the United States, whose Appointments are not herein otherwise provided for, and which shall be established by Law: but the Congress may by Law vest the Appointment of such inferior Officers, as they think proper, in the President alone, in the Courts of Law, or in the Heads of Departments.

Clause 3: The President shall have Power to fill up all Vacancies that may happen during the Recess of the Senate, by granting Commissions which shall expire at the End of their next Session.

Section 3.

He shall from time to time give to the Congress Information of the State of the Union, and recommend to their Consideration such Measures as he shall judge necessary and expedient; he may, on extraordinary Occasions, convene both Houses, or either of them, and in Case of Disagreement between them, with Respect to the Time of Adjournment, he may adjourn them to such Time as he shall think proper; he shall receive Ambassadors and other public Ministers; he shall take Care that the Laws be faithfully executed, and shall Commission all the Officers of the United States.

Section 4.

The President, Vice President and all civil Officers of the United States, shall be removed from Office on Impeachment for, and Conviction of, Treason, Bribery, or other high Crimes and Misdemeanors.

Article III.

Section 1.

The judicial Power of the United States, shall be vested in one supreme Court, and in such inferior Courts as the Congress may from time to time ordain and establish. The Judges, both of the supreme and inferior Courts, shall hold their Offices during good Behaviour, and shall, at stated Times, receive for their Services, a Compensation, which shall not be diminished during their Continuance in Office.

Section 2.

Clause 1: The judicial Power shall extend to all Cases, in Law and Equity, arising under this Constitution, the Laws of the United States, and Treaties made, or which shall be made, under their Authority;—to all Cases affecting Ambassadors, other public Ministers and Consuls;—to all Cases of admiralty and maritime Jurisdiction;—to Controversies to which the United States shall be a Party;—to Controversies between two or more States;—between a State and Citizens of another State;—between Citizens of different States,—between Citizens of the same State claiming Lands under Grants of different States, and between a State, or the Citizens thereof, and foreign States, Citizens or Subjects.

Clause 2: In all Cases affecting Ambassadors, other public Ministers and Consuls, and those in which a State shall be Party, the supreme Court shall have original Jurisdiction. In all the other Cases before mentioned, the supreme Court shall have appellate Jurisdiction, both as to Law and Fact, with such Exceptions, and under such Regulations as the Congress shall make.

Clause 3: The Trial of all Crimes, except in Cases of Impeachment, shall be by Jury; and such Trial shall be held in the State where the said Crimes shall have been committed; but when not committed within any State, the Trial shall be at such Place or Places as the Congress may by Law have directed.

Section 3.

Clause 1: Treason against the United States, shall consist only in levying War against them, or in adhering to their Enemies, giving them Aid and Comfort. No Person shall be convicted of Treason unless on the Testimony of two Witnesses to the same overt Act, or on Confession in open Court.

Clause 2: The Congress shall have Power to declare the Punishment of Treason, but no Attainder of Treason shall work Corruption of Blood, or Forfeiture except during the Life of the Person attainted.

Article IV.

Section 1.

Full Faith and Credit shall be given in each State to the public Acts, Records, and judicial Proceedings of every other State. And the Congress may by general Laws prescribe the Manner in which such Acts, Records and Proceedings shall be proved, and the Effect thereof.

Section 2.

Clause 1: The Citizens of each State shall be entitled to all Privileges and Immunities of Citizens in the several States.

Clause 2: A Person charged in any State with Treason, Felony, or other Crime, who shall flee from Justice, and be found in another State, shall on Demand of the executive Authority of the State from which he fled, be delivered up, to be removed to the State having Jurisdiction of the Crime.

Clause 3: No Person held to Service or Labour in one State, under the Laws thereof, escaping into another, shall, in Consequence of any Law or Regulation therein, be discharged from such Service or Labour, but shall be delivered up on Claim of the Party to whom such Service or Labour may be due.

Section 3.

Clause 1: New States may be admitted by the Congress into this Union; but no new State shall be formed or erected within the Jurisdiction of any other State; nor any State be formed by the Junction of two or more States, or Parts of States, without the Consent of the Legislatures of the States concerned as well as of the Congress.

Clause 2: The Congress shall have Power to dispose of and make all needful Rules and Regulations respecting the Territory or other Property belonging to the United States; and nothing in this Constitution shall be so construed as to Prejudice any Claims of the United States, or of any particular State.

Section 4.

The United States shall guarantee to every State in this Union a Republican Form of Government, and shall protect each of them against Invasion; and on Application of the Legislature, or of the Executive (when the Legislature cannot be convened) against domestic Violence.

Article V.

The Congress, whenever two thirds of both Houses shall deem it necessary, shall propose Amendments to this Constitution, or, on the Application of the Legislatures of two thirds of the several States, shall call a Convention for proposing Amendments, which, in either Case, shall be valid to all Intents and Purposes, as Part of this Constitution, when ratified by the Legislatures of three fourths of the several States, or by Conventions in three fourths thereof, as the one or the other Mode of Ratification may be proposed by the Congress; Provided that no Amendment which may be made prior to the Year One thousand eight hundred and eight shall in any Manner affect the first and fourth Clauses in the Ninth Section of the first Article; and that no State, without its Consent, shall be deprived of its equal Suffrage in the Senate.

Article VI.

Clause 1: All Debts contracted and Engagements entered into, before the Adoption of this Constitution, shall be as valid against the United States under this Constitution, as under the Confederation.

Clause 2: This Constitution, and the Laws of the United States which shall be made in Pursuance thereof; and all Treaties made, or which shall be made, under the Authority of the United States, shall be the supreme Law of the Land; and the Judges in every State shall be bound thereby, any Thing in the Constitution or Laws of any State to the Contrary notwithstanding.

Clause 3: The Senators and Representatives before mentioned, and the Members of the several State Legislatures, and all executive and judicial Officers, both of the United States and of the several States, shall be bound by Oath or Affirmation, to support this Constitution; but no religious Test shall ever be required as a Qualification to any Office or public Trust under the United States.

Article VII.

The Ratification of the Conventions of nine States, shall be sufficient for the Establishment of this Constitution between the States so ratifying the Same.

Done in Convention by the Unanimous Consent of the States present the Seventeenth Day of September in the Year of our Lord one thousand seven hundred and Eighty seven and of the Independence of the United States of America the Twelfth In witness whereof We have hereunto subscribed our Names,

GO WASHINGTON—Presidt. and deputy from Virginia

[Signed also by the deputies of twelve States.]

Delaware

Geo: Read
Gunning Bedford jun
John Dickinson
Richard Bassett
Jaco: Broom

Maryland

James McHenry
Dan of St Thos. Jenifer
Danl Carroll.

Virginia

John Blair—
James Madison Jr.

North Carolina

Wm Blount

Rich^d. Dobbs Spaight.
Hu Williamson

South Carolina

J. Rutledge
Charles Cotesworth Pinckney
Charles Pinckney
Pierce Butler.

Georgia

William Few
Abr Baldwin

New Hampshire

John Langdon
Nicholas Gilman

Massachusetts

Nathaniel Gorham
Rufus King

Connecticut

W^m. Saml. Johnson
Roger Sherman

New York

Alexander Hamilton

New Jersey

Wil: Livingston
David Brearley.
W^m. Paterson.
Jona: Dayton

Pennsylvania

B Franklin
Thomas Mifflin
Robt Morris
Geo. Clymer
Thos. FitzSimons
Jared Ingersoll
James Wilson.
Gouv Morris

Attest William Jackson Secretary

Congress of the United States

begun and held at the City of New-York, on Wednesday the fourth of March, one thousand seven hundred and eighty nine.

THE Conventions of a number of the States, having at the time of their adopting the Constitution, expressed a desire, in order to prevent misconstruction or abuse of its powers, that further declaratory and restrictive clauses should be added: And as extending the ground of public confidence in the Government, will best ensure the beneficent ends of its institution.

RESOLVED by the Senate and House of Representatives of the United States of America, in Congress assembled, two thirds of both Houses concurring, that the following Articles be proposed to the Legislatures of the several States, as amendments to the Constitution of the United States, all, or any of which Articles, when ratified by three fourths of the said Legislatures, to be valid to all intents and purposes, as part of the said Constitution; viz.

ARTICLES in addition to, and Amendment of the Constitution of the United States of America, proposed by Congress, and ratified by the Legislatures of the several States, pursuant to the fifth Article of the original Constitution.

Amendment I

Congress shall make no law respecting an establishment of religion, or prohibiting the free exercise thereof; or abridging the freedom of speech, or of the press; or the right of the people peaceably to assemble, and to petition the Government for a redress of grievances.

Amendment II

A well regulated Militia, being necessary to the security of a free State, the right of the people to keep and bear Arms, shall not be infringed.

Amendment III

No Soldier shall, in time of peace be quartered in any house, without the consent of the Owner, nor in time of war, but in a manner to be prescribed by law.

Amendment IV

The right of the people to be secure in their persons, houses, papers, and effects, against unreasonable searches and seizures, shall not be violated, and no Warrants shall issue, but upon probable cause, supported by Oath or affirmation, and particularly describing the place to be searched, and the persons or things to be seized.

Amendment V

No person shall be held to answer for a capital, or otherwise infamous crime, unless on a presentment or indictment of a Grand Jury, except in cases arising in the land or naval forces, or in the Militia, when in actual service in time of War or public danger; nor shall any person be subject for the same offence to be twice put in jeopardy of life or limb; nor shall be compelled in any criminal case to be a witness against himself, nor be deprived of life, liberty, or property, without due process of law; nor shall private property be taken for public use, without just compensation.

Amendment VI

In all criminal prosecutions, the accused shall enjoy the right to a speedy and public trial, by an impartial jury of the State and district wherein the crime shall have been committed, which district shall have been previously ascertained by law, and to be informed of the nature and cause of the accusation; to be confronted with the witnesses against him; to have compulsory process for obtaining witnesses in his favor, and to have the Assistance of Counsel for his defence.

Amendment VII

In Suits at common law, where the value in controversy shall exceed twenty dollars, the right of trial by jury shall be preserved, and no fact tried by a jury, shall be otherwise re-examined in any Court of the United States, than according to the rules of the common law.

Amendment VIII

Excessive bail shall not be required, nor excessive fines imposed, nor cruel and unusual punishments inflicted.

Amendment IX

The enumeration in the Constitution, of certain rights, shall not be construed to deny or disparage others retained by the people.

Amendment X

The powers not delegated to the United States by the Constitution, nor prohibited by it to the States, are reserved to the States respectively, or to the people.

Amendment XI

[Passed by Congress March 4, 1794. Ratified February 7, 1795.
     Note: Article III, section 2, of the Constitution was modified by the Eleventh Amendment.]

The Judicial power of the United States shall not be construed to extend to any suit in law or equity, commenced or prosecuted against one of the United States by Citizens of another State, or by Citizens or Subjects of any Foreign State.

Amendment XII

[Passed by Congress December 9, 1803. Ratified June 15, 1804.
     Note: A portion of Article II, section 1, of the Constitution was superseded by the Twelfth Amendment.]

The Electors shall meet in their respective states and vote by ballot for President and Vice-President, one of whom, at least, shall not be an inhabitant of the same state with themselves; they shall name in their ballots the person voted for as President, and in distinct ballots the person voted for as Vice-President, and they shall make distinct lists of all persons voted for as President, and of all persons voted for as Vice-President, and of the number of votes for each, which lists they shall sign and certify, and transmit sealed to the seat of the government of the United States, directed to the President of the Senate;—the President of the Senate shall, in the presence of the Senate and House of Representatives, open all the certificates and the votes shall then be counted;—The person having the greatest number of votes for President, shall be the President, if such number be a majority of the whole number of Electors appointed; and if no person have such majority, then from the persons having the highest numbers not exceeding three on the list of those voted for as President, the House of Representatives shall choose immediately, by ballot, the President. But in choosing the President, the votes shall be taken by states, the representation from each state having one vote; a quorum for this purpose shall consist of a member or members from two-thirds of the states, and a majority of all the states shall be necessary to a choice. [And if the House of Representatives shall not choose a President whenever the right of choice shall devolve upon them, before the fourth day of March next following, then the Vice-President shall act as President, as in case of the death or other constitutional disability of the President.—]* The person having the greatest number of votes as Vice-President, shall be the Vice-President, if such number be a majority of the whole number of Electors appointed, and if no person have a majority, then from the two highest numbers on the list, the Senate shall choose the Vice-President; a quorum for the purpose shall consist of two-thirds of the whole number of Senators, and a majority of the whole number shall be necessary to a choice. But no person constitutionally ineligible to the office of President shall be eligible to that of Vice-President of the United States.

*Superseded by section 3 of the Twentieth Amendment.

Amendment XIII

[Passed by Congress January 31, 1865. Ratified December 6, 1865.

Note: A portion of Article IV, section 2, of the Constitution was superseded by the Thirteenth Amendment.]

Section 1.

Neither slavery nor involuntary servitude, except as a punishment for crime whereof the party shall have been duly convicted, shall exist within the United States, or any place subject to their jurisdiction.

Section 2.

Congress shall have power to enforce this article by appropriate legislation.

Amendment XIV

[Passed by Congress June 13, 1866. Ratified July 9, 1868.

Note: Article I, section 2, of the Constitution was modified by section 2 of the Fourteenth Amendment.]

Section 1.

All persons born or naturalized in the United States, and subject to the jurisdiction thereof, are citizens of the United States and of the State wherein they reside. No State shall make or enforce any law which shall abridge the privileges or immunities of citizens of the United States; nor shall any State deprive any person of life, liberty, or property, without due process of law; nor deny to any person within its jurisdiction the equal protection of the laws.

Section 2.

Representatives shall be apportioned among the several States according to their respective numbers, counting the whole number of persons in each State, excluding Indians not taxed. But when the right to vote at any election for the choice of electors for President and Vice-President of the United States, Representatives in Congress, the Executive and Judicial officers of a State, or the members of the Legislature thereof, is denied to any of the male inhabitants of such State, being twenty-one years of age,* and citizens of the United States, or in any way abridged, except for participation in rebellion, or other crime, the basis of representation therein shall be reduced in the proportion which the number of such male citizens shall bear to the whole number of male citizens twenty-one years of age in such State.

Section 3.

No person shall be a Senator or Representative in Congress, or elector of President and Vice-President, or hold any office, civil or military, under the United States, or under any State, who, having previously taken an oath, as a member of Congress, or as an officer of the United States, or as a member of any State legislature, or as an executive or judicial officer of any State, to support the Constitution of the United States, shall have engaged in insurrection or rebellion against the same, or given aid or comfort to the enemies thereof. But Congress may by a vote of two-thirds of each House, remove such disability.

Section 4.

The validity of the public debt of the United States, authorized by law, including debts incurred for payment of pensions and bounties for services in suppressing insurrection or rebellion, shall not be questioned. But neither the United States nor any State shall assume or pay any debt or obligation incurred in aid of insurrection or rebellion against the United States, or any claim for the loss or emancipation of any slave; but all such debts, obligations and claims shall be held illegal and void.

Section 5.

The Congress shall have the power to enforce, by appropriate legislation, the provisions of this article.

*Changed by section 1 of the Twenty-sixth Amendment.

Amendment XV

[Passed by Congress February 26, 1869. Ratified February 3, 1870.]

Section 1.

The right of citizens of the United States to vote shall not be denied or abridged by the United States or by any State on account of race, color, or previous condition of servitude—

Section 2.

The Congress shall have the power to enforce this article by appropriate legislation.

Amendment XVI

[Passed by Congress July 2, 1909. Ratified February 3, 1913.
    Note: Article I, section 9, of the Constitution was modified by the Sixteenth Amendment.]

The Congress shall have power to lay and collect taxes on incomes, from whatever source derived, without apportionment among the several States, and without regard to any census or enumeration.

Amendment XVII

[Passed by Congress May 13, 1912. Ratified April 8, 1913.
    Note: Article I, section 3, of the Constitution was modified by the Seventeenth Amendment.]

The Senate of the United States shall be composed of two Senators from each State, elected by the people thereof, for six years; and each Senator shall have one vote. The electors in each State shall have the qualifications requisite for electors of the most numerous branch of the State legislatures.

When vacancies happen in the representation of any State in the Senate, the executive authority of such State shall issue writs of election to fill such vacancies: *Provided*, That the legislature of any State may empower the executive thereof to make temporary appointments until the people fill the vacancies by election as the legislature may direct.

This amendment shall not be so construed as to affect the election or term of any Senator chosen before it becomes valid as part of the Constitution.

Amendment XVIII

[Passed by Congress December 18, 1917. Ratified January 16, 1919. Repealed by the Twenty-first Amendment.]

Section 1.

After one year from the ratification of this article the manufacture, sale, or transportation of intoxicating liquors within, the importation thereof into, or the exportation thereof from the United States and all territory subject to the jurisdiction thereof for beverage purposes is hereby prohibited.

Section 2.

The Congress and the several States shall have concurrent power to enforce this article by appropriate legislation.

Section 3.

This article shall be inoperative unless it shall have been ratified as an amendment to the Constitution by the legislatures of the several States, as provided in the Constitution, within seven years from the date of the submission hereof to the States by the Congress.

Amendment XIX

[Passed by Congress June 4, 1919. Ratified August 18, 1920.]

The right of citizens of the United States to vote shall not be denied or abridged by the United States or by any State on account of sex.

Congress shall have power to enforce this article by appropriate legislation.

Amendment XX

[Passed by Congress March 2, 1932. Ratified January 23, 1933.
   Note: Article I, section 4, of the Constitution was modified by section 2 of the Twentieth Amendment. In addition, a portion of the Twelfth Amendment was superseded by section 3.]

Section 1.

The terms of the President and the Vice President shall end at noon on the 20th day of January, and the terms of Senators and Representatives at noon on the 3d day of January, of the years in which such terms would have ended if this article had not been ratified; and the terms of their successors shall then begin.

Section 2.

The Congress shall assemble at least once in every year, and such meeting shall begin at noon on the 3d day of January, unless they shall by law appoint a different day.

Section 3.

If, at the time fixed for the beginning of the term of the President, the President elect shall have died, the Vice President elect shall become President. If a President shall not have been chosen before the time fixed for the beginning of his term, or if the President elect shall have failed to qualify, then the Vice President elect shall act as President until a President shall have qualified; and the Congress may by law provide for the case wherein neither a President elect nor a Vice President shall have qualified, declaring who shall then act as President, or the manner in which one who is to act shall be selected, and such person shall act accordingly until a President or Vice President shall have qualified.

Section 4.

The Congress may by law provide for the case of the death of any of the persons from whom the House of Representatives may choose a President whenever the right of choice shall have devolved upon them, and for the case of the death of any of the persons from whom the Senate may choose a Vice President whenever the right of choice shall have devolved upon them.

Section 5.

Sections 1 and 2 shall take effect on the 15th day of October following the ratification of this article.

Section 6.

This article shall be inoperative unless it shall have been ratified as an amendment to the Constitution by the legislatures of three-fourths of the several States within seven years from the date of its submission.

Amendment XXI

[Passed by Congress February 20, 1933. Ratified December 5, 1933.]

Section 1.

The eighteenth article of amendment to the Constitution of the United States is hereby repealed.

Section 2.

The transportation or importation into any State, Territory, or Possession of the United States for delivery or use therein of intoxicating liquors, in violation of the laws thereof, is hereby prohibited.

Section 3.

This article shall be inoperative unless it shall have been ratified as an amendment to the Constitution by conventions in the several States, as provided in the Constitution, within seven years from the date of the submission hereof to the States by the Congress.

Amendment XXII

[Passed by Congress March 21, 1947. Ratified February 27, 1951.]

Section 1.

No person shall be elected to the office of the President more than twice, and no person who has held the office of President, or acted as President, for more than two years of a term to which some other person was elected President shall be elected to the office of President more than once. But this Article shall not apply to any person holding the office of President when this Article was proposed by Congress, and shall not prevent any person who may be holding the office of President, or acting as President, during the term within which this Article becomes operative from holding the office of President or acting as President during the remainder of such term.

Section 2.

This article shall be inoperative unless it shall have been ratified as an amendment to the Constitution by the legislatures of three-fourths of the several States within seven years from the date of its submission to the States by the Congress.

Amendment XXIII

[Passed by Congress June 16, 1960. Ratified March 29, 1961.]

Section 1.

The District constituting the seat of Government of the United States shall appoint in such manner as Congress may direct:

A number of electors of President and Vice President equal to the whole number of Senators and Representatives in Congress to which the District would be entitled if it were a State, but in no event more than the least populous State; they shall be in addition to those appointed by the States, but they shall be considered, for the purposes of the election of President and Vice President, to be electors appointed by a State; and they shall meet in the District and perform such duties as provided by the twelfth article of amendment.

Section 2.

The Congress shall have power to enforce this article by appropriate legislation.

Amendment XXIV

[Passed by Congress August 27, 1962. Ratified January 23, 1964.]

Section 1.

The right of citizens of the United States to vote in any primary or other election for President or Vice President, for electors for President or Vice President, or for Senator or Representative in Congress, shall not be denied or abridged by the United States or any State by reason of failure to pay poll tax or other tax.

Section 2.

The Congress shall have power to enforce this article by appropriate legislation.

Amendment XXV

[Passed by Congress July 6, 1965. Ratified February 10, 1967.

Note: Article II, section 1, of the Constitution was affected by the Twenty-fifth Amendment.]

Section 1.

In case of the removal of the President from office or of his death or resignation, the Vice President shall become President.

Section 2.

Whenever there is a vacancy in the office of the Vice President, the President shall nominate a Vice President who shall take office upon confirmation by a majority vote of both Houses of Congress.

Section 3.

Whenever the President transmits to the President pro tempore of the Senate and the Speaker of the House of Representatives his written declaration that he is unable to discharge the powers and duties of his office, and until he transmits to them a written declaration to the contrary, such powers and duties shall be discharged by the Vice President as Acting President.

Section 4.

Whenever the Vice President and a majority of either the principal officers of the executive departments or of such other body as Congress may by law provide, transmit to the President pro tempore of the Senate and the Speaker of the House of Representatives their written declaration that the President is unable to discharge the powers and duties of his office, the Vice President shall immediately assume the powers and duties of the office as Acting President.

Thereafter, when the President transmits to the President pro tempore of the Senate and the Speaker of the House of Representatives his written declaration that no inability exists, he shall resume the powers and duties of his office unless the Vice President and a majority of either the principal officers of the executive department or of such other body as Congress may by law provide, transmit within four days to the President pro tempore of the Senate and the Speaker of the House of Representatives their written declaration that the President is unable to discharge the powers and duties of his office. Thereupon Congress shall decide the issue, assembling within forty-eight hours for that purpose if not in session. If the Congress, within twenty-one days after receipt of the latter written declaration, or, if Congress is not in session, within twenty-one days after Congress is required to assemble, determines by two-thirds vote of both Houses that the President is unable to discharge the powers and duties of his office, the Vice President shall continue to discharge the same as Acting President; otherwise, the President shall resume the powers and duties of his office.

Amendment XXVI

[Passed by Congress March 23, 1971. Ratified July 1, 1971.
    Note: Amendment 14, section 2, of the Constitution was modified by section 1 of the Twenty-sixth Amendment.]

Section 1.

The right of citizens of the United States, who are eighteen years of age or older, to vote shall not be denied or abridged by the United States or by any State on account of age.

Section 2.

The Congress shall have power to enforce this article by appropriate legislation.

Amendment XXVII

[Originally proposed September 25, 1789. Ratified May 7, 1992.]

No law, varying the compensation for the services of the Senators and Representatives, shall take effect, until an election of representatives shall have intervened.

George Washington's Farewell Address

Friends, And Fellow Citizens

The period for a new election of a citizen to administer the executive government of the United States, being not far distant, and the time actually arrived when your thoughts must be employed in designating the person who is to be clothed with that important trust, it appears to me proper, especially as it may conduce to a more distinct expression of the public voice, that I should now apprise you of the resolution I have formed, to decline being considered among the number of those out of whom a choice is to be made.

I beg you, at the same time, to do me the justice to be assured that this resolution has not been taken without a strict regard to all the considerations appertaining to the relation which binds a dutiful citizen to his country; and that, in withdrawing the tender of service which silence in my situation might imply, I am influenced by no diminution of zeal for your future interest; no deficiency of grateful respect for your past kindness; but am supported by a full conviction that the step is compatible with both.

The acceptance of, and continuance hitherto in, the office to which your suffrages have twice called me, have been a uniform sacrifice of inclination to the opinion of duty, and to a deference for what appeared to be your desire. I constantly hoped that it would have been much earlier in my power, consistently with motives which I was not at liberty to disregard, to return to that retirement from which I had been reluctantly drawn. The strength of my inclination to do this, previous to the last election, had even led to the preparation of an address to declare it to you; but mature reflection on the then perplexed and critical posture of our affairs with foreign nations, and the unanimous advice of persons entitled to my confidence, impelled me to abandon the idea.

I rejoice, that the state of your concerns, external as well as internal, no longer renders the pursuit of inclination incompatible with the sentiment of duty, or propriety; and am persuaded whatever partiality may be retained for my services, that, in the present circumstances of our country, you will not disapprove my determination to retire.

The impressions, with which, I first undertook the arduous trust, were explained on the proper occasion. In the discharge of this trust, I will only say that I have, with good intentions, contributed towards the organization and administration of the government the best exertions of which a very fallible judgment was capable. Not unconscious, in the outset, of the inferiority of my qualifications, experience in my own eyes, perhaps still more in the eyes of others, has strengthened the motives to diffidence of myself; and every day the increasing weight of years admonishes me more and more that the shade of retirement is as necessary to me as it will be welcome. Satisfied that, if any circumstances have given peculiar value to my services, they were temporary, I have the consolation to believe, that while choice and prudence invite me to quit the political scene, patriotism does not forbid it.

In looking forward to the moment, which is intended to terminate the career of my public life, my feelings do not permit me to suspend the deep acknowledgment of that debt of gratitude which I owe to my beloved country for the many honors it has conferred upon me; still more for the steadfast confidence with which it has supported me; and for the opportunities I have thence enjoyed of manifesting my inviolable attachment, by services faithful and persevering, though in usefulness unequal to my zeal. If benefits have resulted to our country from these services, let it always be remembered to your praise, and as an instructive example in our annals, that under circumstances in which the passions, agitated in every direction, were liable to mislead, amidst appearances sometimes dubious, vicissitudes of fortune often discouraging, in situations in which not unfrequently want of success has countenanced the spirit of criticism, the constancy of your support was the essential prop of the efforts, and a guarantee of the plans, by which they were effected. Profoundly penetrated with this idea, I shall carry it with me to my grave, as a strong incitement to unceasing vows that Heaven may continue to you the choicest tokens of its beneficence; that your union and brotherly affection may be perpetual; that the free constitution which is the work of your hands, may be sacredly maintained; that its administration in every department may be stamped with wisdom and virtue; that, in fine, the happiness of the people of these States, under the auspices of liberty, may be made complete, by so careful a preservation and so prudent a use of this blessing, as will acquire to them the glory of recommending it to the applause, the affection, and adoption of every nation which is yet a stranger to it.

Here, perhaps, I ought to stop. But a solicitude for your welfare which cannot end but with my life, and the apprehension of danger natural to that solicitude, urge me, on an occasion like the present, to offer to your solemn contemplation, and to recommend to your frequent review, some sentiments which are the result of much reflection, of no inconsiderable observation, and which appear to me all important to the permanency of your felicity as a people. These will be offered to you with the more freedom, as you can only see in them the disinterested warnings of a parting friend, who can possibly have no personal motive to bias his counsel. Nor can I forget, as an encouragement to it your indulgent reception of my sentiments on a former and not dissimilar occasion.

Interwoven as is the love of liberty with every ligament of your hearts, no recommendation of mine is necessary to fortify or confirm the attachment. The unity of government which constitutes you one people, is also now dear to you. It is justly so: for it is a main pillar in the edifice of your real independence, the support of your tranquility at home, your peace abroad; of your safety; of your prosperity; of that very liberty which you so highly prize. But as it is easy to foresee that, from different causes and from different quarters, much pains will be taken, many artifices employed, to weaken in your minds the conviction of this truth; as this is the point in your political fortress against which the batteries of internal and external enemies will be most constantly and actively (though often covertly and insidiously) directed, it is of infinite moment that you should properly estimate the immense value of your national Union to your collective and individual happiness; that you should cherish a cordial, habitual, and immoveable attachment to it; accustoming yourself to think and speak of it as of the palladium of your political safety and prosperity; watching for its preservation with jealous anxiety; discountenancing whatever may suggest even a suspicion that it can in any event be abandoned; and indignantly frowning upon the first dawning of every attempt to alienate any portion of our country from the rest, or to enfeeble the sacred ties which now link together the various parts.

For this you have every inducement of sympathy and interest. Citizens, by birth or choice, of a common country, that country has a right to concentrate your affections. The name of AMERICAN, which belongs to you in your national capacity, must always exalt the just pride of patriotism, more than any appellation derived from local discriminations. With slight shades of difference, you have the same religion, manners, habits and political principles. You have in a common cause fought and triumphed together; the independence and liberty you possess are the work of joint councils and joint efforts, of common dangers, sufferings, and successes.

But these considerations, however powerfully they address themselves to your sensibility, are greatly outweighed by those which apply more immediately to your interest. Here every portion of our country finds the most commanding motives for carefully guarding and preserving the union of the whole.

The North, in an unrestrained intercourse with the South, protected by the equal Laws of a common government, finds, in the productions of the latter, great additional resources of maritime and commercial enterprise and precious materials of manufacturing industry. The South in the same intercourse, benefitting by the agency of the North, sees its agriculture grow and its commerce expand. Turning partly into its own channels the seamen of the North, it finds its particular navigation invigorated; and while it contributes, in different ways, to nourish and increase the general mass of the national navigation, it looks forward to the protection of a maritime strength, to which itself is unequally adapted. The East, in a like intercourse with the West, already finds, and in the progressive improvement of interior communications, by land and water, will more and more find, a valuable vent for the commodities which it brings from abroad, or manufactures at home. The West derives from the East supplies requisite to its growth and comfort, and what is perhaps of still greater consequence, it must of necessity owe the secure enjoyment of indispensable outlets for its own productions to the weight, influence, and the future maritime strength of the Atlantic side of the Union, directed by an indissoluble community of interest as one Nation. Any other tenure by which the West can hold this essential advantage, whether derived from its own separate strength, or from an apostate and unnatural connection with any foreign power, must be intrinsically precarious.

While, then, every part of our country thus feels an immediate and particular interest in union, all the parts combined cannot fail to find in the united mass of means and efforts greater strength, greater resource, proportionably greater security from external danger, a less frequent interruption of their peace by foreign Nations; and, what is of inestimable value, they must derive from union an exemption from those broils and wars between themselves, which so frequently afflict neighboring countries not tied together by the same government, which their own rivalships alone would be sufficient to produce, but which opposite foreign alliances, attachments, and intrigues would stimulate and imbitter. Hence, likewise, they will avoid the necessity of those overgrown military establishments, which, under any form of government, are inauspicious to liberty, and which are to be regarded as particularly hostile to republican liberty. In this sense it is, that your Union ought to be considered as a main prop of your liberty, and that the love of the one ought to endear to you the preservation of the other.

These considerations speak a persuasive language to every reflecting and virtuous mind, and exhibit the continuance of the UNION as a primary object of patriotic desire. Is there a doubt whether a common government can embrace so large a sphere? Let experience solve it. To listen to mere speculation in such a case were criminal. We are authorized to hope that a proper organization of the whole, with the auxiliary agency of governments for the respective subdivisions, will afford a happy issue to the experiment. It is well worth a fair and full experiment. With such powerful and obvious motives to union, affecting all parts of our country, while experience shall not have demonstrated its impracticability, there will always be reason to distrust the patriotism of those who in any quarter may endeavor to weaken its bands.

In contemplating the causes which may disturb our Union, it occurs as matter of serious concern, that any ground should have been furnished for characterizing parties by geographical discriminations, Northern and Southern, Atlantic and Western; whence designing men may endeavor to excite a belief that there is a real difference of local interests and views. One of the expedients of party to acquire influence, within particular districts, is to misrepresent the opinions and aims of other districts. You cannot shield yourselves too much against the jealousies and heart burnings which spring from these misrepresentations; they tend to render alien to each other those who ought to be bound together by fraternal affection. The inhabitants of our western country have lately had a useful lesson on this head; they have seen, in the negotiation by the Executive, and in the unanimous ratification by the Senate, of the treaty with Spain, and in the universal satisfaction at that event, throughout the United States, a decisive proof how unfounded were the suspicions propagated among them of a policy in the general Government and in the Atlantic States unfriendly to their interests in regard to the Mississippi; they have been witnesses to the formation of two treaties, that with Great Britain, and that with Spain, which secure to them everything they could desire, in respect to our foreign relations, towards confirming their prosperity. Will it not be their wisdom to rely for the preservation of these advantaged on the UNION by which they were procured? Will they not henceforth be deaf to those advisers, if such there are, who would sever them from their brethren and connect them with aliens?

To the efficacy and permanency of your Union, a government for the whole is indispensable. No alliances, however strict, between the parts can be an adequate substitute; they must inevitably experience the infractions and interruptions which all alliances in all times have experienced. Sensible of this momentous truth, you have improved upon your first essay, by the adoption of a constitution of government better calculated than your former for an intimate union, and for the efficacious management of your common concerns. This government, the offspring of our own choice, uninfluenced and unawed, adopted upon full investigation and mature deliberation, completely free in its principles, in the distribution of its powers uniting security with energy, and containing within itself a provision for its own amendment, has a just claim to your confidence and your support. Respect for its authority, compliance with its laws, acquiescence in its measures, are duties enjoined by the fundamental maxims of true liberty. The basis of our political systems is the right of the people to make and to alter their constitutions of government. But the constitution which at any time exists, till changed by an explicit and authentic act of the whole people, is sacredly obligatory upon all. The very idea of the power and the right of the people to establish government presupposes the duty of every individual to obey the established government.

All obstructions to the execution of the Laws, all combinations and associations, under whatever plausible character, with the real design to direct, control counteract, or awe the regular deliberation and action of the constituted authorities are destructive of this fundamental principle and of fatal tendency. They serve to organize faction, to give it an artificial and extraordinary force; to put, in the place of the delegated will of the nation, the will of a party, often a small but artful and enterprising minority of the community; and, according to the alternate triumphs of different parties, to make the public administration the mirror of the illconcerted and incongruous projects of faction, rather than the organ of consistent and wholesome plans digested by common councils, and modified by mutual interests.

However combinations or associations of the above description may now and then answer popular ends, they are likely, in the course of time and things, to become potent engines, by which cunning, ambitious and unprincipled men will be enabled to subvert the power of the people, and to usurp for themselves the reins of Government; destroying afterwards the very engines which have lifted them to unjust dominion.

Towards the preservation of your Government and the permanency of your present happy state, it is requisite, not only that you steadily discountenance irregular oppositions to its acknowledged authority, but also that you resist with care the spirit of innovation upon its principles, however specious the pretexts. One method of assault may be to effect, in the forms of the constitution, alterations which will impair the energy of the system, and thus to undermine what cannot be directly overthrown. In all the changes to which you may be invited, remember that time and habit are at least as necessary to fix the true character of governments, as of other human institutions; that experience is the surest standard by which to test the real tendency of the existing constitution of a country; that facility in changes, upon the credit of mere hypotheses and opinion, exposes to perpetual change, from the endless variety of hypotheses and opinion; and remember, especially, that, for the efficient management of your common interests, in a country so extensive as ours, a government of as much vigor as is consistent with the perfect security of liberty is indispensable. Liberty itself will find in such a Government, with powers properly distributed and adjusted, its surest guardian. It is, indeed, little else than a name, where the government is too feeble to withstand the enterprise of faction, to confine each member of the society within the limits prescribed by the laws, and to maintain all in the secure and tranquil enjoyment of the rights of person and property.

I have already intimated to you the danger of parties in the state, with particular reference to the founding of them on geographical discriminations. Let me now take a more comprehensive view, and warn you in the most solemn manner against the baneful effects of the spirit of party, generally.

This spirit, unfortunately, is inseparable from our nature, having its root in the strongest passions of the human mind. It exists under different shapes in all governments, more or less stifled, controlled, or repressed; but in those of the popular form, it is seen in its greatest rankness, and is truly their worst enemy.

The alternate domination of one faction over another, sharpened by the spirit of revenge, natural to party dissention, which in different ages and countries has perpetrated the most horrid enormities, is itself a frightful despotism. But this leads at length to a more formal and permanent despotism. The disorders and miseries which result gradually incline the minds of men to seek security and repose in the absolute power of an individual, and sooner or later the chief of some prevailing faction, more able or more fortunate than his competitors, turns this disposition to the purposes of his own elevation, on the ruins of public liberty.

Without looking forward to an extremity of this kind (which nevertheless ought not to be entirely out of sight), the common and continual mischiefs of the spirit of party are sufficient to make it the interest and duty of a wise people to discourage and restrain it.

It serves always to distract the public councils, and enfeeble the public administration. It agitates the community with ill founded jealousies and false alarms; kindles the animosity of one part against another, foments occasionally riot and insurrection. It opens the door to foreign influence and corruption, which find a facilitated access to the government itself through the channels of party passions. Thus the policy and the will of one country, are subjected to the policy and will of another.

There is an opinion, that parties in free countries are useful checks upon the administration of the government and serve to keep alive the spirit of liberty. This within certain limits is probably true; and in governments of a monarchical cast, patriotism may look with indulgence, if not with favor, upon the spirit of party. But in those of the popular character, in governments purely elective, it is a spirit not to be encouraged. From their natural tendency, it is certain there will always be enough of that spirit for every salutary purpose. And there being constant danger of excess, the effort ought to be, by force of public opinion, to mitigate and assuage it. A fire not to be quenched, it demands a uniform vigilance to prevent its bursting into a flame, lest, instead of warming, it should consume.

It is important, likewise, that the habits of thinking in a free country should inspire caution, in those entrusted with its administration, to confine themselves within their respective constitutional spheres, avoiding in the exercise of the powers of one department to encroach upon another. The spirit of encroachment tends to consolidate the powers of all the departments in one, and thus to create, whatever the form of government, a real despotism. A just estimate of that love of power, and proneness to abuse it, which predominates in the human heart, is sufficient to satisfy us of the truth of this position. The necessity of reciprocal checks in the exercise of political power, by dividing and distributing it into different depositories, and constituting each the guardian of the public weal against invasions by the others, has been evinced by experiments ancient and modern; some of them in our country and under our own eyes. To preserve them must be as necessary as to institute them. If, in the opinion of the people, the distribution or modification of the constitutional powers be in any particular wrong, let it be corrected by an amendment in the way which the Constitution designates. But let there be no change by usurpation; for, though this, in one instance, may be the instrument of good, it is the customary weapon by which free governments are destroyed. The precedent must always greatly overbalance in permanent evil any partial or transient benefit which the use can at any time yield.

Of all the dispositions and habits which lead to political prosperity, religion and morality are indispensable supports. In vain would that man claim the tribute of patriotism, who should labor to subvert these great pillars of human happiness, these firmest props of the duties of men and citizens. The mere politician, equally with the pious man, ought to respect and to cherish them. A volume could not trace all their connections with private and public felicity. Let it simply be asked, Where is the security for property, for reputation, for life, if the sense of religious obligation desert the oaths which are the instruments of investigation in courts of justice? And let us with caution indulge the supposition that morality can be maintained without religion. Whatever may be conceded to the influence of refined education on minds of peculiar structure, reason and experience both forbid us to expect that national morality can prevail in exclusion of religious principle.

'Tis substantially true, that virtue or morality is a necessary spring of popular government. The rule, indeed, extends with more or less force to every species of free government. Who that is a sincere friend to it, can look with indifference upon attempts to shake the foundation of the fabric?

Promote, then, as an object of primary importance, institutions for the general diffusion of knowledge. In proportion as the structure of a government gives force to public opinion, it is essential that public opinion should be enlightened.

As a very important source of strength and security, cherish public credit. One method of preserving it is to use it as sparingly as possible; avoiding occasions of expense by cultivating peace, but remembering also that timely disbursements to prepare for danger frequently prevent much greater disbursements to repel it; avoiding likewise the accumulation of debt, not only by shunning occasions of expense, but by vigorous exertions in time of peace to discharge the debts which unavoidable wars may have occasioned, not ungenerously throwing upon posterity the burden which we ourselves ought to bear. The execution of these maxims belongs to your representatives, but it is necessary that public opinion should cooperate. To facilitate to them the performance of their duty, it is essential that you should practically bear in mind, that towards the payment of debts there must be revenue; that to have revenue there must be taxes; that no taxes can be devised which are not more or less inconvenient and unpleasant; that the intrinsic embarrassment inseparable from the selection of the proper objects (which is always a choice of difficulties), ought to be a decisive motive for a candid construction of the conduct of the government in making it, and for a spirit of acquiescence in the measures for obtaining revenue which the public exigencies may at any time dictate.

Observe good faith and justice towards all nations; cultivate peace and harmony with all. Religion and morality enjoin this conduct; and can it be, that good policy does not equally enjoin it? It will be worthy of a free, enlightened, and, at no distant period, a great nation, to give to mankind the magnanimous and too novel example of a people always guided by an exalted justice and benevolence. Who can doubt that, in the course of time and things, the fruits of such a plan would richly repay any temporary advantages which might be lost by a steady adherence to it? Can it be, that Providence has not connected the permanent felicity of a nation with its virtue? The experiment, at least, is recommended by every sentiment which ennobles human nature. Alas! is it rendered impossible by its vices?

In the execution of such a plan, nothing is more essential than that permanent, inveterate antipathies against particular nations, and passionate attachments for others, should be excluded; and that, in place of them, just and amicable feelings towards all should be cultivated. The nation which indulges towards another an habitual hatred, or an habitual fondness, is in some degree a slave. It is a slave to its animosity or to its affection, either of which is sufficient to lead it astray from its duty and its interest. Antipathy in one Nation against another disposes each more readily to offer insult and injury, to lay hold of slight causes of umbrage, and to be haughty and intractable, when accidental or trifling occasions of dispute occur. Hence frequent collisions, obstinate, envenomed, and bloody contests. The nation, prompted by ill will and resentment sometimes impels to war the government, contrary to the best calculations of policy. The government sometimes participates in the national propensity, and adopts through passion what reason would reject; at other times, it makes the animosity of the nation subservient to projects of hostility instigated by pride, ambition, and other sinister and pernicious motives. The peace often, sometimes perhaps the Liberty, of nations has been the victim.

So likewise, a passionate attachment of one nation for another produces a variety of evils. Sympathy for the favorite nation, facilitating the illusion of an imaginary common interest, in cases where no real common interest exists, and infusing into one the enmities of the other, betrays the former into a participation in the quarrels and wars of the latter, without adequate inducement or justification. It leads also to concessions to the favorite nation of privileges denied to others, which is apt doubly to injure the nation making the concessions: by unnecessarily parting with what ought to have been retained; and by exciting jealousy, ill will, and a disposition to retaliate, in the parties from whom equal privileges are withheld. And it gives to ambitious, corrupted, or deluded citizens (who devote themselves to the favorite nation), facility to betray or sacrifice the interests of their own country, without odium, sometimes even with popularity; gilding, with the appearances of a virtuous sense of obligation, a commendable deference for public opinion, or a laudable zeal for public good, the base of foolish compliances of ambition, corruption, or infatuation.

As avenues to foreign influence in innumerable ways, such attachments are particularly alarming to the truly enlightened and independent patriot. How many opportunities do they afford to tamper with domestic factions, to practice the arts of seduction, to mislead public opinion, to influence or awe the public councils! Such an attachment of a small or weak, towards a great and powerful nation, dooms the former to be the satellite of the latter.

Against the insidious wiles of foreign influence (I conjure you to believe me, fellow-citizens), the jealousy of a free people ought to be constantly awake; since history and experience prove that foreign influence is one of the most baneful foes of republican government.

But that jealousy, to be useful, must be impartial; else it becomes the instrument of the very influence to be avoided, instead of a defence against it. Excessive partiality for one foreign nation, and excessive dislike of another, cause those whom they actuate to see danger only on one side, and serve to veil and even second the arts of influence on the other. Real Patriots, who may resist the intrigues of the favorite, are liable to become suspected and odious; while its tools and dupes usurp the applause and confidence of the people, to surrender their interests.

The great rule of conduct for us, in regard to foreign nations, is, in extending our commercial relations, to have with them as little political connection as possible. So far as we have already formed engagements, let them be fulfilled with perfect good faith. Here let us stop.

Europe has a set of primary interests, which to us have none, or a very remote relation. Hence she must be engaged in frequent controversies, the causes of which are essentially foreign to our concerns. Hence therefore, it must be unwise in us to implicate ourselves, by artificial ties, in the ordinary vicissitudes of her politics, or the ordinary combinations and collisions of her friendships or enmities.

Our detached and distant situation invites and enables us to pursue a different course. If we remain one people, under an efficient government, the period is not far off, when we may defy material injury from external annoyance; when we may take such an attitude as will cause the neutrality we may at any time resolve upon, to be scrupulously respected; when belligerent nations, under the impossibility of making acquisitions upon us, will not lightly hazard the giving us provocation; when we may choose peace or war, as our interest, guided by justice, shall counsel.

Why forego the advantages of so peculiar a situation? Why quit our own to stand upon foreign ground? Why, by interweaving our destiny with that of any part of Europe, entangle our peace and prosperity in the toils of European ambition, rivalship, interest, humor, or caprice?

'Tis our true policy to steer clear of permanent alliances with any portion of the foreign world; so far, I mean, as we are now at liberty to do it; for let me not be understood as capable of patronizing infidelity to existing engagements. I hold the maxim no less applicable to public than to private affairs, that honesty is always the best policy. I repeat it therefore, let those engagements be observed in their genuine sense. But, in my opinion, it is unnecessary and would be unwise to extend them.

Taking care always to keep ourselves, by suitable establishments, on a respectable defensive posture, we may safely trust to temporary alliances for extraordinary emergencies.

Harmony, liberal intercourse with all nations, are recommended by policy, humanity, and interest. But even our commercial policy should hold an equal and impartial hand: neither seeking nor granting exclusive favors or preferences; consulting the natural course of things; diffusing and diversifying by gentle means the streams of commerce, but forcing nothing; establishing with powers so disposed, in order to give trade a stable course, to define the rights of our merchants, and to enable the government to support them, conventional rules of intercourse, the best that present circumstances and mutual opinion will permit, but temporary, and liable to be from time to time abandoned or varied, as experience and circumstances shall dictate; constantly keeping in view, that 'tis folly in one nation to look for disinterested favors from another; that it must pay with a portion of its independence for whatever it may accept under that character; that, by such acceptance, it may place itself in the condition of having given equivalents for nominal favors, and yet of being reproached with ingratitude for not giving more. There can be no greater error than to expect or calculate upon real favors from nation to nation. 'Tis an illusion, which experience must cure, which a just pride ought to discard.

In offering to you, my countrymen, these counsels of an old and affectionate friend, I dare not hope they will make the strong and lasting impression I could wish; that they will control the usual current of the passions, or prevent our nation from running the course which has hitherto marked the destiny of nations. But if I may even flatter myself that they may be productive of some partial benefit, some occasional good; that they may now and then recur to moderate the fury of party spirit, to warn against the mischiefs of foreign intrigue, to guard against the impostures of pretended patriotism; this hope will be a full recompense for the solicitude for your welfare by which they have been dictated.

How far in the discharge of my official duties I have been guided by the principles which have been delineated, the public records and other evidences of my conduct must witness to you and to the world. To myself, the assurance of my own conscience is, that I have at least believed myself to be guided by them.

In relation to the still subsisting war in Europe, my proclamation of the 22d of April, 1793, is the index to my plan. Sanctioned by your approving voice, and by that of your representatives in both Houses of Congress, the spirit of that measure has continually governed me, uninfluenced by any attempts to deter or divert me from it.

After deliberate examination, with the aid of the best lights I could obtain, I was well satisfied that our country, under all the circumstances of the case, had a right to take, and was bound in duty and interest to take, a neutral position. Having taken it, I determined, as far as should depend upon me, to maintain it, with moderation, perseverance, and firmness.

The considerations which respect the right to hold this conduct, it is not necessary on this occasion to detail. I will only observe that, according to my understanding of the matter, that right, so far from being denied by any of the belligerent powers, has been virtually admitted by all.

The duty of holding a neutral conduct may be inferred, without any thing more, from the obligation which justice and humanity impose on every nation, in cases in which it is free to act, to maintain inviolate the relations of peace and amity towards other nations.

The inducements of interest for observing that conduct will best be referred to your own reflections and experience. With me, a predominant motive has been to endeavor to gain time to our country to settle and mature its yet recent institutions, and to progress without interruption to that degree of strength and consistency which is necessary to give it, humanly speaking, the command of its own fortunes.

Though, in reviewing the incidents of my administration, I am unconscious of intentional error, I am nevertheless too sensible of my defects not to think it probable that I may have committed many errors. Whatever they may be, I fervently beseech the Almighty to avert or mitigate the evils to which they may tend. I shall also carry with me the hope, that my country will never cease to view them with indulgence; and that, after forty-five years of my life dedicated to its service with an upright zeal, the faults of incompetent abilities will be consigned to oblivion, as myself must soon be to the mansions of rest.

Relying on its kindness in this as in other things, and actuated by that fervent love towards it which is so natural to a man who views in it the native soil of himself and his progenitors for several generations, I anticipate with pleasing expectation that retreat in which I promise myself to realize, without alloy, the sweet enjoyment of partaking, in the midst of my fellow citizens, the benign influence of good laws under a free government, the ever favorite object of my heart, and the happy reward, as I trust, of our mutual cares, labors and dangers.

George Washington

United States, 17th September 1796

[Spelling and punctuation have been modernized.]

Index

Y